The
Career
Toolkit

Essential Skills for Success
That No One Taught You

Mark A. Herschberg

Cognosco Media LLC | New York, NY

© 2020 Mark A. Herschberg

All rights reserved. This book or parts hereof may not be reproduced, distributed, posted, stored in any retrieval system, or transmitted in any form by any means—electronic, mechanical, photocopy, recording, or otherwise—without prior written permission of the publisher, except as provided by United States copyright law including quotations, reviews, and certain other non-commercial uses permitted by copyright law. For permission requests, write to the publisher.

LIMIT OF LIABILITY / DISCLAIMER OF WARRANTY. The statements contained in this book are the opinion of the author, and no claims are made. References are provided for informational purposes only and do not constitute endorsement of any websites or other sources, and their correctness has not been confirmed. Readers should be aware that the websites, apps, and other tools listed in this book may change. The contents of this book are provided as is. Every person and situation is unique. Nothing in this book is guaranteed to be effective or suitable for your situation. You are responsible for your own choices, actions, and consequences, and any action you take upon reading this book is at your own risk, and the author and publisher will not be liable for any losses and/or damages in connection with your use of this book. The author and publisher do not assume, and hereby disclaim, any liability to any party for any loss, damage, or disruption caused by errors or omissions, whether such errors or omissions result from negligence, accident, or any other cause. Neither the author nor the publisher shall be liable for any damages, including, but not limited to, special, incidental, consequential, or other damages. No warranty is given, nor may any be created or extended by sales or promotional materials. Specific restrictions and laws may apply based upon your jurisdiction and/or any contracts or other legal agreements you may have signed. The author is not a lawyer or any other licensed professional, and nothing in this book should be taken as legal advice or any other advice from any such a professional; you should consult such a professional when appropriate, as well as before taking action based on statements contained in this book.

Published by

Cognosco Media LLC | New York, NY | www.thecareertoolkitbook.com

Publisher's Cataloging-in-Publication Data
Herschberg, Mark A.

The career toolkit : essential skills for success that no one taught you / by Mark Herschberg. – New York, NY : Cognosco Media LLC, 2020.

p. ; cm.

ISBN13: 978-0-9601007-0-5 (softcover)
978-0-9601007-4-3 (hardcover)

1. Vocational guidance. 2. Career development. 3. Success. I. Title.

HF5381.H47 2020
650.14--dc23   2020903968

First Edition

Project coordination by Jenkins Group, Inc.
www.BookPublishing.com

Interior design by Brooke Camfield

Printed in the United States of America
24 23 22 21 20 • 5 4 3 2 1

Dedication

To my parents, Seymour and Phyllis,
who taught me the value of learning.

Contents

Acknowledgments	ix
Introduction	1
Why This Matters	3
How to Use This Book	5
Next Steps	7

CAREER

Chapter One Career Plan	**11**
Setting Sail	12
Inputs to a Career Plan	13
Nowhere to Go, Just Up	15
Assessment Tools	16
Delayed Compensation	18
Creating a Career Plan	20
Refining Your Career Plan	34
Selecting a Mentor	36
Startup or Large Corporation?	40
A. B. See.	45
Summary and Next Steps	47
Chapter Two Working Effectively	**49**
Learning About the Job	49
The Core Role of a Company	51
Meta-Work	55
Navigating a Corporation	58
Summary and Next Steps	63

Chapter Three Interviewing — 65
- For the Candidate — 66
    - *Create Your Own Opportunities* — 72
    - *HR's Limitations* — 75
- For the Hiring Team — 78
    - *The Airport Test* — 95
- Summary and Next Steps — 99

LEADERSHIP & MANAGEMENT

Chapter Four Leadership — 103
- What Is Leadership? — 104
- Positional vs. Influential Leadership — 104
- Leadership Skills — 106
- Developing Your Leadership — 113
    - *Machiavelli on Change* — 115
- The Myth of the Alpha Male — 117
- The Double Bind — 118
- Summary and Next Steps — 119

Chapter Five Management: People — 121
- Four Roles of a Manager — 121
- Motivation — 125
    - *Flow* — 127
- Teamwork — 129
- Your Obligations to Your Team — 131
- Summary and Next Steps — 133

Chapter Six Management: Process — 135
- The Three Precepts of Management — 136
    - *Managing Imposter Syndrome* — 138
- Meetings — 140
- Communication Channels — 148

Contents

The Project Triangle	150
Process Improvement	153
Hanlon's Razor	156
Leadership vs. Management	160
Summary and Next Steps	161

INTERPERSONAL DYNAMICS

Chapter Seven **Communication**   165

What Is Communication?	166
Meaning	167
Models	169
Shared Understanding	173
Thinking Modes	175
Public Speaking	178
Crafting Your Image	181
Summary and Next Steps	184

Chapter Eight **Networking**   185

What Is Networking?	186
The Wrong Way to Network	192
Stop Trying to Sell Me That You're Networking	194
Who Is in Your Network?	195
The Right Way to Network	198
Health, Wealth, and Family	203
How to Talk to Strangers	204
How Are You?	208
Advanced Techniques	209
I Don't Have Anything to Offer	213
Business Cards	215
Summary and Next Steps	216

vii

Chapter Nine **Negotiation** — **219**
- What Is Negotiating? — 220
- Zero-Sum Negotiations — 222
- Positions vs. Interests — 224
- Stages of Negotiation — 225
  - *Unethical Negotiating* — 234
- Types of Negotiations — 237
- It's All a Negotiation — 240
- How to Negotiate Your Job Offer — 242
- Summary and Next Steps — 248

Chapter Ten **Ethics** — **251**
- Ethics in the Workplace — 253
- Why Not Roll the Dice? — 257
- How Do We Stop It? — 260
- Summary and Next Steps — 266

Epilogue — **269**
- Summary — 269
- Next Steps — 270

Appendix A: **Why Isn't This Taught?** — **273**

Appendix B: **Career Questions** — **277**

About the Author — **285**

Index — **287**

Acknowledgments

To borrow from Isaac Newton, if I have seen farther than other men, it is only because a team of people has led me there even while I was kicking and screaming at times.

Like most people, I learned most of what I know from others. Very few authors actually have radically new ideas, although academics tend to be the exception. Most simply take ideas they have learned from others and apply them to new circumstances or describe them in new ways. Not everyone acknowledges this. A number of ideas came from my fellow teachers, students, co-workers, authors I've read, speakers I've heard, and elsewhere. My original ideas were no doubt influenced by what others taught me.

This book began nearly twenty years ago, right around the time we created MIT's Undergraduate Practice Opportunities Program (UPOP). Both this book and UPOP grew out of the observation that these skills were commonly missing in the workplace. UPOP influenced me quite a lot, and it is the reason certain topics are included in this book. I am especially grateful to the entire UPOP team—faculty, staff, speakers, and fellow mentor instructors too numerous to mention. Most important in that group is my friend Chris Resto, who helped start UPOP. I'm grateful that he invited me to be part of UPOP; his vision for the program greatly influenced this book. Professor Charles Leiserson was one of the early faculty leaders of UPOP and helped to develop many of the modules.

The Career Toolkit

Working with him to develop and deliver those modules was extremely insightful.

Deborah Liverman and her staff at MIT's office of Career Advising and Professional Development, along with the MIT Alumni Association, have been friends and supporters of the talks I gave that were an early version of parts of this book.

Renaissance Weekend, those retreats attended by global thought leaders and changemakers, has also been a source of friendship, learning, and inspiration, and I know many of the people who helped me with this book through that community. The weekends are intentionally held off the record, so I won't specifically call out people and conversations.

Another great resource I'm fortunate to have is the NY CTO Club, a group of New York's most senior technologists. I am grateful for the many talks, and the discussions I've had there, in person and online, with the fantastic and supportive club members.

Throughout my career, I've had some great co-workers and managers. Among them are Jon Christensen, Wendell Brown, George Coll, Brendan O'Donohoe, David Urry, and Dennis Syracuse.

My many fantastic reviewers helped me refine my thinking and offered a number of improvements: Carolyn Purnell, Tai Mong, Jasmina Aganovic, Jennifer Flowers, Dom Ricci, Dennis McLeavey, Erin Holder, Drew Holder, Debra Holder, Yana Shend, and Jim Lambert. I'm also appreciative of my parents, Seymour and Phyllis, who have given me great feedback throughout the process.

I was lucky to have a few domain experts, among them Lawrence Susskind and Deborah Tannen, review specific sections based on their research. Others reviewed specific sections of the book, including Igor Shindel, Andrea Rishmawi, Judy Vincent, Vladimir Baranov, Kevin Shen, Rick Kunin, Deborah Liverman, and Steve Heller. I also want to thank the many people who provided input on my title, subtitle, and cover.

Acknowledgments

Publishing a book is a first for me, and I'm appreciative of the kind help from Dorie Clark, Olivia Fox Cabane, Becky Sweren, and Jill Schiefelbein. Ellen Werther suggested developing the companion app. Peter Winick introduced me to the Jenkins Group and others who have been helpful. I'm very appreciative of my primary editor, Carol Reed, who helped guide this first time author. And my sincere thanks to Robin Colucci, who has advised many successful authors and gave me some fantastic insights on my structure and overall guidance for the book.

A special thank-you to my late friend Melissa Newman, who was always there for me and helped me see the bigger picture.

Finally, a second big thank-you to my parents and my brother, Michael, for teaching me the core values of learning and helping others, which led me to the lessons in this book.

I'll end with apologies to anyone I might have missed.

Introduction

A young professional winds up sidelined in a job that's not developing him, and his career stagnates. A rising manager encounters someone who backstabs her politically and takes over her team. A new employee is unable to negotiate the salary she deserves. A successful individual contributor wants to move into management, but the interviews never lead to offers.

Every one of those stories is true. Those are not a few isolated examples but common career setbacks faced by millions of people every year. The real tragedy is that every one of those situations is avoidable. Despite years of higher education and still more years of experience, few people know how to create an actionable career plan, how to handle office politics, how to negotiate effectively, or how to lead.

Most people had more training in how to tie their shoes than in many of those career skills. You trained for your profession, you practiced your hobbies, and you learned how to drive a car. Outside of formal schooling specific to our degree, most of us never studied or developed skills for our careers. Networking, leading, communication, negotiation, adjusting to a corporate culture. All of these are skills that, we're told, are important, but most of us are never formally taught them.[1]

There's an old joke about two men who are camping in the woods, when a bear comes into their campsite. The first man hears the bear and

---

1. For those who are curious, see Appendix A: Why Isn't This Taught? It explains why.

wakes up. He quickly wakes his friend and tells him they need to get out of there. As the second man starts putting on his shoes, the first man says, "You can't outrun the bear in those shoes!" The second man replies, "I don't need to outrun the bear; I just need to outrun you!"

I am often surprised to discover just how badly many companies are run. The leaders themselves seem to be outclassed by their job descriptions. All of those companies manage to stay in business because they don't have to be perfect. They don't need to outrun the bear; they only need to outrun the competition. Similarly, their semi-competent leaders didn't outrun bears to get those jobs; they just outran their peers.

This book is going to teach you to put on your shoes and outrun everyone else. Much like putting on your shoes, you can learn to do so easily, and with a little practice it will become second nature.

Some of these skills will be ones you've never thought about. Others will be familiar—for instance, everyone knows about networking and communicating—but I'll present these topics in a more powerful and useful way than you've probably heard before, based on my experience teaching for nearly twenty years at MIT's yearlong "career success accelerator" and elsewhere. Although that program was developed for college students, the techniques used in this book will apply, no matter your level of experience, from a soon-to-be college graduate to a seasoned professional.

Each chapter will give you a solid foundation in a core "firm skill"[2] you'll need for your career, along with the most actionable ideas to help you improve. Once you've started applying these techniques, they will be as easy as tying your shoes. The competition is slower than you think.

---

2. We refer to them as "firm skills," since they aren't hard skills like math but more concrete than what are commonly referred to as "soft skills," such as listening, time management, self-motivation, storytelling, and more. The term was coined by former Undergraduate Practice Opportunities Program executive director Susann Luperfoy to identify these as distinct from traditionally amorphous soft skills.

Introduction

Why This Matters

Why should you invest time developing these firm skills rather than getting better at spreadsheets, learning a new design tool, reading another scientific paper, or anything else that more directly relates to knowledge specific to your job? While you should always expand your knowledge in your field, you'll get a much better return on your time by developing these skills.

A common adage stresses the importance of being well rounded, as opposed to possessing narrow and deep knowledge. Consider the following analogy, which I learned from Professor Charles Leiserson of MIT.

Suppose you have a rectangle that's 10 units by 4 units, with an area of 40 units. You need to increase one of the sides by 2 units. Which side should you increase to create the largest area? (This will be the only math problem in the book, I promise.)

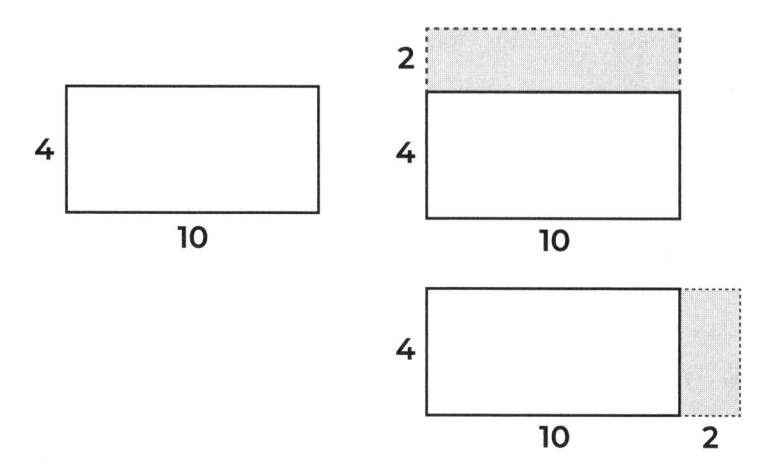

FIGURE 1. Increasing the area of a rectangle

The answer is to increase the short side from 4 to 6 units for a total area of 60 units. (Increasing the long side to 12 units long only results in a total of 48 units.) Conceptually, the reason it makes sense to increase the short side is because every increase in the short side is "amplified" by the greater length of the long side.

Now imagine that the sides of the rectangle represent your abilities—a longer side means more skill. Given a strong skill and a weak skill, which one should you focus on?

The answer is the short side. Let's understand why. It's true that everyone should have some degree of expertise—your core skills, be they marketing, manufacturing, sales, law, or something else. Some people's knowledge is so extensive that that alone makes them valuable. For most of us, we're somewhat interchangeable. Take three hundred directors of finance; no doubt, in terms of financial knowledge, you could substitute at least some of them for others. What makes one candidate stronger than another—in other words, what makes them a better hire for a company—often isn't marginally deeper knowledge of finance, but rather firm skills like leadership, communication, or a strong network.

You already have some functional expertise, such as in marketing, accounting, or another functional area, and you should continue to learn and develop that knowledge. But in terms of impact, you can often get a better return on your time by investing in these firm skills.

Consider the case of a chemist with ten years of experience who has fifty hours to invest in learning. He could learn a new technique or read up on some recent research that will marginally increase his knowledge. Alternatively, he could invest those fifty hours into being a better public speaker. If he's not a strong public speaker, those fifty hours could have a huge impact; every presentation he'll give in the future would benefit from it. In other words, he's increasing his short side and maximizing his overall area.

Obviously, we're more than two dimensions. You get an interview because of your ability to write copy, your knowledge of real estate, or

Introduction

whatever your expertise is, but these firm skills will help you land the job and be more successful in the role.

So, while you should continue to have some domain expertise, be sure to invest time in the firm skills covered in this book. The return on investment from those hours will often yield outsized returns.

How to Use This Book

This book will improve your professional efficacy. It will make you more effective at work, as well as in your personal life. This book, like the MIT class I teach, is a "career success accelerator," putting you on a path to develop these critically important skills. Many of us who created the class did so because we learned these lessons the hard way; this book will provide you with a much easier path.

The book itself covers a number of topics. Any one of them could be a book or a class unto itself. After decades of studying and teaching these subjects, I've distilled the content down to the most salient points for each topic so that you can cover one chapter in about an hour. It's by no means exhaustive, but the concepts that are included will absolutely help you throughout your career.

These skills require practice. No one ever became a great swimmer simply by reading about how to swim. What you'll find is that the application of a particular skill isn't so formally bound. Interviewing isn't only having a conversation about your résumé. Negotiating isn't always sliding a piece of paper with a number across a desk. Leadership doesn't depend on having subordinates. Going through these chapters will expose you to the core concepts and help you start to see opportunities to learn, practice, and build these skills in your current job. Each chapter will open a door and make that seemingly opaque field readily accessible. How far you go beyond this book is up to you.

Equally important is how these skills reinforce one another. Good leaders know how to negotiate. Your career path will involve managerial skills, even as an individual contributor. Networking is helped by solid communication skills. Each of these topics helps support others, and holistically, all of them together make you more effective. A basketball player will practice shooting drills, running drills, and passing drills, but at game time, it's the combination of all these skills that makes someone a great player.

A great way to learn is to form a reading group with your friends or co-workers; meet once a week over lunch to discuss these topics. Each week, just pick one topic, such as a section from a chapter, then discuss it with other people to see how they view it and to broaden your own understanding. You get better at soccer not just by playing a match but also by practicing with teammates and watching other teams. Likewise, even if you're not negotiating or dealing with political issues at work, you can learn by talking through such issues with peers in the reading group who are facing those situations. Let me be clear so this doesn't come off as a self-serving ploy to sell more copies; you can discuss these topics with others even without this book. Everyone picks an article related to the topic, reads it before lunch, and shares ideas they've learned. Then the participants discuss the concepts with each other. No book required.

You can read chapters in almost any order. Each chapter can stand on its own and be read as such, but you will find cross-references because, as noted above, the skills help to reinforce each other. Chapter 1, Career Plan, involves the most self-reflection, so some readers may want to jump ahead to a particular skill and come back to that one later.

Introduction

Next Steps

Chapter 1, Career Plan, is a great place to start, since it provides an overarching framework for the skills in this book. But if you have a particular problem you're facing or know where you're going and how to get there, feel free to jump ahead to the relevant chapter.

As you go through the chapters, consider doing so with a peer group (co-workers or friends). As you explore topics, they can help provide different perspectives to help you arrive at a better understanding. There will also be some additional tools you can find on the book's website at http://thecareertoolkitbook.com.

Download the book's companion app, which provides a "tip of the day" reminder; that will help reinforce the topics as you read them. You can even set the app to just reinforce topics from one particular chapter, or you can quickly use it as a refresher, say, before walking into a networking event or a negotiation.

CAREER

Chapter One

Career Plan

> "Always have a plan. Even a bad plan is better than no plan at all."
>
> —Professor Jason Rosenhouse,
> James Madison University

I used to teach chess to kids. My friend and co-teacher Jason Rosenhouse used to tell our students, "Always have a plan. Even a bad plan is better than no plan at all."

The goal in chess is to capture your opponent's king while protecting your own. Randomly moving pieces doesn't work. Sitting back and playing to simply keep your king from getting captured may prevent you from losing, but it won't help you win. Only by having a proactive plan to capture the opponent's king can you achieve success.

Professor Rosenhouse's advice reminds us that you have to proactively plan to reach your career goals. You don't have to begin with a perfect career plan; it's about having a career plan that's good enough and then improving upon it over time. No matter where you are in your career—just out of college or decades in—having a plan increases your chances of success.

The Career Toolkit

Far too many people have a career plan that ended once they picked a profession. Much like a poor chess player, they simply moved through their careers without a clear goal. While having a plan alone is no guarantee of success, the lack of a plan often ensures failure.

By setting a destination and creating a plan to get there, you greatly increase your chance of success. Better still is enlisting the help of others along the way. This chapter will help you craft a plan, get input from others, and apply the plan effectively.

As you read this chapter, don't feel that you have to have an answer to every question; this is a tool to help you, not a test to judge you. Some people know what they want to do from the age of five, and others figure it out as they go. However far you look ahead, be it two months or twenty years, these tools will greatly increase your chance of success.

Since this chapter involves significant personal reflection, some readers may want to skip ahead to other chapters to focus on specific skills and come back to this later.

Setting Sail

What happens to a ship adrift on the ocean? It will float wherever the currents take it. Sometimes a storm may arise and thrust it in a new direction. That's sufficient navigation if you don't care where you're going or when you get there, but most people have a specific destination in mind.

Your career—and your life in general—work much the same way. You probably have some idea where you want to wind up and what you want to achieve. Whether it's a specific job title or more general goals of impact, power, money, fame, or something else, there is some destination you have in mind. Simply hoping you'll get there won't work. Hope is not a strategy. In the words of Antoine de Saint-Exupéry, "A goal without a plan is just a wish." Sometimes good fortune will find you: A senior person leaves and you get promoted or a new project comes along, giving you an opportunity to stand out. Other times, there will be misfortune, such as a recession and company layoffs. Much like the sailors of old, you need to have a course laid out, and then you can seek benefits and avoid setbacks while you do what you need to do to reach your goal.

Ultimately, a career plan is a set of guidelines, values, and goals—a path you create to help you manage your career. It's navigation for your life.

Inputs to a Career Plan

Before setting sail, you must plan your journey. Obviously, that includes a path to your destination, but it also means deciding what provisions you need along the way so you're not caught unprepared. The provisions for your career are the skills you need to build in order to get your future job.

Creating the plan begins by considering relevant questions. I've listed some common questions below. It helps to answer these questions, not just for today but for your overall career. If you're twenty-two and just out of school, a $70,000-a-year job may seem like a huge amount of money. When you're fifty-two with a mortgage and two kids in college, that may be nowhere near enough. You might discover a new hobby along the way that becomes important. Your spouse may add some constraints about where to live. Try to look ahead five, ten, twenty years into the future. Ultimately, as I've said, this is a tool, not a test; there are no wrong answers.

Much like the plans of a chess player, you can revise yours anytime—and I guarantee that you will. Many people have careers that take twists and turns in unexpected directions, so don't be surprised if your answers change over time.

Appendix B: Career Questions goes into more detail about the questions listed below. It includes more refinement to the questions that you'll likely grapple with as you attempt to outline a career plan.

The Career Toolkit

Try to think about the questions below now. If the list feels overwhelming, just skim it; think about the two to three most important questions, and move on.

Personal Needs
- What are my goals in life?
- What would make me happy?
- What is the purpose of my job?
- What do I like doing?
- What don't I like doing?

Job Requirements
- How many hours a week do I want to work?
- How much travel do I want?
- Do I want to manage people? Be managed? Be independent?
- How flexible does my career path need to be?
- What skills do I want to leverage? To avoid?
- What type of corporate/industry culture do I want?
- What trends can impact my career?

Lifestyle Options
- Do I want a family? If so, when?
- What family obligations will I have?
- Where do I want to live, and what industries are supported there?
- What lifestyle do I want?
- What flexibility is needed?

Financial Needs
- How much money do I want to earn?

Career Plan

Impact
- What type of impact do I want to have in my field?
- What type of impact do I want to have in general?

Ethics
- What are the ethical considerations of the role?
- What are the ethical considerations of the industry?
- What are my limits?

Nowhere to Go, Just Up

Most corporate ladders implicitly assume higher is better. There's typically more pay higher up, because a CEO or a VP has more impact on the company than an individual contributor. It may not feel fair to those who don't want a role managing others, but from the company's perspective, the best return on money is to put the premium at the top. There is some debate about when this no longer generates a return for the company and whether higher pay for those lower down is better than additional executive pay. But that's beyond the scope of this book.

Some companies now recognize that a great individual contributor may not be a great manager. That person might not even want to manage others. Promoting someone like that into a managerial role means the company loses a great contributor and gets a mediocre manager—a double whammy. The tech industry, for example, discovered that some great technical minds would prefer to stay focused on technical problems, not people problems, so they created a separate ladder for individual contributors with equal pay to those in managerial roles.

The Career Toolkit

> Not all industries and careers offer such dual-track options. Even if they do, the nature of the jobs may not lend themselves to similar compensation. The fastest shelf stocker at a supermarket is never going to deliver as much value to the company as the vice president of inventory management, and so that world-class stocker will never earn as much as even an average person in a vice president's role.
>
> If you don't want a role managing others, look at the industry and functional areas you're considering, and make sure you understand both the career path options and the compensation ladder available.

Assessment Tools

There are a number of tools that can be used to help you better understand yourself and subsequently answer the career plan questions. Technical skills, for example, how well you can draft a contract or design a logo, aren't always objectively measured, but corporations will give you feedback on your work product. (Note: Here and elsewhere, the term "technical skills" doesn't refer to your ability with computers but instead describes skills for a particular job function.) Skills such as relationship building and public speaking are fuzzier still to measure, and you are less likely to get direct feedback from your company on these skills.

What can be measured are preferences. There are a number of tools out there to measure preferences, including the Myers-Briggs Type Indicator (MBTI); the Herrmann Brain Dominance Instrument (HBDI); the Big Five personality traits (also known as the "five-factor model" (FFM) and OCEAN, an acronym for openness, conscientiousness, extraversion, agreeableness, and neuroticism); the DISC (dominance, influence, steadiness, conscientiousness) model; BASIS (Business and Attitude Style Information System); the Enneagram; and many others.

These tools can help you better understand who you are. Each measures a number of traits, such as introversion versus extroversion, conceptual versus concrete thought, and risk-seeking versus risk-avoidance behavior.

These are tools, not tests. There is no passing or failing grade. Unlike the SATs, they aren't measuring competence but rather personal preference. As an analogy, it's like asking, "Which classes do you prefer: science, English, math, or history?" rather than, "How good are you at science?"

I've found these tools useful because they've helped me realize why I'm stronger in some areas over others. Once I realized my preferences, I understood why I avoided certain types of activities and consequently, why my skills weren't as strong in those areas. This then directed my plan to allow me to address those shortcomings. Some people are naturally gifted, but for many of us, experience and practice make us better. Aversion to an experience limits our growth and subsequent ability. The tools only show preferences, but preferences become actions (or lack thereof), which over time result in strengths and weaknesses.

As I became more conscious of my preferences, I incorporated actions into my career plan to correct for the limited experience—even if I had to force myself into certain development plans, much like I had to force myself to eat more vegetables. No doubt, you already recognize some of your preferences; for me, no one ever had to tell me I liked quantitative reasoning. But you may not see them all and may not have consciously thought about your aversions. These tools can help give you an understanding of yourself to better address the questions above.

It's important that you never say, "I'm an introvert, therefore I can't do X," because doing so limits you. Instead, recognize this: "I'm an introvert, so I know that when I do X, I should be mindful of Y." As someone who is an introvert, I know that after being around a lot of strangers in an unfamiliar setting, I need some alone time to decompress. This helps me perform better in certain situations.

Some people argue that there is not sufficient evidence supporting the validity of these tools. Personally, I have gotten consistent results across all the tools I have used in my self-assessments, and I have found them useful. At the end of the day, they are tools. If these tools work for you, then use them; if they do not, or if you question their veracity, you don't need to use them.

Delayed Compensation

In almost any industry, as you progress in your career, you'll take more senior roles and earn more money. The financial growth, however, isn't the same in all industries. Some have a large gap between early and late compensation. The common examples are medicine, law, and finance.

All three industries start with relatively low compensation. Top law firms, for example, seem to pay quite well, but they don't pay well relative to future earnings. Entry-level jobs start with a large amount of work relative to the compensation; eighty-hour workweeks are the norm in those roles. There's an expectation in law and finance that many won't make it up the career ladder. Not every first-year law student will make partner, and not every analyst becomes a managing director on Wall Street.

You don't need to make it to a top position to have a very successful career. However, it's important to understand that the nature of some industries is such that you will put in a lot of work for relatively little pay early on. Those who make it through the gauntlet then get financially rewarded later—funded by the work of the next generation of entry-level workers putting in eighty-hour weeks.

There may not be a financial reward at the end. Some universities intentionally hire more associate professors than they have available tenured positions. During their time on the tenure track, the junior faculty put in long hours following the mantra "Publish or perish," which means they must get lots of research published in respected journals, or they'll fail to make tenure with its reward of lifelong employment. If three associate professors are hired, and there's only one tenured role, two will put in long years and wind up short.

The professors who don't make tenure at a top school may find opportunities at lower-ranked universities. Lawyers who don't make partner may still be okay working their own cases at a firm, or they may find an in-house position. If you burn out on Wall Street, however, a $500,000-a-year job may not be available as a fallback.

In medicine, once you graduate from medical school, odds are you'll complete a residency and go on to become a practicing doctor. However, with a general residency and then any additional specialization, it can take years before you earn more than a resident's paycheck. Longer residencies in specialized fields like neurosurgery delay that compensation, but residents are usually rewarded with higher compensation once the training is complete. If you want to go to medical school to become a neurosurgeon, then you need to recognize that when your friend goes off to a job in Silicon Valley at twenty-six and is earning a good salary, you'll still have four years of medical school and many years of residency to go before you start earning a significant income. Money, however, may not be the important factor for those going into medicine.

If you choose to be an artist, recognize that there is less of a formal career path. Classical musicians may move up in the ranks in orchestras. Painters, actors, and aspiring rock stars are more likely to be "discovered," with some of their success dependent on external factors such as cultural trends that align with their style. That's not

> to say that the skills in this book don't apply; successful artists know how to network, negotiate contracts, be recognized in their field, and more. But here again, the financial rewards are non-linear, with most doing poorly, some doing modestly, and a very few doing very well. Financial rewards are rarely the motivation of artists, but it is important that anyone entering or working in a field understand the likely outcomes.
>
> There's no wrong track, but when going into any such field, it's important to go in with your eyes open. Fully understand the time-to-reward trade-off and how much culling takes place as you climb the ranks. Ask yourself at the outset if you honestly believe you're likely to be the one who makes it and whether this pursuit is worth your time.

Creating a Career Plan

Now that you've considered your destination, you need to define a route to get there. This is not a one-off exercise. Like all plans, it will require adjustments along the way.

DEVELOPING THE PLAN

Let's consider a possible career path. You can't become a chief marketing officer right out of school. It takes years of experience and skill building. How do you become a chief marketing officer? You might start as a marketing associate. During that time, you'll learn basic technical skills, like how to manage an ad campaign or run a social media account. You may assist in preparing your team to go to a conference or in making a slide presentation look good. After a time, you'll be promoted to a more senior role and engage in more advanced tasks, such as allocating a client's advertising budget, copyediting, or planning the conference attendance.

Career Plan

As you learn more skills, you'll take on more responsibility. Soon, more junior people may start reporting to you. Over time, you'll move up to become a marketing manager, then perhaps a marketing director where you learn to staff up a team. At that point, you might switch to a new company and become a senior director of marketing and then vice president of marketing, and finally you could be offered your dream job: chief marketing officer of a six-year-old startup managing a team of twenty people.

That's a pretty linear career path—one that applies to most professions. Start at the bottom, do the grunt work, get more responsibility, begin to manage, and finally wind up in a senior leadership role.

Not all careers need to be so linear. Many won't be. You might start as an operations consultant and spend a few years at a large consulting firm. Then you may decide to go in-house and manage operations at a food-delivery company. In those roles, you'll learn budgeting, managing, planning, and hiring. In your early thirties, you may decide marketing is more exciting, so you'll go back to school for an MBA. Upon graduation, you may join a large company as a director of marketing and start advancing, picking up skills like creating marketing plans and managing copyeditors along the way, until one day a friend from high school tells you about her startup, and you leave the corporate world to start her marketing department as a team of one. The company continues to grow, and six years and a few hires later, you're the chief marketing officer managing a team of twenty. You're doing exactly the same job as before, but you followed a very different path to get there, and one certainly not foreseen at age twenty-five.

We can't know ahead of time which path we're going to take. Many have some idea of the general field—for instance, marketing or medicine?—but not the specific path. And that's okay. The goal isn't to have a perfect path but a general plan to navigate your career.

I think of my plan as a decision tree. One of the first decisions you made was to go to college, attend vocational school, or just start working. After finishing school, you choose between different jobs as well as the potential return to grad school. Each time you choose to find a new job, you'll have yet another decision.

CHANGING OPTIONS

Not all decisions are equal. Some are big, some small. Some can be reversed; some have limited windows.

Many people who go to medical school or law school do so just after college or within a few years of graduating. You can go anytime you choose, but there are costs. Going into one of those programs can cost hundreds of thousands of dollars—both in debt you'll have to pay off for the rest of your career and in lost income from not working. The amount of lost income, of course, tends to get higher later in your career. So, while you can attend graduate school at any time, the cost-return evaluation becomes less appealing over time.[3]

Similarly, startups are often created by younger adults, because they can live with roommates and eat ramen noodles. They know that if things don't work out after eighteen months of not taking a salary, they can move back in with their parents. Those options are less appealing to a fifty-year-old with a family. Conversely, a fifty-year-old who has made millions may not need to take a salary for a few years, whereas someone who is twenty-four has to pay off college debt. The catch is that at age twenty-four, you don't know for certain that you'll have millions of dollars by age fifty, but you have a much better sense of whether you can move back home for six months if you go broke.

---

3. Here, we are only considering financial cost. Other factors, such as your happiness and feeling a call to a profession, do apply, and you should take those into account, too. Financial cost is the easiest to understand, since I can't tell you how much happier one path will make you over another, but I can tell you the financial impact.

The above may seem fairly obvious, but other choices and opportunities are more subtle. When I graduated from college, I spoke to a number of consulting firms and Wall Street firms. They didn't care what I had majored in; they just wanted smart people and would train me with the necessary competencies for anything from financial modeling to assessing a client's risk factors. I received a few job offers but decided to pursue a career doing tech startups. Years later, former students of mine were encouraging me to join their large consulting firms. I wasn't certain but thought I'd apply. That time, I didn't even get an interview. It made no sense. I was clearly as smart as before, and now I had experience—maybe not all of it was relevant, and I wouldn't, for instance, be writing software in the jobs I applied for. But I had more experience in managing, working with customers, understanding certain industries, and much more. I had gotten better; why didn't they want me anymore?

After going through some back channels, I learned why. Imagine you have a twin brother, and you both graduate from college with exactly the same major and GPA. You go into software development at startups, and your twin joins McKinsey. A few years later, you're managing software teams at another startup, and your twin has moved to a junior managerial position at Accenture. Ten years into your careers, you both apply for a consulting role at PricewaterhouseCoopers. The two of you are equally smart, and you both have ten years of experience. Who gets the job?

From the perspective of the hiring manager, your twin is the clear choice. Your twin has the proven track record. Worst case, if your twin is hired but doesn't work out, they chalk it up to simply missing something in the interview process or him not being a cultural fit.

What about you? Well, they see that you're equally smart, and maybe you have the right skills or could learn them fast. But maybe not. Why take a chance on someone with a startup background when there are other candidates with consulting backgrounds who are better qualified?

If they do hire you, and you don't work out, your hiring manager will have a lot of explaining to do to his boss: Why did he hire someone who seemed, on paper, less qualified than other candidates? It was an unnecessary risk. Maybe you're a superstar, but you'd have to be enough of a superstar to justify the potential downside of not being a fit for the role. For most hiring managers, it's not worth the risk.

The same issue applies when someone wants to change professions and is willing to take an entry-level role. He may say, "I'm willing to start at the bottom and take an entry-level salary. I'm just like the other college graduates but with more experience, so therefore I'm a better option." That's true in theory, but not in practice. First, he will have formed some habits (bad or simply different) that they would need him to unlearn. New college graduates don't have such baggage. Second, while he may be willing to take an entry-level salary today, two years into the job he may be feeling the financial pressure, and he may need to get back to his prior income track. There's a lower risk of the recent college graduate leaving for that reason. Generally, once you're out of school, you get hired for what you have done in your career, and your schooling becomes less important. That's why people don't ask for your college GPA in interviews once you have a few years of experience; they have much better information by which to evaluate you.

If you become a noted expert in your field, or if you have a close personal connection to people in the firm, and they have enough knowledge about you, they may know that the risks mentioned above don't apply. Those are the rare exceptions, though, not the rule. The point is, as you continue down certain paths, some options disappear, while others become available.

CONSTANT OPTIONS

Some windows are always open. At any point in life, you can become an artist. There's no interview, and there are no minimum requirements, although obviously having some skill is important. Likewise, you can open a bakery or start your own company. Those have some costs, such as buying equipment or giving up a salary. But there's no external decision-maker preventing you from doing so, compared to becoming a doctor, which requires acceptance to medical school. These self-determined elections are open choices that exist throughout your career.

There are also "reset buttons." Typically, that's grad school, particularly getting an MBA. You can be a salesperson, then get an MBA and go into strategy consulting, or an MBA degree can turn a software developer into a marketer. Once you get an MBA, companies are willing to see you as credentialed in your area of concentration. Many people do use an MBA to advance in their field, say, someone in HR getting an MBA to get a more senior role in HR. Likewise, before law school, it doesn't matter if you were pre-med, worked in the Peace Corps, or traded stocks; post-law school, you're a lawyer. These options basically allow you to go from any career path into one or more specific paths after graduate school. This is different from, say, a PhD program in chemical engineering, because those programs will only accept someone with a degree in chemical engineering or the equivalent. Such a degree program will advance the career of someone in the field, but that graduate program required them to be in the field already.

Finally, there are terminal choices. Some jobs don't really have a career ladder. Painters, for example, generally don't advance and become senior painters. A few may get an artist-in-residence or a teaching position, but most painters simply paint. Likewise, if you become a director of a funeral home, that's about it. Maybe from there, you can lead a funeral trade association, but those roles are few and far between, compared to the number of people running funeral homes. If you decide to run a funeral home, there's no next rung on the career ladder. Just to be clear, that's fine. The goal is to have a career that meets your needs, not to climb some arbitrary ladder for the sake of climbing.

PROFESSION VS. INDUSTRY

Note that some professions are industry-specific, while others are not. An accountant can work in almost any industry: law, software, aerospace, government—or in an accounting firm. On the other hand, if you're in hospitality, say you're a hotel desk manager, you're generally going to stay in hospitality. Manufacturing companies will need accountants but not hotel desk managers. Neither option is necessarily better. Even if you can change industries in theory, companies in practice may want someone with industry experience. A lawyer can choose to practice any type of law, but a Wall Street firm looking to hire a lawyer will want one who has experience with securities law, not maritime law.

CAREER DECISION TREE

Given everything we've learned, let's put together a map. A career decision tree will look like those in Figure 2.

ACCOUNTANT

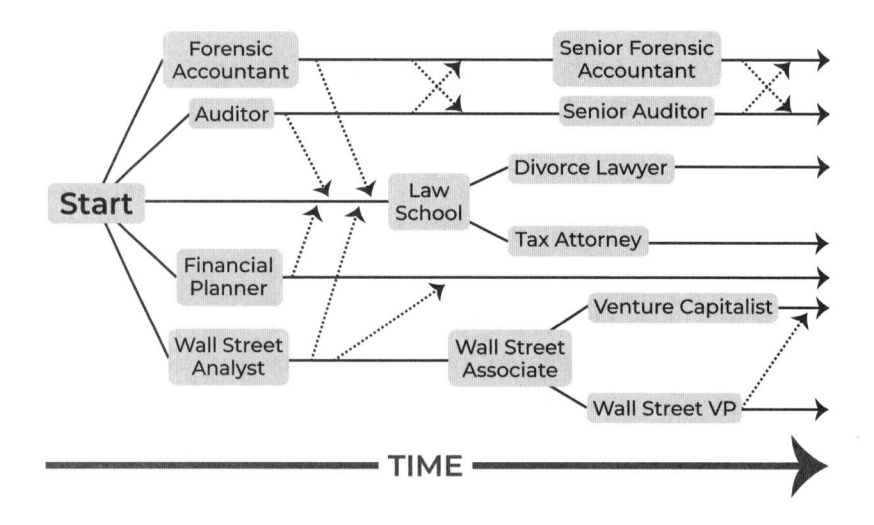

Career Plan

BIOLOGIST

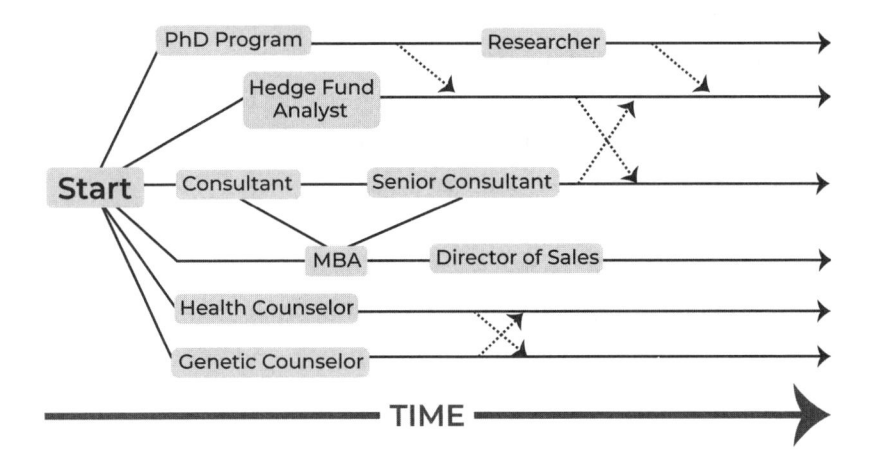

- PhD Program — Researcher
- Hedge Fund Analyst
- Consultant — Senior Consultant
- MBA — Director of Sales
- Health Counselor
- Genetic Counselor

◄──────── TIME ────────►

MARKETER

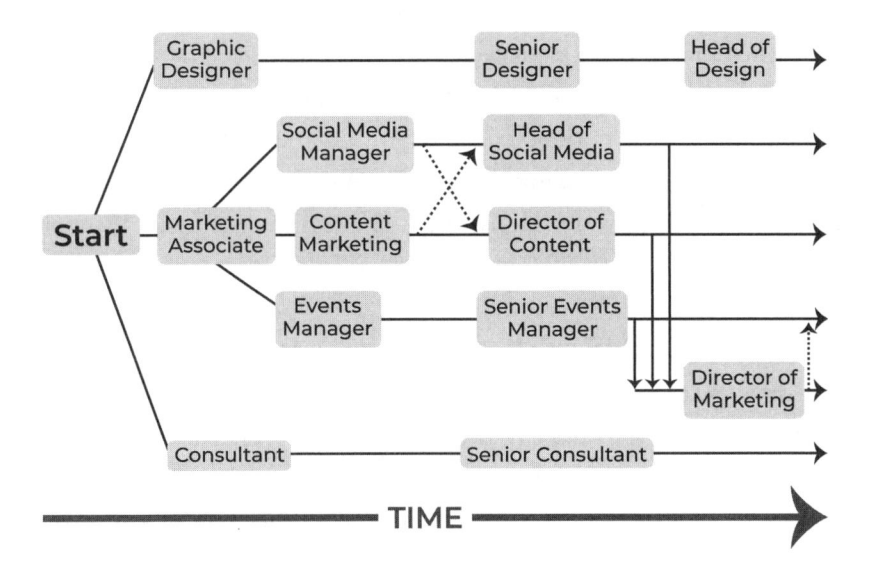

- Graphic Designer — Senior Designer — Head of Design
- Marketing Associate
  - Social Media Manager — Head of Social Media
  - Content Marketing — Director of Content
  - Events Manager — Senior Events Manager
  - Director of Marketing
- Consultant — Senior Consultant

◄──────── TIME ────────►

FIGURE 2. Potential career decision trees

The Career Toolkit

The diagrams in Figure 2 show example career paths for an accountant, biologist, and marketer. In each case, as someone choses a specific path, some options open up, but others become less accessible. In some cases, it's easy to switch, as shown by the dotted line; in other cases, switching is much more difficult. More advanced roles, such as director of marketing, have multiple paths to the role.

These career trees above are by no means exhaustive. Many more branches than can be shown exist for each case, both in terms of career length and number of options at each decision point. The diagrams just show a few options for some hypothetical people. Additionally, but not shown in each tree, open choices are always available, as are the reset buttons.

Readers earlier or less certain in their careers should consider carefully the flexibility afforded by different paths. Some jobs may give you more flexibility, while others may take you down a path with fewer options.

You don't have to perfectly map out your career path. Trying to accurately project a career over decades is simply not feasible; you can't possibly get all the options right. That's not the point; rather, it helps to lay out some of the major choices. You may want to write it down as in the diagrams, or you may just think about it in your head. Whatever works for you.

PLANNING AHEAD

The final piece of the puzzle is in the famous Wayne Gretzky hockey advice: "Good players skate to the puck. Great players skate to where the puck is going to be." As we map out the choices, we need to think about our goal—where the puck is going to be—and head in that direction. The tree is shown from where you are today to where you might wind up. You can also look at it in reverse: Think about a given job you want in the future, and map back likely paths to get there.

Career Plan

There's more to being a chief marketing officer than running marketing campaigns. As you move into managerial roles, you'll need to deal with budgeting, hiring, strategy, and working with both corporate partners and other departments within the company. You may be expected to speak at conferences and to help close sales. You'll need to be not just a manager but also a leader.

But this is not a surprise. Whatever your career ladder, you should look at job descriptions of the more senior roles you hope to hold later in your career. Equally important is to talk to people in those roles and ask them what the job is really like and what skills really matter. For each of the roles along the way, you can list the skills needed for the job—just like the prerequisites for college classes. This technique is especially useful if you're still trying to figure out what you want to do; talking to people who actually work in the field gives you a much clearer picture.

Don't be nervous about asking people about their jobs; it's actually the easiest thing in the world. Most people like talking about themselves; most people also like flattery. When you ask someone about their job, they get to talk about themselves. When you ask for their input as you think about your career, you're saying, "I respect and value your opinion."

When planning your career, you can map out the major requirements for each job as well as what you'll learn from each job. You might also just identify stages along the way and not a specific job title. Note that a general manager of a theater wouldn't necessarily have done acting and lighting and set design and accounting and ticket sales and marketing. You don't need to have worked in every role of the team, as long as you have sufficient knowledge of the field to understand the issues.

Not all skills need to be learned on the job. Leadership, public speaking, writing, negotiating, and even technical skills, where, again, "technical" can mean anything from using manufacturing tools to

The Career Toolkit

learning how to create a budget, can be learned through classes, reading, practice, and other techniques.

So, when we take Gretzky's advice about where the puck will be, and consider what the requirements are for a job we want in the future, we can start to map out the path to where we want to go and what skills we'll need to get there. A career plan can be defined by the following stages.

Short-Term Plan (1–2 years out)

These are your short-term goals. From a job perspective, it might be a specific project or role that you want. From a skills standpoint, it should be fairly clear what those skills are and how to achieve them, be it through work experience, books, courses, coaching, or other methods.

You might decide, for example, that you want to become better at public speaking. To do that, you might take a public-speaking class, read a book containing great speeches, or talk to your manager about having more opportunities to present.

Intermediate-Term Plan (3–5 years out)

This plan usually includes a specific role and an understanding of what skills and experience are needed for that role.

It may not be as concrete as your short-term plan. While your short-term plan may include "Take a class on public speaking," the intermediate plan may not be so specific. That is okay, since you've targeted working on that later, in years three and four. You might put "learn the new accounting system next year" in your short-term plan, while joining the new project team to migrate to the new accounting system as listed in year three of your plan only requires mentioning to your boss today that you'd like to be on the project in the future.

How you achieve your intermediate-term goals is a little fuzzier than with the short-term plan, but what you want should be quite clear.

Long-Term Plan (7–12 years out)

This is where you're headed. It might be a specific job title or more generally a role or set of responsibilities, such as leading a team of thirty people, having the authority to hire and fire, being responsible for a business's P&L (profit and loss statement), or leading partnership deals.

Even if you don't have a specific title in mind, you should have a sense of the skills and experience needed at your desired level. These are the skills you'll feed back into your intermediate-term plan so you can develop them in time to reach this goal.

Vision (15–20 years out)

This part of the plan is more of a guiding star. It's likely to be a title, such as, "I want to be the VP of sales by the time I'm forty-five," although it doesn't have to be. If you can, define the skills and experience needed, but recognize that the role is far enough away that you may not be able to create a complete list. It doesn't matter; this vision is just there to guide you. It helps direct your long-term plan.

As you journey farther along your career path, this goal may shift to "retire," or you may have achieved the title, and then it becomes more about the level of accomplishment. This goal will be the most fluid. At twenty-three, you may set your sights on a goal twenty years out, but ten years later, that goal may change. That is perfectly normal.

The above is just one possible structure. If you do six-month reviews, then perhaps the short-term plan should be a six-month plan. Maybe you prefer three-, seven-, and nine-year plans. Define whatever works for you.

There are two things to remember when creating a career plan. First, the farther out you go, the less detailed the plan. When doing your plan, start with the vision, and cascade back the steps along the way from long term to short term. If you want to be the VP of sales by forty-five, then in ten years (long-term plan), you should be leading a region with some direct reports or closing a certain amount of business or possessing a track record of bringing in two large clients a year. You'll probably need to show not only that you have a solid sales record but also that you can develop a new territory; so then in your intermediate-term plan, you can set "open new territory" as a goal. The requirements for each plan farther out become the development targets for the stage before.

Second, while the above plan is primarily about career goals, don't forget about personal goals. If you're trying to make tenure at a university, there's a very clear clock; if your seventh year is when the decision gets made, then planning on having two kids back to back in years six and seven may be asking too much of yourself (or your spouse). I'm not saying you can't do it, just that you need to account for your personal goals and needs as well.

This can all seem overwhelming, especially if you don't yet have answers. That's fine. Simply thinking about these questions is a good start. Dwight D. Eisenhower famously said, "Plans are worthless, but planning is everything." Don't worry if you don't have a clear plan. Trying to plan is, at times, more important than having one.

DEPTH VS. BREADTH

One common question when making a career plan is regarding depth versus breadth: How much do you need to focus on becoming a deep expert versus developing a wide range of skills?

The answer, as we often see, is: It depends. Einstein was a genius whose abilities far surpassed those of his peers. He didn't have to be a good manager or networker or even be in the field; he began his career as a patent clerk, not a researcher. He was a genius who could do things others couldn't.

A research professor is similar. The primary factor in hiring a research professor is the quality of research. Being a stronger researcher—a deeper expert in a field—is the number-one factor to career success. Even so, in

A PhD Is Not Enough! A Guide to Survival in Science,[4] Peter J. Feibelman notes that having management, networking, public speaking, and other skills significantly helps improve your prospects of success.

Ultimately, it comes down to economics. There was only one Einstein, so he was paid a premium. On the other hand, if you're an accountant, so is everyone else who was in your accounting class—plus all the other accountants who graduated from other schools around the same time as you. Are you really the best? Even if you are, is that something an employer can easily determine during an interview? We can listen to two violinists and know who is better within a matter of minutes; I don't know how to easily compare two accountants in a short time. During an interview, we can distinguish a significantly better one from a much worse one. But how do we recognize in the interview process that one candidate is only 8 percent better than another? It's not likely that such a subtle difference will come across. But your networking will get you more opportunities; your ability to explain how to manage a team will stand out; your knowledge of the sales process will uniquely impress the director of sales, who might be part of the interview process. In these cases where there is a large supply of candidates, and differentiation is harder during the interview process, breadth can help make you stand out against candidates with similar technical competencies.

The exception is if you're known to be an expert in your field. Perhaps you're a leading expert in social media marketing. In that case, you had better know everything you can about the field, because if you're only mediocre, no one will hire you as an expert. Likewise, if you're the leading lawyer specializing in musical copyright infringement, a very small field, then it's less likely you need to be great at the other skills, because people will seek you out as the domain expert.

---

4. If you have a PhD, whether you want to work in academia or industry, this book is a must-read.

Breadth also becomes more critical in more senior roles. The CTO is not the best programmer, and the VP of sales is not necessarily the best salesperson. Top rungs of the ladder require being sufficiently good in the functional disciplines of the role and then having other skills as a force multiplier to make you more effective when leading and managing. It goes back to maximizing the area of the rectangle and being well rounded, described in the section "Why This Matters."

Refining Your Career Plan

Your career plan is not a static plan you create and stick to. It's often fuzzy at best and requires regular input and revisions.

WHO SHOULD HELP?

You do not have to take this on alone. Your life is full of people who are there to help you. In your company, you have your manager, other people more senior to you, HR, and even your peers. Let's consider each.

A manager, in my opinion, has a responsibility to develop the people who work for him. Not all managers agree, and even those who do can get distracted, or worse, just aren't good at it. Your manager should be giving you advice and helping you grow. Whether at formal reviews or just informally with feedback and support, your manager should be aware of your growth goals. If he's not, make sure you speak to him and make him aware.

More senior managers, ideally, should also be supporting you. Someone running a 200-person department won't be able to take a personal interest in each and every employee under her, but someone managing three team leads with four people each should have some general idea of not just who all fifteen people are, but also their strengths, weaknesses, and goals. Even more senior people outside your department who get to know you can be resources.

Career Plan

HR should also help you. I use, "should" because the reality is that many don't. With the gutting of HR budgets, additional requirements of HR, more rapid employee turnover, the shift toward ultracompetitive hiring, and the lack of investment in people, many companies have de-emphasized such support.

Even your peers can be helpful. The goal here is to get input, and they may have perspectives different from yours.

Outside the company, you have friends, family, and mentors. They may also have advice. Your spouse should definitely have some input on your career, since it affects him or her. Other family members may as well (what parent or guardian doesn't like to give advice?), but they are less directly impacted by it. College alumni databases often have people who flag themselves as available mentors.[5]

Finally, you can use third-party resources. Books like the one you're reading can provide guidance. Also consider business articles, industry publications, and podcasts. Someone interested in the travel industry in 2001 would have been wise to look at the rise of the World Wide Web and the implications it would have for travel agencies. Time and again, we've seen industries disrupted by change, whether that means technological improvements or globalization with its global sourcing. When creating your career plan, remember to consider how things will look ten, twenty, even thirty years down the line. You probably won't get it right—almost no one does—but it might help you prepare for a few changes coming down the road in your industry.

When you do talk to people, you can ask questions such as:

- What do you like or not like about your job?
- What does it take to be successful in your job?

---

[5]. I'm listed as a mentor in the MIT alumni network. I get a request maybe once every three to four years, which is typical for most alumni mentors. They are a very underutilized resource.

- What do you wish you knew when you were starting out?
- How do you think the industry will be different in X years?
- What makes someone not just good but exceptional at this job?

Selecting a Mentor

Many companies have advisory boards composed of industry experts, experienced executives, and thought leaders. Individually, most of us would do well with our own advisory boards, or more commonly, with our mentors.

There are no hard-and-fast rules to having a mentor. Most people have one or two. More than three or four, and you're probably spreading your own time and efforts too thin. You can formally ask someone to be your mentor, or it can just be a person you talk to. You can meet with a mentor regularly or just reach out when you need help. What matters is that the relationship works for you and your mentor—it should be a two-way street.

You want a mentor who can help you. That typically means someone with more experience than you have in a given area. While age often correlates with experience, it isn't always the case. It should be someone you respect and trust. Importantly, you two need to be able to communicate well and have similar enough values and approaches that the advice can work for you. If you're a young transactional lawyer who is not drawn to litigation but enjoys exploring the finer points of legal contract negotiations, a mentor whose approach is to go to court at the drop of a hat may not be a good fit. Your mentor may or may not be in the same field, but he or she should definitely exhibit the qualities and values you admire and hope to develop in yourself.

Ideally, you'll have mentors who provide different types of guidance. One should probably be an expert in your industry, another an expert in your functional area. The others may have qualities you admire, such as leadership or networking, or simply fill in the gaps that you don't get from your other mentors. (Note: You don't have to have all these mentors concurrently; your mentors will change over time with your development needs.)

You can keep your mentor as long as you need. Some relationships span lifetimes, others perhaps just a few years. If you do have a formal relationship with a mentor, don't just disappear one day. If it's time to move on, thank your mentor for all the time he's provided, and explain why you're moving on. Doing that keeps the door open, should you need to come back.

Because it's a two-way street, understand why your mentor is doing this. Often, mentors are people who like to help others. Whether it's because they had a great mentor themselves or because they simply felt the desire to help others, they get enjoyment from helping you. Keep them apprised of how you're doing and be sure to thank them, and let them know how they have been helpful. It's unfortunate that most of us never thank teachers or mentors who have impacted our lives.

You would do well to remember that they are giving you their valuable time, so don't waste it by ignoring their advice. This doesn't mean you have to act upon every suggestion your mentor makes, but it does mean you need to make a sincere effort to improve yourself using your mentor's advice. If you find that you routinely don't want to follow the advice offered to you, it's a sign that you shouldn't be mentored by that person.

Many mentors like helping younger people, because it helps them feel younger or more connected to newer ideas. Consider the classic example of a college student being mentored by a professor who

The Career Toolkit

> is in his sixties. The professor probably hasn't kept up with the latest trends in social media, which apps are popular, and how people use them. During your discussions, he'll learn from you which apps students are using and why. It will keep him informed and feeling connected. Don't simply think about what's in it for you; respect and engage with your mentors on topics important to them as well.

NO ONE IS MORE COMMITTED TO YOUR CAREER THAN YOU

The people helping you along the way will offer lots of advice. They do it because they care about you. Even though they are trying to help you, it doesn't mean that you should always listen to them.

Early in my career, we hired a junior developer right out of school. We made her the build engineer. It was a necessary role but not a glamorous or challenging one. Most of us have to start at the bottom.

After six months, I told the director of engineering we needed to shift her to a new role so she wouldn't stagnate. I said that she could still own the process, but we could also rotate in some other people for some of the work. It would be good for the other engineers to be familiar with the build process, and it would be good for her to start developing other skills. We had that same conversation multiple times over a year, but he never moved her. She got stuck in that role for a few years. When she finally got a job at another company, it was still as a build engineer, because that's the only experience she had. It set her career back years.[6] The director of engineering wasn't actively trying to hurt her career; he just never got around to helping her.

Patterns like this abound. Fresh out of college, a man joins a large consulting company. They tell him, "We're going to assign you to an

---

6. There's nothing wrong with being a build engineer, but she wanted to become a Java developer, and at that point in history, Java developer roles were, compared to build engineer roles, better in terms of pay, responsibility, and opportunity.

38

Career Plan

energy project." He's young, naive, and excited, so he works on the project for eighteen months. When he's done and ready for his next project, all that are available are other energy projects, so he dutifully does another energy project for the next twelve months. He realizes that he really wants to do health care, not energy, and he asks for one of those projects, but then a very senior person in the company calls him and pleads with him to do one more energy project. It's a big, important client, they need experienced people, and he's got the right background. The senior person promises his next project will be in whatever field he wants, so he spends another eighteen months in energy.

If he's lucky, the senior person will keep his word, and the young man will shift into another field. But people aren't always lucky. The senior person may have left the company by then, and the next boss might not care about previous promises, even if the young man was smart enough to have an email that recorded the promise and not just his own memory of a conversation. Maybe the company will have layoffs, and he'll be hit. Maybe he needs to move to another city for personal reasons, which requires changing companies. Whatever the reason, when he's looking for a new job, what does his experience show? A background in the energy industry, not health care.

I knew one student who went into consulting and wound up being assigned to energy. Why? Because she had done an internship at Refinery29. It certainly sounds appropriate, except that Refinery29 is a women-oriented media and lifestyle company. Whoever was responsible for the incoming class of college hires that year didn't know that it was a media company and made what seemed like a reasonable, albeit wrong, assumption.

In all these cases, the managers were not ill-intentioned, but the employees wound up following paths they didn't want.

It's not just managers. I once hired a system administrator who was very excited about joining the company. The day after he signed, the recruiter called back and said that the candidate felt horrible, but he was going to have to withdraw. The candidate's son had been born just a few weeks earlier, and his wife, knowing what a workaholic he was and the demands of a dot-com startup, didn't want him taking a job at one.

That was a reasonable ask, but consider this hypothetical situation: You have a choice of two jobs. One pays 15 percent more but requires an extra hour of commuting time each day, and you'll be miserable at the job. The job that doesn't pay as well is closer and would have you excited to go to work every day. The question becomes, how important is that extra 15 percent?

There's no right answer. Only you know how much happier you'd be at one versus the other. You're the one commuting every day, but maybe your spouse is home alone with the kids for that extra hour each day. There's no question that your spouse means well, as do you, but you may each evaluate the situation differently and may each see a different choice as the best option.

I'm not saying that your spouse is wrong or that you must listen to your spouse (or parents or friends or boss); I'm simply saying that they will have a different, albeit well-meaning, perspective. Ultimately, it's your career.[7]

Startup or Large Corporation?

This is a common question that I get from students and even mid-career people. When deciding between two such extremes and the degrees on the spectrum between them, including spinouts, smaller companies, and more, it's important to understand some of the

---

7. It's also your marriage, which lasts longer than a job or even a career. Balance appropriately.

implicit risks and opportunities that come with working at startups and at more established corporations.[8]

Big corporations have more resources, while with startups you get more exposure to people and decision-making. Larger, established corporations can easily spend $20,000 sending a team to a conference, and a "lowly" junior manager may have the authority to approve it. At a smaller company, such an expenditure would be significant and may require executive approval, since resources are often tight.

At a company of twenty thousand people, you may never personally be in the same room as the CEO, or even the same city. The CEO certainly can't have just anyone walk into his office. Startups, on the other hand, pride themselves on open-door policies, usually encouraged by the lack of any doors or even office walls. You can walk over to the CEO's desk and ask her about the latest plans.

These differences are generally well understood. More subtle are the differences in how you might advance your career in each case. In large corporations, HR departments typically work to ensure standard levels of seniority, with corresponding responsibility and pay across the organization. This is partly because, when managing thousands of people, you need such organizational structures, and partly because it helps to prevent risks. For example, if people with similar roles have different levels of compensation or responsibility, even if unintentionally, it opens the company to the risk of lawsuits. A startup may not have an HR department, and even if it does, early on, HR tends to be much more focused on hiring than structural organization.

The implications of these differences will provide particular opportunities. In a large, structured organization, there is often more

---

8. I'm picking two specific cases, but considering differences among companies this way can apply to large or small companies, or established enterprises and young startups.

support for a formal career path. There are a number of more senior roles, and over time those positions will become available. The company itself will have training, either internally or externally, and can work with you to create a career path. The opportunities before you will be clearer. You can see ahead of time the opportunities with different departments and projects and then create a career plan that will expose you to areas of interest as you grow. Some large organizations even have rotation programs.

In an early-stage startup, there's no HR, no support, no training. There's no promise of more senior roles being available, and your job title may not really mean much. Everything is very fluid; the projects and opportunities, and even the very structure of the company, will be changing rapidly. Typically, there will be little or no support for creating a long-term career plan at the company.

On the other hand, there are few, if any, fences. The company will be understaffed across all departments, and getting involved in something is just a matter of walking twenty feet and talking to the right person. If it's a company that's growing, you have the opportunity to grow your career along with it by simply taking on more responsibility as new corporate needs arise and outpace hiring.

My own career developed that way. I would identify problems no one was addressing and say, "I'll do them." Or in some cases, I simply did it and didn't tell anyone until after it was done. After I did it once, it became part of my job, and just like that, my responsibilities (and experience) grew.

Neither way is better. Some people prefer more structured environments with formal paths, and others do better in more amorphous, changing environments. What is important is that you understand which is better for you and include it in your planning.

WHEN TO ADJUST YOUR PLAN

No sailor ever charted a course and then sat back until he arrived. Every voyage needs course corrections along the way, and your career is no different.

Whatever you have planned, things will work out differently. The job wasn't what you expected, or you couldn't get the job you wanted at that point. Recessions come along like a tornado and throw everything into disarray. Or things could turn out better; you might get an unexpected opportunity or develop faster than you planned. You also might change your mind about your interests. Such changes are especially common earlier in your career.

Revisions will help you make both short- and long-term corrections. They'll take into account the realities of what was actually achieved versus what was planned, as well as external changes in the company, industry, your own life, and the economy as a whole. While there's no wrong time to revisit your plan, there are definitely some right times.

At Annual Reviews

You should be reviewing and revising your plan on a regular basis. A good time to do so is to coordinate it with an annual review. Some companies do their reviews semiannually (twice a year) or quarterly. Annual reviews not only help ensure regularity, they're a logical time to do it. There are three parts to your review: planning what to ask for prior to your review, discussing your needs with your manager during the review, and revising your plans post-review.

The annual review itself shouldn't be a one-way street. You can also use it as a time to request new opportunities. It may be asking for a raise or promotion. It can also include asking for training, customer interaction, more exposure to other departments, assignment to a specific project team, or whatever else makes sense in your plan. Prior to your review, look at your plan, and determine how you want to develop over

The Career Toolkit

the coming period. During your review, make sure to voice your desired goals.

As we'll see in Chapter 9, Negotiation, the best way to ask for what you want is to align it to the other party's needs. So, when asking, be sure to explain how such training or exposure will help benefit the company in the long run.

Post-review, you'll have gotten feedback. You may have identified areas of improvement or discovered new areas of interest. You may also have made more progress toward your goals than you realized. (We can't always be objective in our self-reflection.) Take that feedback, and use it to readjust your plan as appropriate.

At Least Once a Year

Even if your company doesn't do an annual review (or if you're a freelancer), feel free to do your own self-assessment and career revision. You can certainly ask your boss for an assessment, even if not part of an official HR program. This also holds true if there's an annual review but you'd like feedback semiannually.

If you don't have a boss, consider asking clients or mentors or anyone else who has seen you over an extended period of time for input. Even if you have zero external input, you should be reviewing your plan at least once a year.

Changing Jobs or Changing Projects

Another logical time is when changing jobs. Your short-term plan may be very different in one job versus another.

Consider the following example. Running a manufacturing floor at a high-growth company with a single product would afford opportunities to gain experience hiring and growing a team as well as scaling up the manufacturing floor. On the other hand, running a manufacturing floor at a boutique custom manufacturing company may allow you more direct

Career Plan

exposure to clients as you work to understand their specific manufacturing needs, but you won't do much in the way of hiring or scaling. Given the job you take, you may want to shift which skills you're focusing on over the next few years.

If you're at a large company, you may keep the same job but shift from one project to another over the years. It's effectively a job change, since the key factor is less about who signs your paycheck and more about specific responsibilities and opportunities.

When New Opportunities Come Along

Finally, make sure you go back to your plan anytime a new opportunity comes along. If someone approaches you for a job or even a promotion, a transfer, or simply a different project team, use your career plan to evaluate the opportunity. If you haven't looked at your plan in a while, first take a moment to update it and think about what you want going forward.

A. B. See.

No matter what path you take, unexpected opportunities and risks will arise. It's important to make the most of them.

No matter how much you love your job, love your co-workers, and love your life, the world is not static. Kodak, GE, Blockbuster, Schwinn, and other companies that once dominated their industries either went out of business completely or are shadows of their former selves. In today's world, it can happen suddenly—consider Enron, Lehman Brothers, or Pets.com. Your job could be gone tomorrow due to a macroeconomic change, a bad corporate strategy decision, or financial malfeasance by someone at the company. Or it could be simply because someone higher up is leaving, and your department is getting reorganized. Even when things go well for the company, they may not go well for you. A company getting acquired

The Career Toolkit

may be a win from the company's perspective, but for those getting laid off because they're now redundant, it's by no means a victory.

In the cinematic classic *Glengarry, Glen Ross*, adapted from the Pulitzer Prize-winning play by David Mamet, corporate big shot Blake, played by Alec Baldwin, gives the famous speech about sales: "ABC. A, always. B, be. C, closing. Always be closing. ALWAYS BE CLOSING." The essence of sales is to always be selling and getting the customer to sign.

I'm going to leave you with a far less iconic mantra: *A. B. See.* A, always. B, be. See, seeing what opportunities are out there. Always be seeing what opportunities are out there.

While this is a terrible strategy for your marriage, where you make a lifelong commitment, your company made no such guarantee. Gone are the days of a thirty-year career at one company. Loyalty is a two-way street; be just as loyal to your company as it is to you.

Even when your company is sincere when telling you that it values you and wants to keep you, things may be outside its control. The company can't control the economy or a hostile takeover or any number of other things that may happen. When something does happen to your job, in some cases, you can still seek other opportunities inside the company. But that is not always an option, and you need to be prepared for such outside events that can impact your job.

Focus on your current job and building a career at your current company. It's often better to stay at a company than to jump around, but you can't completely rely on your company to always be there for you. Soldiers in the nineteenth century were told, "Keep your powder dry." In other words, be ready, because you never knew when the battle might begin. In today's world, the advice is to keep your networks warm, because you never know when you'll need a new job.

Summary and Next Steps

Every journey should have a plan. This holds true for your career as well. The questions and resources listed in this chapter can help you create one. While it doesn't guarantee that you'll get to where you want to go, it certainly increases the odds.

Start by writing down your answers to some of the questions posed in this chapter—somewhere you can find them again, such as a journal or a file in the cloud. You don't need to answer each question formally, but each answer provides some direction for your career.

If you have a clear goal, work backward to develop your short-, intermediate-, and long-term plans. If you don't have a clear goal, then work forward by creating some career-path trees. Don't be afraid to want flexibility early on or to change your mind completely about your goals.

Talk with others to get their input and ideas; their answers might impact your own thinking. As an alumnus, your college may have webinars or other career programs to continue to help you.

Consider using an assessment tool. Your HR department may have some, or you can find links to some free assessments on the book's website.

When your next review comes up, review your career plan ahead of time, discuss your goals during the review, and then revise your plan afterward. If you don't have a regular review, ask your manager for one. As a freelancer, create your own review panel of customers, mentors, or others you've worked with.

Think about finding a mentor. You probably already know someone who would be good. If not, consider looking through your school's alumni database or using online mentor services that can help you find one.

Remember that this is not a one-time exercise. Continually revisit and revise your career plan, and don't be afraid to completely tear up

The Career Toolkit

your plan and start anew. Your preferences will change significantly, especially in your twenties and thirties. It's okay to decide you want to go in a new direction, but when you do, don't go in blind. Create a new plan, because, as Professor Rosenhouse said, "Always have a plan. Even a bad plan is better than no plan at all."

Chapter Two

Working Effectively

> "Great things are done by a series of small things brought together."
>
> —Vincent van Gogh

Congratulations! You've landed your dream job. Now what? Most people work hard, try to do a good job, and simply hope for a promotion. While not wrong, such a standard approach results in missed opportunities to accelerate your skills and your career.

The question you should be asking yourself (and others) every day is: "What can I do to be more successful in this role?" While the question itself is open-ended, no matter your job, the following techniques will help you become more valuable to your team, your manager, and your company, thereby enabling you to become more successful and accelerate your career advancement.

Learning About the Job

You may be good at what you do, but there is far more to know about your job than simply how to do it.

LEARN YOUR ROLE

Learn everything you can about your role, inside and out. First, acquire technical competence. In other words, learn the functional skills your job requires.

Then, understand the purpose of your role. Why does it exist? It might seem trivial—to sell products or to tally invoices—but ask that question on a deeper level. Why are you needed at all? How important is what you do to the company's core function? Are there similar teams (in other departments or even other companies)? If so, how are they the same or different? Why are you organized as you are? In some companies, IT is under the CFO, while in others under the COO or CEO. Some organizations have marketing under the vice president of sales, but in other companies they're peer departments, both reporting directly to the CEO. Why did your company choose its current operating structure? What are the benefits and trade-offs it offers?

How much value do you create? That's easy for those in sales (revenue); for other roles, not so much. The farther you are from a customer (for example, in finance or manufacturing), the harder it is to measure your direct value. You don't need an actual amount to the penny, but if you understand your value, then you can start to understand how to be more valuable.

Paleontologists can reconstruct dinosaurs and tell whether they were carnivores or herbivores by looking at their bone structures. Looking at the structure of your organization can give you insight as well. For example, say your company has a ratio of one account representative for every five customers—so it must need to provide a lot of customer support. Why is that? If you're not sure where to start, look at other companies. How does your corporate structure differ from theirs? They'll all have the same basic areas—marketing, finance, sales, IT, and others—but how big those departments are and how they are organized will likely vary quite a bit.

The Core Role of a Company

It's helpful to understand the core functionality of a business. That may seem obvious—and it is in most cases—but still, many people miss it. The core business is the part of the company that drives the revenue. Everything else is support.

At a financial trading firm, the core business is trading. The valuable people are the traders. Everyone else supports them. Investor relations brings in money to trade, accounting makes sure the numbers add up, the IT department makes sure the systems are running, and the cleaning staff keeps the office clean, but it's the traders who generate the revenue. The other departments, generally, can only hurt revenue, not increase it. If the cleaning staff doesn't take out the trash, and the office smells, the traders get distracted and don't perform as well. If the accountants don't tally the numbers correctly, it costs the company time and money. IT might help a bit by providing faster systems, but the bulk of the value comes from the traders themselves. Contrast this with algorithmic trading, where the bulk of the value comes from the tech department. In such companies, IT writes code that selects the trades, while in non-algorithmic firms, the traders select trades, and the code simply executes them.

At an accounting firm, the accountants are the core function, since their accounting services provide the revenue. Marketing, IT, legal, and the other departments all support the company but don't generate revenue. At most non-accounting firms, accounting is a support function.

Each company has generally one, sometimes two core functions.[9] Nike and Coca-Cola are marketing-oriented companies. Yes, they

---

9. A case of two core functions might be a company that designs and manufactures high-tech wind turbines; the engineers who design it are key, since the engineering differentiates the turbines, and the employees in manufacturing make the actual product being sold, which is not mass produced. The other departments are support.

have significant manufacturing and distribution challenges, but at their core, it's about marketing. They focus on finding market opportunities and convincing customers to buy product based on their product branding. R&D, HR, finance, and more all support that core competency.

This is important because you need to understand the opportunities and limitations and where you sit. At the hedge fund, you can wind up leading marketing, but the marketing team is small and secondary; a hedge fund VP of marketing will never become the CEO, but the CMO at Coca-Cola could.[10] At Coca-Cola, you can lead logistics, and while it may not be the primary function, that company is probably one of the most complex logistics organizations in the world. "Secondary" doesn't mean "bad" or "less desirable."

I'm not saying you have to work in the core function. You can have a successful career and great growth opportunities at times when working in a non-core function. However, it is important that you recognize where you are and whether that's the right role for this stage of your career.

THE BLIND MEN AND THE ELEPHANT

It helps to look at things from multiple perspectives. An old Indian parable tells of a group of blind men who come across an elephant. The first, touching its ear, describes it as soft and flat. The second, grabbing the tail, says it's thin, long, and hairy. The third, feeling its leg, describes it as wide, firm, and rough; the three begin to argue about who is right. Each is correct from their own perspective, but none of them can see the complete picture.

I can't tell you how many people I've met who don't understand what the people sitting thirty feet away from them do. Once, in a company

---

10. Becoming the CEO isn't necessarily the right goal for most people; the role is being used here to illustrate a point.

Working Effectively

of only fifteen people, I asked each person what the company did. I got very different answers across the departments—everyone only saw their piece of the elephant.

Most engineers I know can't explain how marketing works beyond "They do our website and run ad campaigns." While it's true that they are responsible for the website and advertising, they also commonly generate leads, promote the brand, create marketing partnerships, oversee PR, define market segments, perform customer research, and do so much more.

Why are they promoting this product more than that one? Perhaps the market changed, or a new competitor entered. Why is this product sold through online ads, but those products are sold through channel sales? It may have to do with how the customer buys or deploys the product.

I picked marketing for this example, but it could be any department. You don't need to be deeply knowledgeable about every function in your company, but you should have a general idea about what those departments do. In theory, leadership coordinates across the departments to make the company operate in unison. In reality, it's a complex and difficult task that is imperfect at best. Everything you can do to help them coordinate—that is, to help your team operate in a manner more in line with the larger goals of the company and the challenges and limitations of other teams—helps the company and makes you stand out as a better employee.

On my teams, I always emphasize how important cross-department knowledge-sharing is. In some cases, at my department's monthly meeting, I'll bring in an executive from another team to share with my own what her department is focused on and why.

Another common approach is a "lunch and learn." Having a weekly or monthly lunch where a team presents what it's doing to anyone else in the company who is interested in learning helps to break people out of the department bubble and start to see the rest of the elephant.

The Career Toolkit

If your team doesn't do this, ask HR or start it yourself. All you need are a conference room and people willing to present what they do. If the company can't afford to sponsor lunch, just have folks bring their own to the meeting.

LEARN YOUR ECOSYSTEM

Just as you learned about different groups inside your company, you should learn about the different entities outside your company. It begins with your customers. Your company wouldn't exist without them.

You don't have to personally know your customers; you may not be in a role to personally meet any. It does mean that you should understand who your customers are. What are their characteristics? Why do they buy your product? What does it do for them? Why do they choose your product over your competitor's product? What motivates them? Is it to make more money? Save money? Fix a problem? Prevent a problem? Could you recognize a potential customer? What would disqualify someone as a customer?

Consider your suppliers and partners. Who are they? Why are they working with you? Why did your company pick them and not an alternative option? While customers, suppliers, and partners are not directly part of a company, they are integral to its success. You learn more about your company by understanding its larger ecosystem—the industry and the other organizations within it.

Your industry will change over time. Technology will disrupt your business in part or in whole. A policy (legal) or regulatory change can have a huge impact. Each and every change is both a risk and an opportunity. Staying on top of changes helps you lead change and brings value to your company.

Change impacts not only your industry but also related industries that your company works with. It can be pretty broad. For example, McDonald's is not just fast food and restaurants but also farming, ranching, electronic payments, home food delivery, social media, and much more. Changes in the farming industry impact supply; food delivery by rideshare services will impact how the company interacts with customers.

Consider not just your industry but also your functional area. You may work at McDonald's, but your role is very different if you're a cashier, accountant, or marketer. Cashiers may get replaced by automation; accounting can be done by lower-cost offshore teams, and radio marketing budgets were gutted by TV, TV by the web, and the web by social media. When learning about your industry, track both the industry your company is in, based on the product or service, and also the functional "industry" your job is in. Both will change over time.

The unemployment line is filled with people who didn't see change coming and thought their job was going to be in demand for decades to come. The executive suite is populated by people who saw the change coming and got ahead of it, leading their companies to capitalize on new opportunities. If you're not watching the road, it's much harder to stay on it.

Meta-Work

Learning will make you more effective, but ultimately you need to execute. This will vary greatly based on the nature of your role, but there are some fundamental techniques that will apply to all situations. These will help you be a better team member and deliver more.

MANAGE YOUR MANAGER

Knowing how to manage your manager is extremely powerful but is often overlooked. There are two parts to doing this effectively.

First, understand what would make your manager successful. Most work in corporations is done by teams. Even if you're the sole person

The Career Toolkit

working on something, that something is part of something larger. Whether it's your manager or a team leader, someone is ultimately responsible for it, and his career will benefit or suffer based on the success of the project. How can you help that person be more successful? Understand his goals: What makes him successful in his job? What's his career path?

Why should you care? Because when he gets promoted, he will be rewarded with more work and more responsibility. A smart manager will know that you helped him be successful. Don't help in secret; make sure your manager is aware of how much you contributed to his success. He'll be wise enough to bring you along to the next project and will know to keep you happy with promotions so he can continue to rely on you. It's not uncommon for a senior manager to move to a different company and bring top performers with him.

That may sound Machiavellian, but if you're a key contributor on a team, any manager worth his salt will want to reward you for it and keep you around. That's not Machiavellian, that's business. It's no different from the reason you keep going back to the restaurant you like because of its good food and service.

Second, learn how to work with your boss. Understand her style. Does your boss prefer long discussions or brief emails? Does she like to get notified immediately of an issue, or does she have strong boundaries about not being contacted outside of work? Does she like to stick to a meeting agenda or let the discussion go where it may?

Then there are process questions. Does she prefer to get input from others when making a decision? If so, can you get that input for her before asking her to make the decision, making her job easier? Does she like to review pros and cons? If so, always bring her pros and cons when you're pitching an idea.

Everyone is different; recognizing those differences helps you communicate more effectively. I know my style and process, and when

I join a company or make a new hire, I am explicit with them about what I expect of my team and its members, how I lead, and how best to communicate with me. If there's ever a question, my team knows they can ask me. You can always ask your boss, "Do you prefer this or that?" Even if she's not sure how to articulate what she wants, you can intuit clues by seeing how she reacts to different approaches. You're not going to figure this out in a day, so keep your eyes open, and learn over time.

By working more effectively with your manager, you become a more effective part of the team. These techniques can be applied to more than just your manager; learning how best to interact with your teammates and others in the company also increases your effectiveness across your team. One question that Diane Lampert taught me to ask when I join a company is, "What can I do to make you more successful?" It's a friendly and supportive way to ask how best to work together.

BE PROACTIVE

Companies often say they want people who are proactive and take initiative, but what does that actually mean? It's not simply about taking action, but rather solving problems before they begin.

There's an expression in software that "a good programmer is a lazy programmer." The thinking is that a lazy person will find a way to automate as much of the task as possible to minimize the overall work; the ironic motivator is that laziness brings out the best effort. It's a variation on the famous "Work smarter, not harder."[11]

I describe myself as a lazy manager. I try to make as few decisions as possible. Every time I'm needed to make a decision, it means I was needed at that decision point, which means I could not have been doing something else at that moment. If there is any way I can empower

---

11. "I choose a lazy person to do a hard job. Because a lazy person will find an easy way to do it" is often misattributed to Bill Gates, but the closest origin to that phrase comes from Frank Gilbreth Sr., who pioneered time and motion study.

someone on my team or create a process to make the decision instead of me, I do. Then it's one less thing I have to do and more free time to do other things I can't delegate.

Tim Ferriss, author of *The 4-Hour Workweek*, discovered this for himself when he realized he was spending much of his time dealing with customer-service issues. He realized that below a certain dollar amount, he could empower his team to make decisions, and that freed him up to do other things.

Those are both examples from the managerial side, but it applies even if you're not managing. What can you do to anticipate and then solve problems or create opportunities for your team without being asked?

Being proactive isn't just about not waiting to be asked to do something. That's only step one. The next logical step is to create systems—processes, rules, empowered people—that can execute before you even become aware of it. Decisions get made, and problems get solved, before they start. Now you're solving problems with reduced effort and can use the freed-up time and energy to do more and become a bigger, and more valuable, contributor to your team.

Always remember that while you can delegate some of your authority, your responsibility is never diminished. If the system or empowered people get it wrong, it's still on you.

Navigating a Corporation

No matter how much you have worked to see the bigger picture and how well you execute, some things will always be outside your control. Most people outside the executive team don't have a good grasp of the big picture, and even then each executive is looking mostly at one part of the elephant. Things can come at you out of the blue and impact your career, for better or worse. You need to be prepared.

WATCH FOR SIGNALS

At one of my first companies, the co-founders, unbeknownst to me, had a falling-out with each other, something I've learned is surprisingly common. When my CTO called me into his office to ask me to join him as he departed to start a new company, he began by saying, "This may come as a surprise to you, or maybe not, but I'm leaving the company." It was a surprise to me, but it shouldn't have been.

During the previous months, I had noticed the senior team having a lot of meetings, more often than usual. The body language and facial expressions of people going into and out of the meetings had shown a little more stress than usual. I had noticed, but I had never really taken note. Those were very obvious signs that something was happening. It turned out that there was a falling-out within the management team, and the company split in two. Luckily for me, the outcome gave me opportunities (both groups wanted me). But not all signals are so obvious, and not all outcomes are so positive.

Signals can come in many forms. It may be a case of who is meeting with whom and when. This could be people around the office, or it could be people from another branch. If you notice a group of people in suits coming to the office, it could be a sign of a partnership, a large sale, a corporate acquisition, a lawsuit, or something else. Even if you don't talk to them and don't know where they are from, you might be able to see whom they are meeting with. Are they seeing folks in business development? Legal? Finance? Simply knowing whether it's the same people each time gives you some information.

When your company sends messages, either public press releases or internal announcements, what are they saying? Just as important, what *aren't* they saying? Why is this being said now? Most executives don't really step down to "spend time with their family." This is yet another reason to build relationships outside your department; others in the

The Career Toolkit

company may see or interpret their part of the elephant differently and can help you see the bigger picture.

I'm not suggesting that you live a life of corporate intrigue. This is a very small part of your job, less than 1 percent. Do remember, though, that chance favors the prepared, so pay attention to what is happening around you. If you're struggling with this, *The Ropes to Skip and the Ropes to Know*, by R. Richard Ritti and Steve Levy, is a great read.

CORPORATE POLITICS

Office politics permeates most corporations, but its workings remain opaque to many. Most people hate politics. I've met more than a few who have refused to play. I used to be one of those people until I lost a few battles, sometimes battles I didn't even know I was in. The higher up the ladder you go, the more others will want what you have.

Politics is like the ocean current; you can refuse to deal with it, but it is going to affect you just the same. You can choose to be passive but recognize that that is a conscious choice, and you will still be impacted by the political games in the office, simply with a limited voice of your own. Ignoring it won't make it go away.

In their fantastic book *Survival of the Savvy: High-Integrity Political Tactics for Career and Company Success*, Rick Brandon and Marty Seldman provide a great model for understanding the political spectrum, from apolitical to overly political people. Simplistic models view political people as Machiavellian, or apolitical people as inept, but these models fail to recognize important nuances in interpersonal communication and relationships. Instead, recognize that different people have different views about the value of ideas versus the value of relationships. They describe the political-styles spectrum as ranging from "power of ideas" (less political people) to "power of person" (more politically oriented people). The differences manifest themselves as follows:

Power of Ideas Style focuses on . . .	Power of Person Style focuses on . . .
Substance—values facts, logic, analysis	Position—values status from job title
Learning—looks for input and feedback	Image—values how he or she is perceived; focuses on reputation
Doing the right thing—puts team and company interests first; uses proper channels	Getting results—compromises, works the system, appreciates the art of the possible
Openness—values being transparent	Private agendas—believes knowledge is power, and knowledge sharing is more limited
Meritocracy—believes the ideas themselves matter most	Relationships—believes relationships are critical to success and may be more important than the best idea
Self-evidence—lets the results speak for themselves	Self-promotion—makes sure every success is noticed

TABLE 1. Political styles defined by Brandon and Seldman

Two people on opposite sides of the spectrum may evaluate something differently, based on both the content of the message and how it is presented and perceived. Likewise, they will undertake different actions, based on how they prefer to move forward with projects. People who have more of the power of person style may recognize that time is of the essence on a project and will undertake an action thinking it's better to ask forgiveness than permission when permission will take too long. In the same situation, a power of ideas person would rather follow the set procedure, even if it means the project will be late.

One side isn't necessarily more self-serving or inept than another, and neither approach necessarily means crossing ethical lines. Office politics is simply a tool. As with any tool, the tool itself is neutral. It is the employment of the tool toward an end, good or bad, that colors our view of its use.

Some people focus on their careers to the detriment of the team and company. They may backstab you for selfish reasons. Others may seemingly believe that what you see as backstabbing is actually something they feel is best for the company, just as the thief may simply be greedy or may be stealing bread to feed his hungry family. Living in the modern world requires some commonsense safety precautions against low-probability but highly negative risks, such as locking your door, not walking down a dark alley at night, or carrying something for self-defense. Working in the corporate world also requires some basic precautions and some planning to defend yourself against the occasional threat.

Many of the skills in this book will help you, especially for those on the less political side of the spectrum; but the skills do apply to people all along the spectrum. You'll start by managing your reputation (see "Crafting Your Image") and being recognized for your success so that you have a positive reputation inside the company, one that aligns with the corporate culture. In Chapter 7, Communication, we look at how best to communicate with different people. Those techniques can be applied in your communications with people on both sides of the political spectrum that's described above. In effect, look at the characteristics in Table 1, and communicate in a manner relating to those styles. Building a strong network inside the organization (see Chapter 8, Networking) will give you support during a conflict, political or otherwise. Having a mentor (see "Selecting a Mentor") who is senior in the organization can provide the counsel you may need. All of these techniques will help strengthen your standing without compromising any of your values.

I cannot possibly do justice to the subject matter as well as Brandon and Seldman do in their book, but I want to emphasize the importance of corporate politics. It exists, and it is not as black and white as thinking that the only people who engage in corporate politics are inherently self-serving. Rather, people on opposite ends of the spectrum have different visions of how to achieve their goals.[12]

Managing corporate politics is critical if you wish to move up the ladder. That doesn't necessarily mean you need to shift where you are on the spectrum. Most important is that you understand the different styles along the political spectrum: Recognize your own, and identify those of the people you work with. This means developing the tools to engage with people all along the spectrum. If corporate politics feels at all foreign to you, I highly recommend reading *Survival of the Savvy*.

Summary and Next Steps

While being effective at your tasks is of primary importance to your job, these additional techniques will help you become exceptionally effective in your role. Understand your ecosystem, including other departments, customers, partners, and suppliers. Learn how you fit into the larger picture, which part of the elephant you touch. One good way to start is to regularly read articles about your industry or have coffee or lunch with people from other departments. Consider reading a book

---

12. Just as in actual politics, people on different sides of an issue tend to agree on the goals. These could be, for example, economic prosperity or national security. But these same people disagree on prioritization, trade-offs, implementation, and more.

The Career Toolkit

or taking an online class in a business discipline other than your own. To help improve my knowledge of marketing, I took some online courses, had lunch regularly with friends from marketing to learn from them, sat in on some marketing meetings, and got involved in hiring people in marketing—all of which helped expose me to the field.

Learn the work style and goals of your manager and of other team members. Manage your manager, and become a valuable team member. A good manager will want to bring you up the ladder with him. Be proactive in your work; try to systematize what you do or find ways to empower others to make decisions on your behalf. This frees you up to do more, thereby helping you become more valuable.

Navigate the currents of your company by learning the signals that get sent out. Look for trends, opportunities, and risks. Your connections to people in other parts of the company will help expose you to signals they see but that you may not.

Build relationships inside and outside the company. Get to know people not only in other departments but also in other companies in your industry and among suppliers and customers. It's fine to have friends at competitors as well, as long as you both respect appropriate corporate confidentiality. The more people you interact with, the more parts of the elephant you will see.

Recognize that politics is part of office culture—a dislike of it or a refusal to engage in it doesn't make it go away. It simply reduces your ability to be effective. The higher you go, the more important it becomes, so consider reading up on it in books and articles. Find some training courses, or get a mentor who can help guide you.

Chapter Three
Interviewing

> "If opportunity doesn't knock,
> build a door."
>
> —Milton Berle

Finding opportunities and being an effective interviewee are critical to getting the jobs you want and advancing your career. Being an effective interviewer when you're part of a hiring team is an equally critical skill that most people don't even recognize, let alone try to develop. For a leader, hiring the right people is just as important as setting the right goals.

It's unfortunate how little training people get when the opportunity is all around them. Suppose you want to become a great public speaker, but you aren't able to watch a tape of yourself or watch any other public speakers. Instead, all you can do is give talks and never get feedback. How good could you become? Good public speakers have learned by watching themselves on tape. The same challenge applies to interviewing, although with interviewing you don't get to record your interviews.[13]

---

13. You could, however, record a mock interview with a friend or mentor.

The Career Toolkit

Watching other people interview can be a powerful way to improve your own interviewing skills.

One of the best things to happen to me in my career was being asked by my boss to interview two candidates for a software engineering role. I had zero training, other than having been a candidate myself. Far too many people have the same experience.

The first candidate was clearly more intelligent and technically stronger. The second candidate was not as smart, but he was much more personable. It was like night and day. I knew the first candidate was smarter and better at writing code, but I was drawn to the second candidate . . . . What to do? I realized what I needed to do was to understand why. It wasn't just about raw IQ; there had to be a more holistic evaluative model.

This chapter begins from the candidate's perspective. It walks through the essence of what you're trying to achieve during the interviewing process and what you need to convey as a candidate. We then switch to the hiring team's perspective and walk through how to define a role and qualify someone for it. Members of the hiring team should understand what the candidate is trying to be hired for; likewise, the candidate should know how the hiring team is thinking about the role. Whichever side you're currently on (and in the course of your career, you'll be on both sides, even if you never plan on becoming a manager), looking at it both ways will help you be more effective.

For the Candidate

A good salesperson knows that in order to get someone to buy, you need to understand the client's needs and then sell into those. You are selling yourself to the company. In order to be effective, it helps to understand the needs of your "buyer" (in this case, the hiring manager and HR).[14]

GETTING HIRED

Submit a résumé, get an interview, impress them, and get a job offer. Let's think about this process in reverse. You want an offer. To get the offer, you need to impress them; to impress them, you need to have them learn about you; to have them learn about you, they need to want to invest time to meet you; and to want to invest time in you, they need to know who you are. Each step of the process is designed to simply get you to the next step, until you get to the actual goal: a job offer. In reality, it's not quite so gated, but conceptually, that's roughly how it works.

The very first step is to get noticed, usually by submitting a résumé. The primary purpose of your résumé is to get you to the next step of the process. Given that there could be scores, even hundreds, of applicants, most résumés are skimmed for about ten to fifteen seconds on average. Usually the résumé is viewed before the cover letter—if the résumé isn't good, I'm not reading the cover letter. But you need to send a cover letter anyway, because if they like you, they may want to see what else you wrote, and it's another chance to stand out. Be specific by emphasizing how you'd be great for the role. You need the résumé to be thorough for later interviews, but you also need it to quickly convey enough information to get you past the first gate.

This is the reason your résumé should follow a fairly standard format. Every second spent trying to find information on your résumé, such as education and job titles, is a second less spent getting to know you.

---

14. Throughout this chapter, and the book, we use the term "HR" for human resources. "HR" is now sometimes called "people operations," "talent management," and other names. In some companies, it has also been divided into separate groups for hiring, training, benefits management, and more. To keep things simple, we use "HR" to refer to the organizational unit that helps with recruiting or with training and development.

The Career Toolkit

If you do break with convention, it should be because you really want to highlight something, and that something should be compelling enough to get you to the next stage. For this reason, bold or slightly larger font sizes are used for job titles and company names to draw the reviewer's eye to them. Consider also using bold within the résumé to emphasize a success you had; for example, "Led sales team to **150% YoY growth for 3 years**." Alternatively, use a summary section on your résumé that shows the key selling points.

This is why going through your network is often helpful. As we'll learn in Chapter 8, Networking, when you come in through a trusted channel, you often get moved right to the next stage.

Once you're interviewing, you have one job: To convince them that you're the best candidate for the role. That's all. Having good answers to their questions helps, as do dressing the part and being polite, but those aren't the goal, and many candidates lose sight of the goal. Convince them that you are the best choice. It's what you say, it's how you say it, it's how you act, it's what you've done, it's even the little pauses before you answer a question. It's anything and everything. But there's really only one question the hiring manager needs to answer: "Is this person the best candidate for the role?"

There are two parts to that question. First, you need to get the hiring team excited about you; this could be due to your knowledge and experience, energy and passion, diligence, or positive attitude. You need to sell them on your ability to do this job better than anyone else.

Second, remove as much as you can any misgivings they may have as to your fit. This is different from "Can you do X?" Rather, you're answering, "What may go wrong?" Your experience, answers to questions, and ability to think all help to eliminate the possibility of risk by addressing questions such as the following: "Will she be able to balance three simultaneous projects?" "Can he gain the trust of the team?" "Will she burn out traveling 50 percent of the time?" A genius who can't communicate

Interviewing

well may not be seen as a good hire despite being capable on paper. A good candidate sells strengths but then also addresses any concerns. These are often unspoken, so you need to read between the lines.

A quiet mentee of mine had been an analyst on Wall Street and was applying for a competitive VP role at his company. He asked me to help him with a mock interview. He was smart, and his ability to answer questions wasn't in doubt—certainly not to those who had worked with him for nearly two years. I told him that to prepare he needed to watch *Mad Men* and channel Don Draper. What was going to make him or break him in the interview wasn't a single question they were going to ask, but the underlying question: "Can this person lead projects and close business in the culture we work in?" Conveying the Don Draper traits of confidence, command, even a little cockiness (the opposite of who the otherwise humble candidate was) was necessary for him to get the job, because in that company's culture, those traits were valued. He brought out his Don Draper and got the job.

If you can sell them on you and remove their doubts, then you're 90 percent of the way there. The last 10 percent is something most candidates fail to do: differentiate themselves. I ask most candidates, "With all the candidates I have, why should I pick you for this role?"[15] About 95 percent of candidates respond with some combination of: "I'm smart, I work hard, and I learn fast." When I point out that other candidates have said the same thing and ask them to try again, most are unable to come up with anything more.

Those answers aren't wrong, but they don't help a candidate stand out. It's better to show, not tell. Candidates need to answer in a way that not only sounds good, but in a way that no one else can. "I'm a fast learner. When I joined a project at Harvard Business School, I had never taken a single econ class, but I asked the professors to help train me.

---

15. If you use this question, tone is important. Don't phrase it as a challenge, but rather, with a tone similar to, "Help me see how you stand out."

The Career Toolkit

Over the first two weeks, I read three finance books, and we did a tutorial session every day. At the end of two weeks, I was ready to build a trading platform, which is now used in many of the top business schools."

Many can say they're a fast learner, and they may all be right, but I'm the only person in the world who can tell that story. Every answer you give should convince them that you and only you can do what they need. Don't just say it—prove it.

Some interviewers dislike the "Why should I hire you?" question. Beyond the fact that it can often be said in an arrogant tone (even though it shouldn't be), they feel it's too general. They feel the better question is, "What are some past experiences relevant to this role?" The second is more direct, but I prefer the former because it's less direct. Some interviewers like intentionally general questions and prompts, such as, "Walk me through your career," because a job isn't like a test with clear questions but real life with open-ended problems. No matter how general the question, it always comes back to you, as the candidate, convincing them that you're the most qualified person for the role. Every answer you give needs to lead the interviewer in that direction.

As a candidate, you should never be surprised by an interview question. You may not know the specific questions ahead of time, but you'll know the types of questions. (See Interview Questions.) You also know your answers. You have past accomplishments you can discuss, failures you've overcome, things you've learned, difficult problems you've solved. As we'll see in Chapter 7, Communication, interviews are a form of public speaking, and you should treat them as such. Before giving a talk, you'll practice your speech, but not to the point that it's memorized word for word. Likewise, you should practice your answers to these types of questions, but not so much that your answers are mechanical. You can easily find interview questions online, and you can practice your answers at home, waiting for the subway or while

Interviewing

taking a shower. As you practice your answers, you'll gain confidence in giving answers and will come off better in an interview.

SHOW WHAT YOU CAN DO

The very best candidate I ever hired was a nineteen-year-old HR intern. During the interview, she answered the questions fairly well. Then she astounded me. She said, "I looked at your job requirements for a software developer. Here's a list of twenty candidates I found on LinkedIn who I would target for this role, and here's a sample outreach letter I would send them." In over two decades of hiring, I have never seen any other candidate take that much initiative.

It instantly answered three questions. Is she a hard worker? Absolutely! Will she take initiative? No question! Is she competent? While at that moment she hadn't yet brought in any new hires, neither had any other candidate for the job. She proved beyond a doubt that she understood what we were looking for and could send an appealing cold outreach. Other candidates might have been able to do so as well, but with her, there was no doubt.

Was it unusual? Yes. It definitely stood out. There's nothing to stop you from walking into an interview and saying, "Here's my ninety-day plan" or "This is my two-page marketing strategy" or "Here's a three-page summary of how I turned around the sales department at my previous company."

If you choose to do this, just think about the timing. Doing it in the first round helps you stand out. But you don't know much about the company, so it works best when you provide a detailed summary of something you've already done.[16] Alternatively, wait a round or two, after you've had the chance to ask questions and better understand the needs of the company. Then send over your plan for how you would address them. You'll be saying, in essence, "My plans aren't perfect (I've

---

16. Be careful to respect any confidentiality agreements with previous employers.

had limited exposure to the company during the interview process), but I'm one of the only candidates who has a plan, and that sets me apart." This is less relevant for some individual contributor roles, but as you get more senior, showing that you have proactive plans to solve their needs really stands out.

Create Your Own Opportunities

Most of your job-search effort will involve applying to existing roles online. But don't limit yourself to roles that exist. At least a third of the jobs I've held, full-time and contract, were ones I created. Prior to meeting me, the company wasn't looking for me and had no idea that they should hire someone like me.

To create your own role, you need to do two things. First, you need to cast a wide net. Having a large network helps, and in Chapter 8, Networking, we talk about how to build one. But you can also use cold outreach. I once saw an interesting startup company with a job posted for software developers. While that role wasn't an appropriate level for me, I thought the company's focus was interesting, so I reached out to meet with them. From the outset, I made it clear that I wasn't looking for a software developer role. I didn't want to mislead them or waste their time. Once we met, they were impressed and brought me on as an adviser to the company. Later, they hired me as a full-time executive.

Once you've got the meeting, you need to ask questions and listen. Everyone has a problem. It could be hiring more people, closing more business, dealing with a dysfunctional culture, trying to select a vendor, and more. Most problems are small, and often the company can solve them on its own. Every so often, someone has a problem that is sufficiently big or that they lack either the time or expertise to solve.

Interviewing

When you find one of those problems, that's an opportunity for you. They need help.

Once you discover that someone has a problem, explore it. Understand as much as you can about the problem. Then figure out if you can help solve it.

That's really all that employees are: problem solvers. The need for more sales is commonly solved by hiring more salespeople to close business, or more marketing people to drive leads. If you are drowning in receipts and billables, hiring for your accounting department will help you manage that. If you need to automate something with software, hire a software developer.

Not everyone knows their needs. This is especially true when someone has a problem outside their domain. The head of DARPA, the federal government's Defense Advanced Research Projects Agency, once told me a story about a biological researcher, a computer engineer, and a gamer who were standing in a hallway. It sounds like the start of a bad joke, but it led to an amazing innovation. The first two were discussing protein folding. Understanding how protein folding works for a virus was critical to understanding how to stop it. Unfortunately, it's a really difficult problem to solve, even using complex computer simulations. The gamer heard them and said, "That sounds like a video game." Think of it like a three-dimensional version of Tetris. It's very hard for computers to solve this problem, because of the complexity, but this is something humans are good at (think jigsaw puzzles). This insight led to Foldit, a DARPA initiative where biological problems are turned into video games.

Players playing games actually solve complex scientific problems. Most researchers never thought about it as a video game, and most video game developers never thought about making video games out of science problems. The point is, people may know they have

The Career Toolkit

> a problem, but they don't always know what the solution looks like. Listen carefully, and keep an open mind.
>
> It's not always so easy. You need to find the right person at the right time, who has a problem that you can solve. Even then, that person may not have enough money to pay you to do it. You should still be submitting résumés and using your network, but part of your search strategy should also be a little more outside the box.

YOU'RE ALWAYS INTERVIEWING

Remember that an interview begins long before you meet the interviewer. After an interview, I would always ask the company receptionist about her impression of the candidate. Was he polite to her, or did he feel she was beneath him? Did he seem nervous or anxious before I walked in? There was a CEO who, in the days before profiles and photos on the web, would send a limo to pick up a senior candidate from the airport and take him to the company. The limo driver was actually the CEO, and he liked to catch a candidate off guard in interviews. Another CEO would take a candidate out to breakfast and, as part of the interview, have the waitress (whom he tipped very well) intentionally screw up the candidate's order just to see how the candidate reacted to the problem and how he treated her.

The interview begins even before you set foot in the corporate office. You have a presence in the world. Even if you have no online profile, you have a reputation. In a given city, within a given industry, there is probably someone whom you and the interviewing team have in common. This reputation precedes you and could be why you got the interview. (We discuss how to deliberately create that reputation in "Crafting Your Image.")

The truth is, you are constantly interviewing—all day, every day. If I need to fill a role tomorrow, I'll need to review the submitted résumés and interview the candidates. If a woman who worked with me a

Interviewing

few years ago calls me up and says she's interested, I may not need her résumé or an interview at all—or at least my questions will be more limited. Perhaps I'd just ask about her experience in an area relevant to this role. Her real interview took place during the years we spent working together.

When you speak at a conference, you're interviewing. Everyone in the audience gets to know a little more about you, hopefully with a positive impression. When you meet someone at an event for a few minutes, you leave them with an impression. When my students are taking my class, they are interviewing with me, even though none of them knows it. Most I'll never hire, simply because their careers and my companies don't overlap. But some do. Some of my students made good impressions, and in the future, I'll recommended them for jobs—often jobs they didn't know existed and weren't applying to. Outside of friends and family who see you enough that any particular moment won't matter, every interaction with someone is part of the interview process. Most won't lead to any jobs, but some will. The catch is that you don't know which ones will. By the way, when I'm teaching, I'm also interviewing for future jobs with my students—even if they don't know that either.

There's no need to be nervous about it. You don't have to be on guard all the time or feel like you're under the microscope. Be yourself. Live your life. This should be seen as an opportunity, not a risk. But recognize, too, that the opportunity, the interview, is happening all around you.

HR's Limitations

HR is responsible for all things people-related. In the mid-twentieth century, when you joined a company and stayed there for decades, HR was your guide. Things have changed since then.

First, as the company-worker social contract of long-term job tenure eroded, corporations were investing less in employee career development. Certainly, some companies focus on retention and training and a long-term career path within the company, but they are much fewer today than decades ago. It made sense for employees who would be with a company for twenty years—not so much for employees who are only around for four.

Second, HR's resources have been spread thin. HR itself is often one of the first places cut in a recession, because it's seen as a short-term cost center, not to mention that whenever there are layoffs, no hiring is likely to happen. With employment law becoming more complex and litigious,[17] HR has become more focused on hiring processes, so more resources are focused there. Similarly, in a competitive hiring market, additional benefits, flex time, child care, and corporate gyms all require HR's time to plan and execute. Sadly, this is exacerbated by many companies not investing in HR in the first place, even if they have the resources to do so.

Third, HR no longer has the time or, in some cases, the interest to understand the roles within the company. I've been at many software companies where an HR person doesn't understand which technologies may be relevant to the roles in the company. Some HR people couldn't tell you the different career options between being a forensic accountant and doing treasury work, even though their company employs people in both roles.

You might be lucky to be in a company with competent HR and an executive team who values what HR can do, but regrettably, most organizations see HR more as a necessary bureaucracy than as a key driver of corporate value. This is why people often talk about applying directly to the hiring manager via their network and bypassing HR.

---

17. This isn't a bad thing. We're all better off in a society that prevents hiring discrimination and with companies that won't tolerate harassment.

Interviewing

All too often, HR doesn't have the capability to recognize a qualified résumé if the wording is different. For example, if the job description says, "Two years of experience using Microsoft Dynamics GP," you should be qualified if you used the Sage package over the past three years. But an HR person might not realize the two programs are similar enough. They might not even consider you if your résumé lists Great Plains, even though Microsoft Dynamics GP is just the new name for the very same software. Even if people in HR would recognize that, the ATS—the applicant tracking system, which is the software that receives résumés and manages applications—isn't going to suggest alternatives when someone types in certain keywords.

There are some phenomenal people working in HR and recruiting who take the time to understand the terminology, culture, and true needs for a particular role. I don't mean to paint everyone as incompetent. Unfortunately though, a very large number of people are, and you don't want to miss opportunities because someone in HR doesn't understand the role as well as they should.

In fairness to HR, in addition to the increased burdens above, the process of applying to a job shifted from typing and mailing a résumé in the twentieth century to the single click of a button in the twenty-first. Consequently, HR receives a rather large number of résumés from unqualified applicants. I am sympathetic to the avalanche of résumé spam that they get. (I've gotten it myself when hiring.)

Nevertheless, if you think you are qualified but don't quite match the exact description, I'd recommend trying to communicate directly with the hiring manager, ideally through your network. You'll likely have to submit a résumé and follow the HR process eventually, but that way, the hiring manager will be keeping an eye out for you, and if he doesn't see you, he'll likely ask HR explicitly to bring you in. Remember, the goal of submitting a résumé is to get the interview,

> and sometimes that means getting the résumé to the right person, even if it means bypassing HR.
>
> Likewise, if you're a hiring manager, have a conversation with the person in HR who is reviewing the résumés. Spending an hour or two walking them through terminology and showing them good and bad résumés is well worth it. That time can later save you countless hours of interviewing mediocre candidates.

For the Hiring Team

Being able to hire is a critical skill every manager needs, but one rarely ever taught. A team that can't effectively hire will not hire effective people. Even as a candidate, understanding how the hiring team thinks gives you a huge advantage during the interview process.

DEFINING THE ROLE

The first thing you need to do when hiring is to understand your needs. That seems easy: I need a forensic accountant. Okay, great. That means you won't accidentally hire a violinist for the job, but there's a lot more to it.

There are two parts to any role: abilities and personality traits. Abilities include the technical skills, such as knowing how to post on social media or how to prepare a budget. It also includes the firm skills discussed in this book, such as leadership, negotiation, and communication. All of these skills can be learned.

The second part comprises personality traits, such as drive, relationships with others, integrity, work style, and cultural fit. It could be something concrete, like how often the candidate seeks input from others, or something as intangible as a sense of humor. The term "personality traits" is being used here to encompass characteristics, abilities, network, and other attributes.

Interviewing

Companies have long been good at defining lists of experiences or abilities required for a job (for example, "Ten years of experience with injection mold design"). They have only recently been learning to define the personality traits necessary for success in a job.

It may seem that personality traits should align with the corporate values of the company or department. Generally, they should; a company valuing teamwork and direct communication shouldn't hire a lone wolf who hoards information. But the appropriate personality traits could also be unique to a role. For example, a company may value directness, efficiency ("Around here, we like to get straight to the point"), and formally defined processes. However, when this company hires someone to do business development in certain regions, the person best suited to the role may be a schmoozer. That quality may not align with the values of the company, but it does align with the needs of the role. Ideally, the candidate can alternate between the two cultures, just as someone who is bilingual can easily alternate between two languages.

Companies often do a poor job when defining the role. Job postings follow a format of 1) job title, 2) prose about the company and role, 3) list of responsibilities, 4) required skills and experience, and 5) application information. All are valid, necessary components of a job description, but two things are missing.

First, the personality traits should be included in the rubric. This may not be practical for in-demand jobs where there is intense competition for a limited number of candidates, and the hiring manager is lucky to see more than two résumés. But when supply outpaces demand, personality traits should be considered.

Second, the public job posting should include a weighting of all those requirements, based on the relative importance or time spent on those activities. A job description may list six to eight responsibilities, but the employee won't divide his time among them equally. For junior

The Career Toolkit

roles, this may be somewhat well understood without further details, but for more senior roles, it can vary.

Consider a chief technology officer (CTO). Typical responsibilities include technology selection, architecture and planning, hiring, corporate strategy, and external relations.

A CTO running a team of twelve would be fairly involved with the code, perhaps sitting in on code reviews. She would be personally responsible for the system architecture. Corporate strategy means working closely with the four other department heads to develop and promote the product lines.

Contrast this with a CTO running a team of twelve hundred people. Her architecture decisions relate to questions about key technology partnerships, like choice of cloud provider. Not only is she not looking at code, but her direct reports might not even look at the code. The corporate strategy involves a total of eighteen other executives, who may each have an office staff, so close coordination with the other departments isn't practical. She's part of a team running an aircraft carrier, not a sailboat.

Twelve compared to twelve hundred is obviously quite a range, chosen to accentuate the differences, but the concept is the same across all sizes. Even two teams of the same size can have significant differences in the weighting of tasks. At some companies, the CTO never speaks to customers or outsiders. In others, she regularly speaks at conferences and helps close major sales. Every CTO knows they get called in when large deals have technical topics, but how often and to what extent they get involved can vary.

You may choose to be explicit about these personality traits in the public job description, but it's not always necessary or even advantageous to do this. For personality traits, when the demand for a role exceeds the supply, as with software engineers today, you may need to cast a wide net. Likewise, when hiring at a director or VP level, you may be open

Interviewing

regarding how to divide up the time and may even adjust the role to fit the candidate.

Whether or not you state it explicitly in the job description, you absolutely must define the weighting internally. Otherwise, in the case above, one interviewer might overweight technical architecture, when supporting technical sales is really the more important skill. One interviewer might be looking for a great public speaker, when having a strong network matters more. Internal alignment to these requirements is critical.

Many companies fail to define weighting adequately. Without a clear rubric, inexperienced interviewers often leave the interview with thoughts such as "He seemed good" or "I think I could work with her." While having an opinion is the desired outcome, all too often the opinion is formed based on intangible feelings. When pressed further on their opinions, inexperienced people stick to those generalities.

Both abilities and personality traits need to be specified. Then weighting needs to be applied to those items. You could prioritize them, weight each with a value, or define the role by percentage of time devoted to each task. It doesn't matter how you do it; what matters is that everyone on the interviewing team understands what the weighting is so that all candidates are evaluated by the same rubric.

One interview question I often ask senior candidates is, "In your ideal role, how do you see yourself dividing your time in a typical week?"[18] It's remarkable how varied the answers will be. It's helpful because if I expect a director of product to be writing product specifications 50 percent of the time, but the candidate wants a role that only spends 10 percent of

---

18. If you use this question, be prepared for about half the candidates to push back, claiming that no week is typical. While that's true, that's not the point, and I rephrase: "Over a year, break down where you spend your time by percentage. For example, a director of product might spend 20 percent of his time writing product specifications, 20 percent hiring, 30 percent working with clients, 15 percent on marketing, and 15 percent on other tasks. Don't worry about these adding up to 100 percent. I just want to get a sense of your weighting in your ideal role."

The Career Toolkit

their time writing specifications, the job may not be a good fit for either party. All too often, statements like "I enjoy . . . ." or "This role requires a lot of . . . ." are too vague and open to different interpretations regarding the amount of time and effort required.

When you meet with the team to discuss the candidate, don't allow statements without justification. There needs to be a reason for an opinion, supported by evidence. "She seems smart" becomes "She seems smart, because she gave really great technical explanations for the complex problems we presented." Or "He's nice" becomes "He was very polite, for example, he thanked each person individually in each round of the interview process." Maybe that's not a good definition or justification of "nice," and that's the point. The other interviewers can now decide whether he's "nice" by their definition, or they can choose to disagree with the assessment.

Offering your feelings is fine, as in "My gut says to hire her," but even then your gut has a reason: ". . . because she handled herself well in a three-on-one interview, and her experience over the last five years is very relevant." You can even mention reasons that are not in the job description. You might not have asked for a good public speaker, but post-interview you comment, "He's really well-spoken, and he's experienced at public speaking with all his conference talks." It might not be what you were looking for initially, but the group can now explicitly decide whether that's a relevant factor or not.

Define the role in terms of both abilities and personality traits. When you advocate for or against a candidate, it needs to align with these requirements. Now everyone is on the same page, and you're not simply taken in by someone you want to grab a beer with. As a candidate, it's often acceptable to ask what traits would make someone successful in this role if they're not explicitly listed.

HIRING TRIANGLE

Suppose your boss says she wants you to hire a director of marketing who has fifteen years' experience and knows all the social media tools; has B2B and B2C experience; has run conferences; and knows channel marketing, direct marketing, branding, product marketing, and more. The salary is 20 percent under market rate, and she wants this person to start in one month. Go!

What you should do is go look for a new job. It's unrealistic to think that you'll find that needle in a haystack to work for that low compensation, and in only one month. If money were no object, you could offer $600,000 plus have recruiters search as well (for their additional commission). That would get qualified candidates in the door fast. Alternatively, if the money is fixed, it's just a matter of finding someone who would be excited by the appealing mission of your company. Someone may take the job at that salary eventually, but you'll need many months to find that person. The third option is to loosen the constraints. Maybe only ten years of experience would be sufficient, or perhaps the candidates don't need both B2B *and* B2C experience.

Every manager would love to hire the perfect candidate tomorrow, for low pay.[19] But that just doesn't happen. Time is how fast you need to find the candidate. Cost is how much you're willing to pay, including the cost of benefits as well as the cost of job posts and external recruiter fees. Qualifications are how close they come to meeting or exceeding the job requirements.

Time, cost, qualifications—you can only pick two. When hiring, the more you strain two dimensions, the more you need to be flexible in the third.

---

[19]. The low pay isn't necessarily because they're being greedy jerks; lower compensation can allow additional hires for the team.

The Career Toolkit

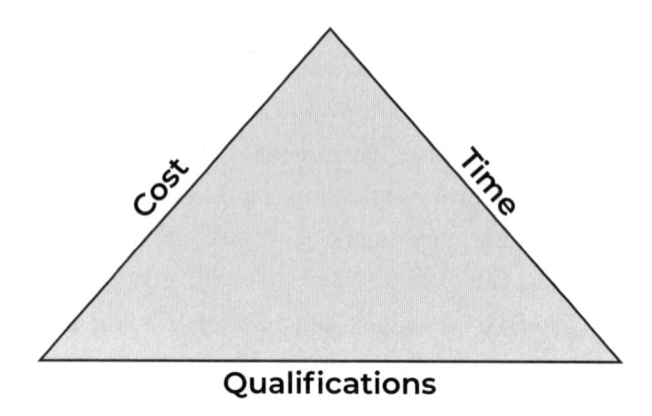

FIGURE 3. The hiring triangle

The triangle above shows the three sides you're trading off. You can't fix all three dimensions. Don't fix two and blindly hope to get lucky in the third dimension. Recognize that the more you constrain two dimensions, the more flexibility you need in the third. As we'll see later in this chapter, we can actually add more sides to the triangle by looking at other things we want in a candidate.

When hiring, think consciously about what's important and where you have flexibility. If you need someone yesterday, throwing money at the problem can help attract more candidates. If money is fixed, and time is an issue, perhaps you can be more flexible about the requirements, and you could train someone up. There's no right answer, but the wrong answer is to have unrealistic expectations across all three dimensions.

A DIFFERENT TYPE OF DIVERSITY

When hiring, diversity is a topic commonly discussed in corporate circles. Everyone wants diversity, but identifying it isn't always so obvious. I promise this isn't the same as the "Hire more than just white men" advice you always hear.

Interviewing

Let's start with the obvious though. We commonly hear "diversity" in terms of gender, race, religion, and sexuality. Some people feel this is necessary, because certain categories have historically faced discrimination. Others see diversity as code for so-called reverse discrimination, which takes jobs from those who are more qualified.

Any competent investment manager will tell you to diversify your portfolio with stocks and bonds and other assets across a variety of industries. Changes in a company, industry, or economy won't affect all assets equally, so by having a diverse portfolio, you get exposure to more upside possibilities and reduce the risk of catastrophic loss. For long-term investing, portfolio diversity is a must.

This same rule applies to your team. An African American woman will have a different set of experiences from a Caucasian man. Even if they both grew up in the same neighborhood and went to the same college with the same major, they will have had other experiences in life that are different. More generally, someone who grew up in a different culture has different stories, views, traditions, and ways of thinking about situations.

I can talk to African American female friends about their experiences, but I cannot truly understand what it is like to live life as an African American woman or a Muslim or a member of the LBGTQ community. I've never been judged that way. I've never had to wonder, "Will this person think differently about me if they know my sexuality?" I've never had to worry about my safety because of whom I choose to date. Those experiences and that mindset *do* make a difference on the team. The impact of diversity is direct, in that you'll have a voice on the team who can speak for those communities, and it is indirect, in that it serves as a reminder to others on the team that not everyone is the same. There will be diversity among your customers, so you need to align your company to address it by having diversity on your team.

The Career Toolkit

Age diversity is also a common problem, especially among Silicon Valley companies. Physical impediments, in the cases of those who are differently abled,[20] falls under another type of diversity. National origin is yet another, which is especially important for companies with a global presence.

All of these categories tend to be on the radar of HR. I'm going to assume that you generally understand why diversity in these categories is important. If not, please do have a conversation with people from those groups, and ask to learn about their experiences in the workplace. Or you could speak with HR or those with diversity-training backgrounds. No one should ever chastise you for asking questions and trying to understand someone else's perspective.

Then, there's another important, overlooked category that my colleague Chuck McVinney named "mental diversity."[21]

Let's start with an extreme example. Professor Temple Grandin, named to *Time*'s 2010 list of The 100 Most Influential People in the World, has autism. She exhibited many symptoms at a time when it was not widely understood. Her schoolmates ridiculed her, and the recommended course of action in those days was to put her in an institution. Luckily for society, she continued with her studies and went on to earn a PhD in animal science. Her paper "Livestock Behavior as Related to Handling Facilities Design" was the first to note that livestock are very sensitive to light and sound. For example, dangling chains, common in such facilities, were disturbing to animals. Most humans working in such facilities quickly learned to tune out such distractions. Grandin's autism

---

20. Commonly referred to as "people with disabilities," this term is recommended by Eric S. Raymond, author of the great book, *The Cathedral and the Bazaar*.

21. I intentionally use the term "mental diversity" as distinct from "neurodiversity." The latter refers to more formally diagnosed and recognized conditions such as ADHD, autism, dyslexia, and other neurological outliers. Although I begin with an example of someone with autism, most of this chapter is about less formally defined neurological differences. That said, I support neurodiversity as well as mental diversity.

Interviewing

prevented her from tuning it out as easily as others did, which allowed her to notice the issue. The tuning-out by non-autistic people made it that much harder for them to recognize the issue and evaluate its impact on animals. Grandin attributes her ability to see things from the animals' perspective to her autistic mindset. What was once labeled a defect by society has allowed her to see things in a way that few others, if anyone, did.

Some people are very analytical; others are good with people. Some are great communicators, and other folks are just full of positivity and are helpful to have on your team when things look bleak. There is no shortage of ways to divide up people's personalities. What does matter is that you have people with those different perspectives. Obviously, you can't possibly have every perspective in a team of ten or even fifty people. They still need to be qualified for the roles and available to work for your company. What is important is that you try to foster diversity as much as possible: both the traditional types of diversity and mental diversity.

When I build a team, certain core functional skills are required. But there are other areas where I explicitly want diversity. Suppose I'm hiring a team of ten software engineers. Obviously, all need to know the software language we are using. Having one or two people with really deep technical knowledge provides expertise; I don't need everyone to be an expert, but one or two can help others when they're stuck. It's helpful to have a few team members who are good at explaining complex ideas to non-technical people; they're the team members I bring to meetings with clients or other departments. I'll need a few prolific coders, people who I know can power through an assigned task and churn out code. It might not be the most beautiful or most efficient code, but it will be working code; essentially, they get things done quickly. Not everyone needs to be a deep expert, or a strong communicator, or highly productive, but having some of each gives the team flexibility when facing different stages of the project.

The Career Toolkit

Hiring for racial, cultural, and mental diversity across any of the standard categories helps you see new risks and opportunities and makes your team stronger.[22] Of course, that hiring triangle can already feel pretty tight, and adding more constraints only makes it harder.

INTERVIEW QUESTIONS

Once you, as a hiring manager, have identified the type of candidate you want to hire, you then need to conduct the interview. You're likely familiar with interview questions. Unfortunately, given the lack of interviewer training, many people simply ask the questions they like, with little consideration as to organization or purpose. Rather, given the rubric you created for the role, you now need to design a series of questions to evaluate against that metric.

Questions should be selected against one or more of the abilities or personality traits you're looking for, to systematically determine the candidate's fitness. Nearly all interview questions fall into one of six categories. Some may fall into multiple categories.

Values

These questions seek to explore a candidate's values or cultural fit with the role or organization. They may be direct, such as asking about qualities a candidate admires, or indirect, for instance, asking for a decision on something and then asking for the reasoning behind the decision. The *why* is key, so make sure the candidate always gives you the reasoning; ask if the candidate doesn't immediately offer it.

---

22. There are some drawbacks relating to conflict, but the general wisdom is that these are outweighed by the benefits. See, for example, *Evan Apfelbaum, interviewed by Martha E. Mangelsdorf*, "The Trouble With Homogenous Teams," MIT Sloan Management Review (Winter 2018). https://sloanreview.mit.edu/article/the-trouble-with-homogeneous-teams/. I believe that as we continue to view the world around us as more diverse, as younger employees grow up with that being the norm, the drawbacks will continue to diminish.

Interviewing

There aren't necessarily objectively right and wrong answers to most questions, but for a given company, certain traits may be preferred. A single question alone doesn't tell you everything, but the answer starts to give the interviewer a perspective from which to drill in.

Examples:
- What are the qualities you value in your co-workers?
- What did you like or dislike about previous corporate cultures?
- If you could have a superpower, what would it be and why?
- What public figures do you admire and why?
- Would you rather face one horse-sized duck or a hundred duck-sized horses?[23]

Situational Questions

These questions explore decision-making and practical problem-solving. They describe a problematic situation and ask the candidate to recommend corrective action. Such questions may be based on previous circumstances or hypothetical situations. Some companies ask about current challenges they face.

These questions can overlap with other categories. How a candidate would handle a situation speaks to her values. For example, how did she reach consensus during a disagreement? Did she become an expert? Did she go to her network? Build prototypes? Flip a coin? Similarly, how she chooses to explain her answer displays her communication. See whether the answers given to these questions are consistent with those to other questions in other categories.

---

23. This sounds like a situational interview question that explores decision-making and problem-solving abilities. But our question actually goes to values. In essence, it asks: "Do you prefer facing one big problem or lots of small problems?"

The Career Toolkit

Candidates, when answering these questions, focus on explaining the situation. One common technique is STAR: Situation, Task, Action, Result. Explain the situation, talk about what was needed, how you did it, and then describe the result. Candidates often leave out important details in the situation or forget to explain the result. The candidate has all the context; the interviewer has none. So, candidates should learn to be explicit. Interviewers should ask clarifying questions if needed.

Examples:
- Tell me about a time you failed.
- What was your biggest challenge?
- Please walk me through what you did on this project.
- Let's say your team needs to change from a direct sales approach to a mix of direct and channel sales; how would you approach the change in terms of team organization and incentives?
- Suppose your team is divided on the solutions, with one group wanting . . .
- You're two weeks away from launching your company's new marketing campaign, featuring more powerful motors in your next generation of scooters, when suddenly you learn that you need to recall 10,000 of your current generation's units. Do you make any changes to the marketing launch, and if so what are they?

Communication

Communication is a key skill for most roles. That includes communication with peers, bosses, subordinates, other departments, customers, suppliers, partners, competitors, and media.

Interviewing

We explore effective communication in Chapter 7, Communication. Those guidelines apply to both interviews and day-to-day communication.

Examples:
- Explain this project to me.
- Can you explain how this software works to someone with no technical background?
- How would you explain the recent changes in the corporate tax code to the director of marketing?
- Read this, and provide a four-bullet summary.

Technical Skills

These are the actual skills required by a job, such as being able to spot-weld, typing at a certain speed, having knowledge of SQL databases, or being familiar with GAAP accounting standards. The questions will vary significantly, but they ultimately demonstrate knowledge or ability. One alternative to asking these questions is sometimes to have the applicant do a problem at the whiteboard or in a take-home assignment; sometimes it may be part of a situational question. These are the most common type of questions, especially for more junior roles.

Examples:
- When would you use ... ?
- Compare the following two tools . . . .
- Explain how ... works.[24]
- How would you design ... ?
- Do the following . . . .

---

24. In this case, the interviewer is trying to understand what you've done. When this question is asked in the context of communication, the interviewer is looking to see how the candidate can explain a complex idea to someone with a different domain of understanding. In such a case, it's less about what was done and more about how it's conveyed. Knowing what is being asked should be clear from the context ("How would you explain ... to someone who ... ?"), but if in doubt, ask.

The Career Toolkit

Analysis

These questions focus on how a candidate thinks, generally seeing how she would approach or solve a problem. These questions are more abstract than technical or situational questions and include brain teasers or case studies. They focus on core critical thinking skills and are common in consulting, finance, and engineering companies.

Examples:
- How many Ping-Pong balls fit into an airplane?
- Your friend wants to open a seafood restaurant in this part of town and asks you to help him figure out whether he should. What is your process?
- If one and a half chickens lay one and a half eggs in one and a half hours, how many eggs do three chickens lay in two days?

One common mistake interviewers make is to ask a question with a "binary" answer. Asking the classic "Why are manhole covers round?" means the candidate either has the right answer or does not. There's no partial credit. Contrast this with asking for the number of Ping-Pong balls that can fit in an airplane, which should be answered as follows:

> *Let's see, an airplane is about 300 feet long, and I guess maybe 20 feet wide and 10 feet high. So, it's 300 x 20 x 10 or 60,000 cubic feet. About 200 Ping-Pong balls fit in a cubic foot, so 60,000 multiplied by 200 is 12 million.*

That answer could be better, for example, considering whether the seats take up space or inclusion of the cargo space; and the estimates are not correct. But the approach is, and it's the thought process that's the point of these questions. Companies don't care whether the candidate

Interviewing

knows the exact length of the airplane (other than that it isn't three feet or three million feet) but rather how the candidate approached it. She'll get a lot of "partial credit" for how she thought it through, as opposed to saying, "Um . . . one million?" in which case the interviewer can't see her thought process. As an interviewer, ask questions that allow for a thought process and not simply whether the candidate can guess the right answer.

As a candidate, remember to talk through your answer. It's okay if you make some mistakes along the way in a brain teaser; interviewers understand that some people are nervous. What matters is that they can see how you think, so think out loud. It's okay to go down a wrong path, but talk it through. The worst thing to do is sit there silently for two minutes and then give an answer. If it's wrong, there's no "partial credit" for seeing how you thought about it; if it's right, the interviewer doesn't know whether you have critical thinking skills or simply guessed and got lucky. Interviewers should ask candidates to talk through their process if they sit thinking in silence.

Personal Preferences

These questions ask about a candidate's personal opinions and preferences. While the questions are personal in nature, they are being asked to understand values and cultural fit.

I sometimes use personal questions to get to values. Asking someone about their strengths leads to some pretty banal answers, since most people know how to answer with positive qualities. Asking, "If you were to hire a more junior person in your department, what would you look for in that candidate?" provides more insightful answers with its indirect approach. Generally, people who look for expertise value having expertise and have invested in building their expertise; those who answer "a good team player" value teamwork and likely have tried to ensure that they are a good team player.

The Career Toolkit

Example:
- What do you like to do on weekends?
- What's your favorite book?
- How do you go about learning a new subject?
- What are your weaknesses?

Illegal Questions

In the United States, certain questions are simply illegal. I'm not a lawyer, but I do know that these include questions about your race, religion, ethnicity, country of origin, physical measurements, gender, sexual orientation, marital status, family status, citizenship, or other EEOC-protected classes. In other countries, these questions are not necessarily prohibited.

Note that a candidate may volunteer such information but is not obligated to do so, nor can they be penalized for not doing so. For example, I often ask candidates about hobbies and activities they enjoy and get answers such as, "I enjoy taking my kids fishing." I didn't ask about his children, and I may not ask follow-up questions like, "How old are they?" and I may not use the fact that he has kids as a factor in evaluating him, but I can't unknow that he has children. I simply move forward with the interview and won't factor the parental status into my decision.

Assignment

For some roles, it makes sense to have some part of the process take place outside of the office. This might be due to time constraints or because some people get nervous in a face-to-face interview. Or perhaps some needed information isn't available until after at least one in-person meeting. An assignment is essentially a longer-form "question." It could take place during the onsite interview or outside of it. The assignment is then reviewed, possibly during a later stage, face-to-face interview.

Interviewing

Examples:
- Please write code to do the following . . . .
- Given what you learned about the company goals, how would you allocate a million-dollar marketing budget?
- Please write an essay on integrity.
- What would be your ninety-day plan?

It's important to keep in mind that as roles get more senior, the weighting of a job's requirements and corresponding interview questions shifts from more emphasis on technical skills to the firm skills discussed in this book. It also means the "right fit" is harder to find, since now there are more constraints. A sales coordinator job, which is an entry-level role, requires someone who can send emails and coordinate schedules. You can easily find a dozen qualified people in a major city. Finding a CEO for a midsize food-distribution company is not so easy. The candidate should have the right executive experience in the food industry; the "right" experience may mean someone more oriented toward operations or turnarounds or overseas expansion. The executive also needs to fit in with the culture and interact well with the other executives. Technical skills were sufficient for the sales coordinator (assuming no glaring personality issues), but the CEO role is much more complex.

The Airport Test

The airport test is an unstated interview question going back many decades. Note that the question was originally asked before we all carried the Internet in our pockets. Imagine you're stuck in a small regional airport with a co-worker, and your flight is delayed three hours. You're stuck with nothing to do but talk to your co-worker.

The Career Toolkit

How do you feel about that? The thinking is that you want co-workers you'll enjoy spending time with.

It matters because you're going to spend forty or more hours a week with your co-workers. You're also going to have some long days and late nights, and if you're stuck in the corporate foxhole with someone, you'd rather it be someone you can relax and feel comfortable with.

On the other hand, it doesn't matter, because this might not be someone you personally work with that directly. Or it might be that they are hired for some specific expertise. Your co-workers don't need to be your friends, just people you can respect and get along with. Some of my co-workers have become lifelong friends. Others are good people I want on my team, but I wouldn't choose to spend time with them outside of work.

Many companies use the airport test. As a candidate, it's better to pass it than not. As an employer, consider how important a factor it is for this particular role.

CULTURAL FIT

When hiring, companies often proclaim, "We want someone who is a cultural fit." But what is that? Most people follow the philosophy of U.S. Supreme Court Justice Potter Stewart: "I know it when I see it." But as we've already discussed, a "gut feeling" isn't enough.

To most people, a cultural fit means aligning with the company values. A company that is extremely customer-centric generally wants people who are very focused on the customer.

That's mostly true. But you may not want this trait in *everyone*. Companies all too often suffer from groupthink. If you're running a hotel chain, certainly you want the people who interact with the customers—like reception, room service, maid service, and managers—to all convey that highly customer-focused attitude to customers. It's important that it be a general attitude around the company. If it's not a value lived and

Interviewing

demonstrated by higher-ups, who may not interact with customers but who need to lead by example, then the value isn't promoted along the team.

But there is value in having some people who don't quite think the same—this is the mental diversity we discussed in the section "A Different Type of Diversity." If you're a delivery service with the corporate value "Never be late," no one in the company might think to propose a lower-end product with a variable delivery time that might appeal to a different market segment. A company that always values consensus might have people yield too quickly to get buy-in when, in a few cases at least, they should be standing their ground.

Pure iron is very soft, but it becomes strong steel by mixing in a little carbon. With groupthink, everyone sees the same opportunities and risks—and in a self-same way, they all miss other opportunities and risks. Different ways of thinking—adding that little bit of carbon—makes the team stronger.

It's up to you how much divergence from cultural fit is appropriate, both in quantity of hires and the extent of their divergence The answer will likely vary by function and level within the organization. Certainly in some areas, the answer is zero. Highly complex systems like rocket launches and nuclear power plants do well with a culture that emphasizes safety and following the rules and doesn't deviate from that thinking.

The need for alignment typically has more to do with communication than values. Some cultures like to have open debate in meetings. Others prefer consensus-building in private one-on-one sessions prior to the actual decision meeting. The meeting is the final coming together, not the actual debate. Some teams like to communicate face to face; at other companies, people sitting five feet from each other send emails and instant messages back and forth. It is much more critical to be aligned on these communication issues. If everyone communicates by instant message, then the person who prefers to walk over to someone's desk will be annoying his co-workers and not checking his instant messages in a timely matter. That's a problem.

Likewise, in an on-time delivery company, being late for a meeting would be a big cultural faux pas. (Everyone should be on time in the office in such a culture.) Someone who is regularly late to meetings just doesn't fit into the team, but that's different from someone who proposes products with intentional uncertainty in their delivery.

Imagine someone who comes from a culture of backroom political deal-making and relationship-based horse-trading joining a company where disagreements are raised openly and directly between people and evaluated based on merit. This new hire might be perceived as sneaky or not a team player. If the situation were reversed, the new hire might be seen as unable to build a coalition. Both people are effective, but only within a certain type of culture. If they can't adapt to the other culture, it will not be a fit, no matter how intrinsically capable either may be.

One of my friends told me of a company he worked at where whoever yelled the loudest won. In that culture, if you're not a confrontational person, it doesn't matter how much you "put the customer first" or whatever the official corporate values may be. If you're not ready to shout, you're not going to be effective there. (I'm certain that "yelling" wasn't listed on the corporate values webpage.)

GE evaluated people along two dimensions: skills and cultural fit. People were rated low or high in each dimension. Obviously, the low-lows were not hired or were let go, and the high-highs were desired. What about people who were high in one category and low in another?

Those who were cultural fits but lower performers were given training. If they improved, they moved into the high-high category; if not, they were let go. Employees who were not cultural fits were let go, even if they were good performers.

Interviewing

Skills can be learned. In addition to the technical skills of a profession, there are the many skills in this book, all of which can be learned. The thinking is that cultural fit cannot be. People's values can change, but it's far less common than improvement of their technical skills or firm skills. Some people are adaptable, but those people are usually astute enough to recognize the culture and will find a way to fit in. GE's thinking was that investing resources into improving an employee's skill would likely lead to a high-high employee, but investing in someone to change their cultural mindset had a low chance of leading to a high-high employee, making it more efficient to simply find a better cultural fit in a new hire.

You have to find what works best for your company and culture. Generally speaking, rather than alignment with corporate values (cultural fit, for example), communication and interpersonal dynamics matter more.

Remember the hiring triangle: Cost, time, qualifications—pick two. It was hard enough to begin with, and now we're adding "cultural fit" (or deviance from it) as another requirement. This is good to keep in mind, but you won't always have the luxury of optimizing for it when hiring.

Summary and Next Steps

Hiring is complex, across both sides of the table. Taking a moment to plan ahead helps both a candidate and an interviewer to be more effective. Understanding what the other side is thinking helps in most situations, including during the hiring process.

As a candidate, you need to sell yourself as being able to deliver value while assuaging any concerns the hiring team may have. Your answer to every question, whether specific or broad, needs to lead the interviewer in that direction. Doing a little extra work to demonstrate your abilities can make you really stand out.

Remember that opportunity is all around you. You're always interviewing, even if neither you nor the hiring manager knows it at the time. There are also hidden opportunities for you that aren't posted and that the company may not even consciously realize. Only by exploring can you discover them. Ask and listen.

When it comes to hiring, begin by defining the role, including both the abilities and personality traits you need in a candidate. Make sure the whole team is clear on what these are and their relative weights. As a candidate, you can ask what a typical week is like and what skills or qualities are important.

The hiring triangle teaches us that we can't get the ideal candidate in the door tomorrow. Of cost (compensation, recruiter fees), time (how long to hire), and qualifications (candidate's profile), the more you constrain two, the more the third needs to be flexible.

Diversity has been shown to help teams make better decisions. Mental diversity is equally important.

There are six different types of interview questions: values, situational questions, communication, technical skills, analysis, and personal preferences. As an interviewer, understand how to use each type of question to assess the skills and qualities you are looking for in a candidate. As a candidate, recognize what each question is asking you for. Practice your answers to these types of questions ahead of time so that when you get them, you can immediately and confidently jump to your answers.

Cultural fit is often misused and really should be a question of communication. Both the company and candidate should understand what values are important and make sure they are aligned.

Consider doing a mock interview with co-workers, as either a candidate or hirer; recording the interview can let you watch and learn. Watching others in their (mock or real) interviews is also valuable. Ask whether you can sit in on some interviews that your company conducts.

LEADERSHIP & MANAGEMENT

Chapter Four

Leadership

> "Leadership is about vision and responsibility, not power."
>
> —Seth Berkley

Leadership is a necessary skill for those who want to climb the corporate ladder. Many mistakenly believe that leadership comes from having a leadership role. In truth, a leadership role is earned by having already led. You need to learn to lead before you are given a leadership role. While that may sound like a catch-22, your current job, even if not a leadership position, is teaching you to lead—you just need to know where to look.

Understanding what leadership is guides you to the skills you need to develop. Once understood, you'll see how to develop those skills, even if you're the most junior employee at the company. Equally important is to avoid picking up bad habits in your leadership development. This chapter provides a basic leadership framework and outlines how you can develop your leadership abilities, no matter your role. Two common leadership obstacles are also presented.

The Career Toolkit

What Is Leadership?

The core question when studying leadership is, "What does it mean to be a leader?" The simplest definition is, "A leader is someone who has followers." That's it. If no one is following you, you're not leading.

While the definition may seem tautological, it is practical. Asking, "What is leading without followers?" is like asking, "What is the sound of one hand clapping?" Leadership does not work in a vacuum, because it inherently involves others. As you develop your leadership, you may prefer more sophisticated models, but this basic definition is a good place to start exploring the core principles.

Positional vs. Influential Leadership

The next logical question is, "What does it mean to have followers?" Here we get into the crux of the question. The concept of having followers is an important definition to remember and not just a word game. Without followers, you aren't a leader. In order to answer this question, we'll first examine what is often mistaken for genuine leadership: positional leadership.

The old adage in the military is that when an officer says, "Jump!" the enlisted men ask, "How high?" The military is the ultimate example of positional leadership. Someone with a higher rank can command those in a lower rank. No debate, no questions asked. The more junior person may not like or respect the more senior person. He may disagree with the order, but he must obey it. This is known as "positional leadership," although "positional authority" might be a better name for it. The authority comes from the position (the rank in the military). Those in the military accept this rule without question.

The workplace is a less extreme example, but we see some examples of positional authority. The CEO may decide to move the office. You may

Leadership

agree or disagree with that decision, but it's her decision, and she has the final say. Why? Because she's the CEO. The company's owners or board granted her that authority.

Your boss may assign you to a project, ask you to work late, or tell you to do something. Unlike the military, you won't be court-martialed for non-compliance, but you're likely to be doing it, at least partially, because of the authority granted to the office your boss holds.

Consider two cases. In the first, your boss asks you to get something done by Friday. That may mean staying late or doing extra work. If you don't, you may get fired. Even if you won't be fired, certainly your boss will remember that you didn't get it done. Alternatively, he'll remember that you stayed late and got it done. Either way, it can impact your future at the company.

In the second case, your co-worker in a different group has to complete something by Friday and asks you for help. You have the skills and experience to help significantly; perhaps your help will impact whether it gets done on time. This co-worker has no authority over you and will in no way affect your promotions or lack thereof. Do you help?

If you helped in both cases, was it for the same reason? You may genuinely like to help others, but there are times, say, a busy week at home with the kids while your spouse is away, when you're more likely to do it because your boss asked than when your co-worker asked. That difference is the positional authority your boss has in relation to you. While some may qualify this as leadership, it is not how we define true leadership. That's positional authority as distinguished from influence-based leadership.

In the military, leadership is mostly positional. At the other end of the spectrum, in a group of volunteers working together, leadership is highly influential. In the workplace, it's a combination. If your co-worker needs your help, you may do it because you're nice or to help the team, but also because you know that good relationships with peers will reflect well on you in the long term. Whether they'll return the favor directly or you'll become known as a team player, it will have a positive impact. There's nothing immoral about this; you can still be a good person and act based on potential future rewards from positional authority, even when the other person is only a peer.

The key takeaway is that while some leadership or authority comes from a position, true influence-based leadership is not tied to an office. In his struggle for equal rights, Dr. Martin Luther King Jr. opposed the most powerful government in the world but never held any governmental position or authority. Although he eventually led the Southern Christian Leadership Conference, that was a civil rights group with no governmental authority. His election as president of that group was because of, not the cause of, his leadership within the community. Through his efforts, he convinced others to support the civil rights movement, from volunteers who marched for civil rights, often risking their own personal safety, to changing the hearts and minds of much of America. His leadership was persuasive in nature.

For the rest of this chapter, when we discuss leadership, we will be referring to influential leadership, based on persuasion, and not positional leadership, based on a job title.

Leadership Skills

The standing question is then, "What does it mean to have followers?" You likely already have some intuitive sense, because all of us have led, or have been led, at some point. Take a moment to consider the following questions.

- Whom did you follow and why?
- What was it that caused you to want to follow that person?

Leadership

- When did you lead and how?
- What was it that got others to follow you?

We often hear talk about a coach or player "leading" a team to victory. What does this mean? The coach can direct the players both in training and on the field. In American football, a quarterback will call the plays, and the other football players follow the called plays, because the middle of a football game is not the place for debate. Is that leading?

No, directing isn't leading. But when on a team, whether it's a sports team or a project team, we see in leaders both guidance and inspiration. People rally around them to work together to achieve a goal. It may seem hard at first to qualify what exactly a good leader does when leading. Thanks to work by many leadership researchers, we do know how to model it and subsequently learn what we need to know about becoming effective leaders ourselves.

VISION

Every leader has a vision. You must have a goal. The vision could be changing the law, winning the basketball tournament, developing a new product, or increasing revenue.

A leadership vision is a potential future state that requires the efforts of one or more other people working together. "Let's build a pillow fort" is a vision—it might be easy to achieve, but it involves people working together to create it. "Let's all go get Chinese food" is not, since it does not require the group to work together. Simply saying to your sales team, "Everyone, increase your sales by 5 percent this quarter" isn't leadership. That's a directive. On the other hand, calling the team together and saying, "We've been asked to increase sales by 5 percent; let's figure out a way we can achieve this," and then executing that plan, is an example of leadership.

The Career Toolkit

In general, you should avoid negative goals. "Let's not lose the tennis match" just isn't as inspiring as "Let's win the tennis match." If you find yourself saying, "Let's not . . . ," try to reframe your goal in the affirmative.[25]

There are also goals that work to keep the status quo. "Let's prevent the big box store from opening in our town" is a "negative" goal, in that it prevents something and is, in fact, a desire to preserve the status quo. These preventive visions are usually less powerful than affirmative visions. While preventing something bad is often valid—think global warming, an invasion, or a fire—they suffer from two problems.

"Let's not have the house burn down" focuses on a specific issue at the risk of losing sight of others. You may be so focused on preventing the fire that you don't think about protection from floods. "Let's keep the house safe and secure" is a better affirmative vision.

The second issue arises because things are rarely static. As two countries gear up for war, "Let's prevent that country from invading us" is focused on the here and now. You might deter them by threatening to cut off trade to their key partner. Ten years later, the trade flows may be different, and it no longer works as a deterrent. You are right back where you started. "Let's create long-term peace between the two nations" would be a better vision, because it creates a new affirmative state, as opposed to avoiding a negative state.

Your vision should be inclusive. The leader sets it, but if you want others to follow you, it needs to incorporate their needs and goals. For a sports team, the goal may be obvious (win); for a company, the vision needs to be one that everyone can buy into. "Make lots of money" may appeal to the investors, but "being the number one company in X" or "transforming how people do Y" is a vision the employees are more likely to get behind.

---

25. Note that "Let's tear down the abandoned building" is an affirmative goal. Even though the action is "negative" because it's removal, it's an active change.

Likewise, the vision needs to be relatable. Setting a dream goal that doesn't seem achievable may not only fail to inspire, it can do the opposite, because people may see it as unattainable. Curing cancer seems very difficult but possible; altering our DNA to be able to breathe under water seems more like science fiction.

The vision should be relatable to each team member in their own way. Going to Mars may seem extremely difficult, but it is possible, and everyone, from the pilot of the spaceship to the people who order office supplies, can understand how their contributions help make that vision a reality.

It's important to note that a vision is not a plan. It is an end state. It should be an achievable end state, even if it seems like a stretch. While the plan is important to the achievability (no one will buy into your vision if they think it is impossible), the plan itself is not part of the vision.

There are many other aspects that leadership experts will debate about a vision. At its core, a vision needs to be an affirmative future state that the team members can get behind. They need to be able to see themselves contributing to its success.

INFLUENCE

Having a vision isn't sufficient to be a leader. Once you have a destination, you need to convince, not command, people to follow you there. As we said earlier, the opposite of positional authority is influential authority.

When Gandhi began protesting against British rule, he held no office and had no authority. Through nothing more than persuasion, he convinced others to join him in the protest, risking physical harm and prison time in the process. He had no authority to command them to take part.

Google traditionally gave zero positional authority to product managers. While in some companies, product managers create specifications that the software engineers must follow (positional), Google offered product managers no such authority. Rather, the product managers had to convince the software engineers that their proposals, say, a new feature or changing the color, were worthwhile.

Influence can be done by logical argument, emotional appeal, citation of a standard, philosophical point of view, or just about any other reasonable means you can think of, including actions like trading favors. Plenty of politicians have gotten legislation through by trading votes on other issues.[26, 27] True influence does not come from positional authority or coercion like threats of penalty or retribution.

Once you have a vision, you need to persuade people to agree with it and then to follow you in executing it. Employing inclusiveness and relatability will help you be persuasive.

ADDITIONAL ATTRIBUTES OF A LEADER

From a philosophical perspective, having a vision and convincing others to follow you in pursuit of that vision is sufficient to be a leader. Practically speaking, there's a lot more to it.

It's analogous to saying that five people make a basketball team. While technically correct, any team hoping to win anything more than a social game also has practices, drills, plays, and coaching. So do most leaders, in their own way; they have more in their toolbox than simply a vision and the power of persuasion.

---

26. There is a subtle difference. Paying money to do something isn't persuasion, it's purchase. On the other hand, promising some benefit in the future, such as "We'll all have clean drinking water once we get a new water treatment plant," is common. Where to draw the line between the two is a more advanced topic.

27. Note that these same techniques also apply to negotiations. When trying to convince the other party to accept your proposal, consider using any of those approaches.

Leadership

Some of the other skills and attributes that are desirous in leaders include the following:

Listening
A good leader should listen to her followers and others and take their needs and opinions into account.

Empathy
A good leader should empathize with those on the team and those affected by the changes being brought about. By better understanding their concerns through empathy, a leader can more effectively address them.

Competence/Intelligence
Most of us want a leader who is sufficiently competent for the task. The more complex the situation, the more competence and intelligence are important to make sure circumstances and solutions are well understood.

Respect
People won't follow a leader they don't respect. While people may respect someone's commitment or ability, they also need to have an overall general respect for the leader.

Inspiring/Motivating
Influential leadership is asking people to do something. Everything has a cost. In extreme cases, it is risking injury and liberty, or it may just be asking for time and money. No matter what the case, a leader asks followers to do something they might not do on their own and so has some cost to it. Influence often begins with inspiration.

Responsible

No one wants to see their efforts wasted. Followers must believe that their leader is responsible and will make good use of the resources being given and not squander them, even if those resources are simply the time and emotional commitment of the followers.

Good Communicator

A leader who can't communicate well has a much harder time inspiring. It's important to convey the vision, motivate followers, and organize the team.

Trustworthy/Ethical

No one will follow someone they can't trust. Whether it's trusting them with the bank account or trusting that they will keep their word once the goal is achieved, an effective leader is trustworthy.

Dedicated

Nothing's more demoralizing than working long hours, only to find the person who asked you to do so is loafing about, not doing any meaningful work. The person who hired you to mow his lawn may do this, but he's employing you, not leading you. People want a leader as dedicated and hardworking as they are.

Clearly, this is not an exhaustive list. Which skills matter most can vary, depending on the situation. The point is, there is more to being a leader than simply telling others what to do and hoping that they'll listen.

It should be noted that not all leaders excel in every area. Many politicians use speechwriters to help with their communication. A chief of staff can help someone be more organized and responsible. Even trustworthiness may not be as critical as we'd think (or like). Many leaders have cheated on spouses or have been caught in lies, but people still follow them. It's not about overall trustworthiness but whether there is trust in the ability to execute a given plan and achieve the vision. Each skill must be manifested, whether innately by the leader or through delegation, in a manner appropriate to the leadership situation at hand.

The plan is not part of your vision. But for a complex vision, most people will want to see a plan to know that it is achievable and that you can achieve it. The skills above will help you develop your plan. In some cases, the plan may not be completely clear; for example, we may not fully understand what is needed to support a Martian colony, but we will still follow leaders who we believe can figure it out along the way.

One common question at this stage is to ask the difference between leading and managing. It's subtle, and the line between the two blurs: A good leader has managerial skills, and a good manager has leadership abilities. For this type of book, we explore both without worrying about where to draw the line. As a starting point though, my favorite succinct differentiation comes from the brilliant computer pioneer Rear Admiral Grace Murray Hopper: "You cannot manage men into battle. You manage things; you lead people."

Developing Your Leadership

Individual contributors—a term for people who aren't in managerial roles—often think, "Leadership may sound well and good, but I'm a junior employee and won't have a chance to lead for many years." This is wrong on two counts.

First, they are thinking of leadership in terms of positional leadership. From that perspective, it is true that they might not hold a position of authority for some years to come, but that is not the source of leadership we seek.

The ability to provide influential leadership is always available. When you sit in a meeting with others, you have all the tools you need to propose an idea and convince others to go along with it. That is leadership. You may not be given the job of guiding the team through all stages of execution (management), but you have proposed a vision (your idea) and have talked followers into agreeing with your vision (influence). That's influential leadership.

Second, consider a case where you're building a team. You get to pick half a dozen people to be on your team and follow you. What qualities would you look for? Take a moment to think about it before reading further.

Did that list include people who are dedicated? How about good listeners? Should they be trustworthy and ethical? Motivated and hardworking? If you go back to the list above, you'll realize that every one of the qualities that makes someone a good leader also makes someone a good follower. Take the list you came up with; do those qualities also make someone a better leader as well as a better follower?

Companies often have junior team members give presentations. The thinking is that this helps develop that skill for when they become more senior, and presenting to others will be important for their future roles. Similarly, much of what you do every day when not leading (that is, as a follower) is practice for being a leader. In these everyday tasks, you will develop the skills you need to be a leader.

Your leadership training doesn't begin with a job title; it began the day you started interacting with others. There's no secret handshake to learn when you assume a leadership position; it's simply the application of everyday skills that you're already using. To train to be a good leader, work on being a good follower. When the time comes that you have a vision to communicate to a group, those skills will apply to your leadership abilities. Even if you never want to be a leader, these leadership skills will serve you every day in your career as part of a team. Equally important, these skills as a good leader or follower don't apply only to the workplace. You can develop and use these skills outside the workplace, too.

> ## Machiavelli on Change
>
> One key pillar of leadership is envisioning a new future state. It is important to understand the implicit challenges in doing so.
>
> *It must be remembered that there is nothing more difficult to plan, more doubtful of success, nor more dangerous to manage than a new system. For the initiator has the enmity of all who would profit by the preservation of the old institution and merely lukewarm defenders in those who gain by the new ones.*
>
> —Niccolò Machiavelli
>
> No matter what you're proposing, it's likely that someone will oppose it. The status quo exists for some reason, although sometimes that reason is inertia. The decision to do nothing is still a choice, even if only by default.
>
> Certain people who benefit from the status quo will be worse off after the change. In some cases, it's obvious. Diverting a river clearly moves water from one area to another, and that can be better or worse for different parties. Allocating a budget is no different. Providing resources to one group means fewer resources for others.
>
> Sometimes it's not so obvious. Even if other parties don't view the change negatively today, an allocation decision may prevent future opportunities for them, and so they might oppose the change

just to keep their own options open. For example, the new product you propose could possibly be expanded into a product line they may want to control in the future. They don't want to take that chance, so they oppose your proposal today.

Those benefiting from the status quo have a very clear picture. They know exactly their benefits and costs, the risks and opportunities. That is reality. The new state you are envisioning has the promise of becoming something else, presumably involving more benefits and opportunities or fewer costs and risks, but they are still only promises. Anyone who was ever involved in a big project knows that it never works out exactly as planned, and so the end result may not be as promised. There is risk in the path to, and final delivery of, the future state, contrasted against the near certainty of the current state.

In order to overcome the objections of those who will lose out as the status quo goes away, you need a future state that is valuable enough to those who will benefit, even with the risks of variance inherent from the process and implementation. Sometimes this may be so trivial as to be ignored; for example, "Let's do a monthly team happy hour to help people get to know their teammates better" takes so few resources, there won't be many objections. Other times, it makes all the difference. For example, suppose the head of sourcing proposes that changing to a new supplier will result in significant cost savings, which makes his team look better, because they're saving money, but the manufacturing team questions the quality of the new supplier. Even though the contract specifies quality standards, if those standards are missed, it's more time and work for manufacturing, not the sourcing team, to fix the problem. Manufacturing sees little direct benefit but bears most of the risk. In this case, the head of sourcing needs to make sure that manufacturing achieves more benefit, or takes less risk, in order for the department to buy into his vision.

The Myth of the Alpha Male

There is a siren's song luring many novice leaders down a bad path. If you watch many mid-century American movies, you'll see the classic "alpha male." The man in charge (back then, it was always a man) is dominant, commanding, unerring, unemotional, never doubting, aggressive, and often belligerent, especially to those who question him. His authority is not to be challenged; his decisions are always right. That's why he's in charge, and not you. To question him is to invite his retribution, which is clearly unpleasant, or at least that's what's implied.

The very concept of an alpha male comes from the animal kingdom. In some species, there's a single male in the group who is the most dominant. This dominance affords him certain rights within the group. The non-alpha males bide their time, and some eventually challenge the alpha male. Rams and other horned animals literally ram their heads into each other, while gorillas and kangaroos "box." The winner of the fight is the alpha, and the loser is badly bruised.

Whether it comes from the animal kingdom or from the mid-century stereotype, too often, people mistakenly identify such behavior as that of the alpha male.

Ultimately, a true alpha (male or female) is a leader as we've defined it. Alpha males may be decisive or not. (They won't be indecisive, but they may not make snap decisions.) They could be unemotional or not. They could also be soft-spoken, very open to feedback, and humble. Alpha men and women are our leaders, although each may have a personal leadership style. Thankfully, in the modern world, unlike in the animal kingdom, leadership is not determined through combat.

Many people, however, don't recognize that we've left the animal kingdom. They see a man (it's still almost always a man) who shouts at, degrades, antagonizes, or threatens others, and they see it as a sign of being alpha. They see what appears to be decisiveness ("He makes up his

The Career Toolkit

mind quickly, and when he does there's no changing it"), lack of emotion, arrogance, or someone who is demanding of subordinates as signs of an alpha. While an alpha may exhibit these behaviors, good or bad, exhibiting them does not necessarily make one an alpha. It's akin to the logic, "Some primates have tails, but not everything with a tail is a primate."

Many people see someone commanding others as a sign of being the alpha (rather than asking politely). Again, some alphas bark orders, and some don't, but not everyone who does is an alpha.

All too often, bullies and other types of insecure leaders, co-workers, and people we meet in our daily lives exhibit such behavior because they lack confidence and capability in their leadership. They mask their fear and uncertainty by parroting what has been seen in the past as classic alpha behavior. They are false alphas, hiding their lack of true leadership ability behind behavior attributed in the past to alphas.

If you understand what leadership is, it becomes easier to recognize a true alpha leader. Don't be fooled into following someone because they exhibit stereotypical alpha behavior, and don't be a leader who refuses to show emotion, have doubts, ask politely, contemplate before deciding, or do anything your leadership style naturally embodies, simply because you believe it's not an alpha behavior. To be an alpha is to lead—no more, no less. Evaluate leaders by their influential leadership, as we've defined it, not a particular action like volume of voice or speed of decisions.

The Double Bind

A second challenge for today's leaders and followers is what Georgetown University professor and author of *Talking 9 to 5*, Deborah Tannen, describes as a double bind faced by women. In an email to me, she wrote, "Being in a double bind means you're required to obey two mutually exclusive commands: Anything you do to fulfill one violates the other. All women in authority are subject to these two demands: Be a good leader!

Be a good woman!" The more a woman exhibits the traits often associated with being a good leader, such as being direct, confident, unemotional, and ambitious, the more she violates the societal expectations we have of a "good woman," meaning gentle, self-deprecating, emotional, and supportive.

This applies not only to leading but also to daily interactions with peers. One woman's male boss offered her advice on dealing with people who were not providing answers to the questions she asked, sharing with her what he does in those situations. After applying the suggested techniques, she received negative feedback about her approach, even though the very same technique had helped her boss succeed. The same actions reflected positively on him but negatively on her.

I don't have a good answer for this, other than to raise awareness within your organization. Women, unfortunately, have to walk this fine line. Men and women both are biased (it's not just men) and need to be aware of the double bind. If you find that a female co-worker or manager is "difficult," take a moment to picture the same words or actions coming from a male colleague, and see whether you'd feel differently.

Summary and Next Steps

Positional leadership comes from a job title. Influential leadership is based on having a vision and persuading people to follow it. You can lead even without a leadership title, and if you want a leadership title in the future, you should begin to lead today, no matter your role.

Your vision should be affirmative, inclusive of the interests of your followers, and relatable, so the team can buy into it. Other attributes of leaders include empathy, intelligence, respect, inspiration, good communication, trustworthiness, and dedication. The plan itself is not part of the vision, but having a plan for complex or difficult goals helps people buy into your leadership. Further exploration of leadership, such as

The Career Toolkit

reading books and articles on the subject, reading biographies of leaders, or discussing these books with your reading group, can help uncover other attributes that are important to your particular style of leadership.

The qualities that make someone a good leader also make someone a good follower. You can develop your leadership skills as a follower. Even if you don't want to lead, these skills make you a more effective team member. Include improving specific leadership (follower) skills as part of your career plan, and work to actively develop them.

Change, such as that created by your vision, is often a challenge because those who prefer the status quo can envision the downside better than those who benefit from the upside can see the opportunities. There is risk in the implementation, so the upside needs to be sufficiently beneficial to overcome any such risks. When proposing such a change, be sure to understand how it impacts everyone, and work to mitigate the downside.

Leading is about having a vision and persuading people to follow. Behavior that includes being commanding, domineering, and belittling, or qualities such as decisiveness, being demanding, or arrogance, do not make one a leader. Beware of associating leadership with such actions.

Women face a double bind, in that our societal expectations of women are in direct conflict with our expectations of a leader. When working with a "difficult" female co-worker, envision the same behavior coming from a man to see whether you would still feel the same way.

The model of leadership discussed here is a basic starting point. Many other models exist, including servant leadership, situational leadership, holistic leadership, and transformational leadership. Many top business schools and leadership institutes have their own models. You can explore these concepts in books, articles, and training.

As you begin to lead, be sure to get input from your mentors or boss as well as from followers so that you can continue to learn and improve.

Chapter Five

Management: People

> "So much of what we call management consists in making it difficult for people to work."
>
> —Peter Drucker

Like leadership, management is not only for those with a "manager" title. All of us engage in management activities on a daily basis. Knowing how to manage, even as a non-manager, makes you more effective. And if you want to "skate to the puck," as described in the section "Planning Ahead," and become a good manager, this chapter and the next will lay out the core skills you will need.

Management is fundamentally about the people you manage. Understanding people, their needs, and how best to help them is the basis of all management.

Four Roles of a Manager

The naive view of management is that the manager tells the subordinates what to do. This model came out of the Industrial Revolution, when

The Career Toolkit

most workers performed manual labor. The manager's job was to tell the workers which tasks needed to get done and to encourage or chastise them, depending on their performance. Managers directed; workers produced.

In today's information-based economy, the roles are not so black and white. The "workers" often have knowledge and skills that the "manager" does not, and vice versa. The goal isn't to have each worker produce some individual output but rather to have the team, working together, create an output that none alone could have achieved. If you manage a team engaged primarily in physical tasks, such as produce pickers, then you may find yourself primarily directing, rather than managing. In this book, we look at management in the context of the modern office.

When you hold a senior role in an organization, you take on four roles. The weighting of each will vary, depending on how senior the role is and the importance of the role to the company.[28]

STRATEGIST

You will be involved in activities that involve cross-functional teams. As the representative from your department, you need to convey your department's expertise—the opportunities, risks, understanding, and more. Ultimately, you need to help develop the shared vision and strategy for each project and, at the top levels, for the company as a whole by providing your unique perspective. This is based on your role (department) and building a shared vision incorporating the views of everyone else at the table.

Likewise, given a strategy, you need to apply it to your team. A corporate goal results in different specific goals and actions for each team.

---

28. Consider the difference between being a marketer at a steel mill and a marketer at a women's fashion house. In the latter, marketing is a core component of the business. In the former, marketing is needed, but it's not a key function.

TRANSLATOR

As we'll learn in Chapter 7, Communication, not everyone sees the world the way you do. Your domain knowledge and experience give you a unique perspective, as does your position in the company. One subtle but crucial part of the job is translating what is seen and understood by your department into a language and model understood by others. Likewise, you need to take what information others provide and translate it back to your team.

PLANNER

There is day-to-day work expected from your team that you need to plan and supervise. This is the aspect of the role that most people intuitively understand. These are the daily project-management tasks, including project plans, meetings, and budgets.

COACH

Hiring the right people (see Chapter 3, Interviewing) can make all the difference; the wrong people can hamper the team. Just as important are mentoring and developing those who work on your team and helping them develop the skills in this book, as well as other professional skills. Building a cohesive team is important at every level of management, which requires supporting people individually and as a team.

Being a planner is more common among junior managerial roles, and as you move up, the role will expand to being a strategist and translator. The coach role remains constant throughout, although it is often not as well understood or executed by those in more junior positions due to their limited experience. Leadership is an important part of each role, although it is more commonly recognized in the strategist and planner roles.

The Career Toolkit

The reality is that most of the challenges of management are about people. In their seminal book *Peopleware: Productive Projects and Teams*, authors Tom DeMarco and Timothy Lister astutely note that most software projects fail, not due to technical complexity but rather due to people issues. While they focused on software projects, this is true for almost any type of project and team. Many managers will tell you that the most challenging part of their job is managing people, not budgets, timelines, or domain-specific issues. Modern office management is all about people. Don't just take my word for it, ask a manager.

We touched very briefly upon strategy when discussing a leadership vision in Chapter 4, Leadership. Translating will be covered in Chapter 7, Communication. This chapter will focus on people issues, and the next will be on planning and process.

In this book, there are separate chapters for management and leadership. In the real world, it's rare to be in a position where you lead but don't manage. Managing with only minimal big picture-type leadership is more common than the opposite, for example, a project manager who simply focuses on daily tasks. Still, most people in management roles generally engage in some degree of leadership.

Practically speaking, the distinction is somewhat arbitrary. In your career, you will need both leadership and management skills. Effective managers make better leaders, and good leaders know how to manage.

Lest it be assumed that management isn't as important as leadership, we'll contrast Grace Hopper's quote from the last chapter, "You cannot manage men into battle," with another famous military quote often attributed to Napoleon: "An army marches on its stomach." A military leader can inspire his troops to fight, but without proper management (in this case, the project planning and logistics of the food, transportation, and materials that the troops need to advance), the army functions ineffectively, if at all, no matter how inspired its solders may be.

Motivation

One of the key people-related tasks, but one so rarely understood, is that of motivation. The early-twentieth-century model of people doing what they are told, simply for a paycheck, is outdated. Even if pay is a motivator, many of today's knowledge workers perform better with additional motivation beyond their paycheck.

Whether you're a manager trying to motivate your team or even a peer trying to get people to join your project, realize that motivation is a useful tool. That said, there are a number of theories as to what motivates employees. Here are a few.

THEORY X AND THEORY Y (DOUGLAS MCGREGOR)

The Theory X model assumes that workers dislike their work, are not motivated to do it, and so need close supervision. Motivation is accomplished through carrots, such as compensation, and sticks. The Theory Y model assumes that workers are self-motivated and interested in their jobs. They want to be engaged and take ownership of their work.

THEORY Z (URWICK, RANGNEKAR, AND OUCHI)

Combining Japanese and American management approaches, Theory Z is based on strong shared values across an organization and a blending of individual and organizational goals. The model promotes consensual decision-making and long-term relationships between the employee and the organization.

NEEDS THEORY (MCCLELLAND)

People can be motivated by achievement, affiliation, and power. People who need achievement are driven by calculated risk-reward trade-offs. People who need affiliation value relationships with others and with the organization, and they emphasize collaboration. People who need power want to "win" in a zero-sum way and thrive on competition.

EXPECTANCY THEORY (VROOM)

In this theory, people are motivated by their belief that their efforts will produce an outcome leading to a reward they value. For example, a salesperson makes more calls, which leads to hitting sales goals, resulting in a bonus. Setting up the right structure and weighting of factors motivates the employee (or fails to motivate when wrong).

Other models include Porter and Lawler's expectancy theory of motivation, Maslow's hierarchy of needs, Alderfer's ERG theory, and Herzberg's Two-Factor theory.

No matter which model(s) you subscribe to, it's important to recognize that different people are motivated by different things; sometimes the same person is even motivated by different things at different times. As you work with individuals, adjust your motivational style to their specific motivational needs.[29] One size does not fit all when it comes to motivation.

Ideally, you should align what you need them to do (the team goals) with their own goals. Whenever I hire people, I ask about their career goals and personal-development plans. I keep those goals in mind because, whenever possible, I link the projects I assign them to their individual goals. The only way to do this effectively is to literally ask your team members about their goals. Similarly, by getting to know them individually, I start to formulate who took this job for the money, who is motivated by the mission, who values collaboration or winning, and the like.

---

29. Check with HR. Giving some employees a reward of money, others a reward of days off, and others lunch with the CEO can potentially be an HR violation.

Management: People

When creating incentives, keep in mind the advice in *Punished by Rewards*, by Alfie Kohn. Most reward techniques motivate people to get the rewards; that may or may not be sufficient for your team. Equally important, misaligned rewards can do more harm than good. If your team just worked late nights for two weeks straight, and you give them all basketball tickets, that might be great for a sports fan, but for someone who couldn't even tell you the name of that city's team, the reward says, "I may be your boss, but I don't know or care about what you like. You just worked hard for me, but I wasn't willing to put any time into thanking you."

Flow

Flow occurs when you're in a mental state that is very focused or engaged on the task at hand, allowing you to be very efficient at it, colloquially referred to as "being in the zone." It's also experienced in sports, music, and dance. If you're not sure whether you've ever felt it, just think of a time when you had a couple uninterrupted hours of extremely productive work.

As a manager, you can't get people into the flow state, but you sure can get them out of it. Answering emails, phone calls, meetings, and people dropping by your desk all break your flow. Anything that is not the task at hand breaks flow. Once broken, it takes time to get back into flow. (Different estimates put it at anywhere from ten to thirty minutes.) One of your responsibilities as a manager is to protect the flow of your team. Somewhat paradoxically, the more senior you become, the more time you spend jumping from task to task—meetings, emails, phone calls—typically across more diverse issues, limiting the amount of time you personally will be in a flow state. Just because you don't achieve flow doesn't mean you shouldn't be trying to maximize the flow of your team members.

To foster flow among your team, it's important to recognize the circadian rhythm[30] of the team. For example, in many companies, inside sales consist of sales reps talking on their phones, "smiling and dialing" all day long. Generally, they sit in bullpens, cubicles next to each other, where people can overhear each other. The thinking is that the salespeople feed off each other's energy. Even though they each sell independently, they motivate each other by being nearby. Hearing peers celebrate closing a deal helps energize the team. Imagine putting a team of editors, who need extended periods of quiet focus, next to the sales team. The editors suck the excitement away from the sales team, and the sales team's noise distracts the editors.

Legal, marketing, and other teams each have different rhythms, sometimes needing group input for discussion, sometimes working side by side for quick collaboration and interaction, and sometimes being isolated to focus their thoughts. The rhythm itself can even change from one project phase to the next.

As a manager, your job is to understand the cycles of your team and protect the flow. This may mean taking all incoming requests rather than have non-team members constantly interrupt your team, or setting "quiet hours," establishing, say, 2:00 to 4:00 p.m. as a window when there will be no scheduled meetings and no expectations that anyone must answer phone calls or email.

Protecting your team means protecting their productivity. Understand how they need to work, and create an environment that fosters that, which usually means minimizing interruptions and busywork.

---

30. The circadian rhythm is the internal process that regulates the sleep-wake cycle in living things. Here, we're looking at the corporate equivalent.

Management: People

Teamwork

Even when people are motivated individually, it doesn't mean they can automatically work together as a high-performance team. Everyone wants to be part of a team that works well together, but unfortunately, there's no magic wand you can wave to make it happen instantly. As a manager, or even a team member, you can foster the stages of team formation described by Bruce Tuckman.[31] He defined them as: forming, storming, norming, performing, and adjourning, the last of which he added later. When you find a team that is struggling, this framework helps you understand where they are and where they need to go.

FORMING

This is the first stage. People are usually excited and motivated about the potential prospects of the team and project, although this isn't always the case. They might not know many details about the project, for example, the goals, challenges, or resources available, or even their fellow team members. At this stage, orientation is key, which facilitates learning about the project and each other. Hold group activities to get the team familiar with each other and the project.

STORMING

Storming happens when a team begins to work but isn't fully coordinated. Much like a baby learning to walk, it can feel difficult and frustrating. Team members may have different styles or norms of operating that are misaligned. There could be interpersonal conflicts, mistrust, jockeying for position on the team, or territorial disagreements. This stage is marked by conflict and stress. A team should pay close attention

---

31. Bruce Tuckman, "Developmental Sequence in Small Groups," *Psychological Bulletin*, 63. no. 6, (1965): 384–99.

The Career Toolkit

to the team problems (not the project problems, but the meta-problems the team deals with) to understand what needs to be addressed.

NORMING

As the team moves from storming to norming, working together is normalized, conflicts will be resolved, team behaviors will be standardized (for instance, everyone is in by 9:00 a.m., or everyone uses standard templates), and interactions will become smoother. Team contracts are sometimes used to formalize the agreements. There's not a sudden switch from storming to norming; it tends to be gradual. A setback, new issue, or change in a team member, such as a new hire, could temporarily have the team reverting to storming. If so, the manager should step in and get the team back on track.

PERFORMING

The team now knows how to effectively work together and performs well. Coordination issues are fewer than during previous stages. Again, a surprise issue could revert the team to an earlier stage, but a performing team has seen how it can perform and often knows how to get back to this state.

ADJOURNING

All projects eventually end. Whether the project was a success or a failure, it's important to recognize this end state, also referred to as "mourning." If a team spent six months on a project, and it suddenly got canceled or, in some cases, finished successfully, simply telling them, "Come Monday, you'll do something different" can be a rough transition. Even a small ceremony, such as a final group outing or a celebratory cake, helps them recognize the change and make the transition, and leaves them with a positive experience.

Management: People

While the steps are always the same, the amount of time required will vary. In a corporate training exercise of five strangers, you may go through the stages in a matter of hours. Of course, then you're "performing" at the level of corporate training exercises and not at the level of, say, the Blue Angels flight team. Larger teams, more divergent personalities, complex issues, geographic dispersion, and more can all impact how quickly a team goes through these stages. Your job as a manager is to help foster the team through each stage until you reach performing, and then protect that state.

Your Obligations to Your Team

In Spider-Man's origin story, Peter Parker's Uncle Ben famously said to him, "With great power comes great responsibility." It must be remembered that when you hold such a position of authority, you have many obligations.

The most obvious is the obligation to the company. An officer of a corporation has a fiduciary responsibility—that's a legal obligation—to act in the best interest of the company and shareholders.

A leader has an obligation to those she leads. As a leader, you will rally people around a vision, and you have, de facto, promised to make that vision a reality. Members of your team could have chosen not to follow you and invested their time, their energy, and even their hope into someone else, or even into not trying. You have asked them to believe in you, and you have a moral obligation to keep that commitment. If you cannot, you need to say so to your followers.

Less lofty in scope, but perhaps far more a reality for most of us, are the obligations you have as a manager. In your more senior position, you will have access to information and people that others working for you do not. You will also have power and influence that others at lower levels do not. You need to use your power on behalf of those who report to you.

The Career Toolkit

You have an obligation as a manager to look after and develop the careers of the people who report to you. Obviously, you cannot force anything upon them, and if they don't want your advice, that is their right. However, many people would like help from their managers and simply don't know how to ask or even what to ask for. You need to support and help guide them, and to develop their skills and their careers.

The best managers know that, in extreme cases, supporting an employee can even mean suggesting they leave the company for a better opportunity elsewhere. While it might be harder on the team in the short run, and it may seem like that hurts the company, in the long run it's often more than offset by the trust the remaining employees have in their manager and by the long-term relationships that allow the manager to attract talent.

You also have an obligation to fight for your team. This might mean trying to get resources, such as a training budget. It could mean trying to get someone who reports to you placed on a company project that would be good for his career. Remember that these decisions often get made in meetings or office conversations that your subordinates are not even aware of. They are depending on you to speak on their behalf, even if they don't know it.

Obviously, you need to do what's right for the company. You shouldn't put someone on a project if it will help them personally but harm the project or company. After the basic conditions of "What does the company need?" are met, then you, as a manager, need to compete with all the other managers and fight for your team. This is the obligation you accepted when you became a manager.

One question that should be asked of every manager is, "Does he care more about the people above him or below him?" He needs to satisfy his bosses, but a manager should be equally concerned with his subordinates. Whether or not you're a manager, ask yourself how your team would answer this about you, and how much you care about those above you versus those around and below you.

Summary and Next Steps

The line between leading and managing is blurred in the real world. Good managers lead, and good leaders manage. Managers divide their time among strategizing, translating, planning, and coaching.

Each employee has unique motivations. While the motivational tools may be set by the company, your application of them must be done individually, since everyone is different. Try to align project goals with the career goals of the individuals on the team.

Protect the flow state of the team; you can't create it, but you can destroy it. The team itself goes through several stages: forming, storming, norming, performing, and ultimately adjourning. You can't force the progression through the stages, but you can encourage team development and help foster the progression. Any team member, including a non-manager, can recognize which stage their team is in and help it advance to the next stage.

A manager has an obligation to her team members to develop them. She will often be in meetings acting on behalf of the team or its members for things like resources and promotions. A manager should care as much about the people below as the people above.

To continue to develop your management skills, you can read books and articles on management. As you begin to take on managerial responsibility, have your manager and mentors provide guidance and feedback. Even as a non-manager, you can ask your managers and mentors for examples of how they faced managerial situations, or offer to help support some of your managers' tasks in order to gain exposure to them. As a member of a team, you can also employ these techniques to improve team performance, protect flow, and much more.

Chapter Six

Management: Process

> "Knowing is half the battle."
>
> —G.I. Joe

The previous management chapter was all about people and their needs. This chapter is concerned with process and tools. Unlike the many other publications focused on a single process or project-management approach, this chapter discusses the underlying concepts that apply to all of them.

Fundamentally, being good at project and process management is a question of managing information. The labor force has transitioned from the farm and factory to the office. Office workers manage knowledge—they create it, discover it, organize it, and share it. During the industrial age, information was generated by changes in the physical world, whereas in the information age, information causes changes in the physical world. Today, work is information based, and managing that work means managing the flow of information. Looking at a project from the standpoint of information flow allows you to better organize and coordinate a team.

The Career Toolkit

The Three Precepts of Management

On a daily basis, when engaging in planning and execution tasks, a manager needs to do three things: set goals, foster collaboration, and provide support. These three tasks are essentially about coordinating information flow among the team members.

SETTING GOALS

Setting goals means defining the desired outcome. It could be a regular activity, such as selling a product or producing monthly financial reports. It could also be a one-off activity, such as winning a lawsuit or providing a report to upper management. The goal may be a leadership vision or small goals, such as having salespeople hit monthly quotas. Either way, an outcome is set by the person in charge of the team. Note that leaders set goals, while a manager may be given a goal from above and then sets the goal for the team.

Big projects may require intermediate goals. Whatever sub-goals are needed will vary by project. A good manager will set the goal and let the team figure out how to achieve it. The intermediate goals may constrain the "how." Similarly, your knowledge and experience might suggest that certain paths are better than others to guide the team. That is why you're managing. Still, there's a fine line between providing guidance and micromanaging. If you're doing the latter and not letting the team make any of the decisions, it will generally remove the motivation of most knowledge workers. (See "Motivation.")

FOSTERING COLLABORATION

A manager in the knowledge economy is responsible for making sure the right people have the right conversations at the right times. Your team needs to share information and make decisions. Those conversations will have time constraints, such as getting the results of the product

Management: Process

evaluation prior to signing the contract. Coordinating those discussions (and other means of communication) is your job; in other words, the manager needs to manage the flow of information.

The cardinal failure of a rookie manager is the belief that a manager must have all the answers. It goes back to the Industrial Revolution view that a manager orders the subordinates around and, therefore, must know what to order them to do. Under this antiquated view, admitting that you don't know something or aren't certain means that you aren't up to the task of managing. Insecure managers will blindly pick a path and go forward, right or wrong, rather than admit they don't know what to do. That isn't managing, it's covering up a lack of knowledge.

You don't have to have all the answers. Rather, you need your team to get the answers they need, when needed. Maybe you know the answer, maybe someone on the team knows the answer, maybe the team can figure out the answer, or maybe you can get the answer the team needs from someone else in the company. It's not your job to always have the answer but rather to know which of those paths gets you the answer and to support the team in obtaining that knowledge.

Most of the time, that means setting the right coordination structures. It could mean a daily sunset meeting or a weekly status report. It might be getting folks into a room together to figure out a key issue, or choosing an instant messaging channel for the team. Picking the right communications framework, which includes organizational structure, meetings, and communication mechanisms (see "Communication Channels"), is what allows the right people to have the right conversations at the right times.

If the right people aren't getting the right answers at the right times, it's your job to understand why not. Do you have the right people in the right meetings? Maybe you have the wrong people in the wrong meetings. Maybe meetings aren't the answer, but simply having everyone work in close proximity to foster "watercooler conversations" will help. If you have a distributed team, should you do video conference calls?

Would getting everyone working in the same room help? Maybe the right people are having the wrong conversations, and they need guidance. These are the important decisions a manager needs to make.

Sometimes there won't be an answer; in those cases, it's your job to guide the team toward an answer; for instance, "Whatever approach we take, we need to see evidence that it might work within three months so we can know whether to commit to that decision or not."

Use this to guide your operations. What meetings do you need? They should be ones that help generate and distribute information. Who should be on a team? The right people will bring the right information to the team, where "information" could be things they know, will know, or will produce, in the forms of answers, reports, and output. Ultimately, if you can understand the questions and information flows of the project, it becomes much easier to pick the team and set the process.

Managing Imposter Syndrome

Many people have experienced imposter syndrome at one time or another. Imposter syndrome is the belief that you are not worthy of your achievements, you just got lucky, and you were hired for the position you hold by mistake. College students wonder whether the admissions office made a mistake. Employees and even managers fear that it's just a matter of time before the company realizes they aren't as good as everyone else, and they'll be fired. That's imposter syndrome.[32]

If you've ever experienced it, don't worry; it's remarkably common. When you experience impostor syndrome, it becomes harder to admit you don't know something. ("They'll finally realize I don't know what I'm doing and will fire me!") Do a web search for people with imposter

---

32. Note that this is not a formal mental disorder recognized in the *Diagnostic and Statistical Manual of Mental Disorders*.

syndrome, and you'll find that a surprising number of corporate leaders and celebrities have talked about having it.

If, for any reason, you're hesitant to reveal that you don't know the answer, one useful technique is to get input from the team. The U.S. Supreme Court has a tradition whereby the justices cast votes in ascending order of seniority. That is, the most junior justice votes first, and the most senior justice votes last. The thinking is that they don't want more junior justices to feel biased by a more senior justice's opinion.

I lead my teams in the same vein. It works even if you don't have impostor syndrome. My teams know that I don't offer my opinion until I've heard from others. Many times, I do think I know the answer; often I do, but sometimes I don't, or I realize that someone else has a better answer. If so, well, no need to waste the team's time with my dumb idea. Speaking last, as the most senior person, is a great technique in general to make sure you don't overshadow the voices of your team. As a bonus, if you are worried about revealing that you don't know something, it's a good way to calm your nerves and help you overcome your concerns.

PROVIDING SUPPORT

A manager needs to support her team. Support comes in many forms. I like to think of it as being a defensive lineman in American football—keeping out things that can harm your team. The form this support takes will vary from one organization to the next. Generally, it means getting the team the resources it needs, such as information, tools, or access, and protecting the team from distractions.

For example, in many companies it's common to have salespeople regularly coming to the software engineers for questions and sales support; consequently, the software engineers are interrupted throughout the day, making it hard for them to focus. (See the section called "Flow.")

The Career Toolkit

The manager can mitigate this by queuing all requests. Either the manager answers the questions and takes a hit to her own flow, or she queues it up and has the team address it at an appropriate time that's convenient in their work process.

It may be that someone on the team needs a tool or other resource to do his job; if that person doesn't have access or authority, then you need to get it for him. Does he need input from legal? If he cannot get help from legal by himself, then you need to set up a meeting with legal and get the right people to attend it.

I prefer to think of organizational charts upside down, with the CEO at the bottom. As a CTO, I generally don't write much code, but my team does. It's the code (or its output) that the customer is buying—not my meetings, plans, management, or emails. The VP of marketing isn't standing on the corner convincing people to buy the product; it's the marketing campaigns that are created and run by the VP of marketing's staff. It's the people at the opposite end of the organization chart from the executives who do the bulk of the work. A manager's job is to support them. Philosophically speaking, workers with no managers may be inefficient and disorganized, but they will still provide the product or service. Executives with no workers would sit in meetings all day but produce nothing of direct value to the customer. Workers do the work; management creates the environment to make it happen.

Meetings

Fostering collaboration often involves meetings. Many corporate workers spend a significant amount of time in meetings. We attend them, we plan them, we hate them. Far too often, a meeting that begins for one purpose becomes a zombie meeting that hangs around far too long. This section provides a framework to help your team avoid unnecessary meetings.

Management: Process

TYPES OF MEETINGS

Meetings are simply a channel to create and convey information. Fundamentally, there are three types.[33]

1:N Meetings

One person (or a small number of people) will convey information to a larger group. Common examples include status updates, report presentations, town hall meetings, and training. Typically, presenters provide information to the audience, optionally including audience questions. The outcome is that people leave more informed, based on the information presented.

N:N Meetings

Similar to 1:N meetings, here the majority of the people, likely everyone, will be providing information; multiple people (N) presenting to multiple people (N).[34] Common examples include a weekly executive meeting in which each department head gives an update, a daily scrum in which each team member reports the daily plan, or regular meeting in which project team members check in with updates. The main differences between these and 1:N meetings are twofold. While 1:N meetings follow more of a broadcast style, these meetings are often smaller and likely have more interaction among the attendees. Who attends is much more impactful. When the CEO addresses the company, it doesn't matter much if a co-worker is out sick. At an N:N team update, if your teammate doesn't attend, everyone may miss her updates for the week.

---

33. We're excluding 1:1 meetings, since we're looking at organizational information flow, not private conversations.

34. Strictly speaking, 1:N doesn't mean there can only be one person presenting, rather it means a limited number of people presenting to others. Similarly, at N:N meetings some relatively large percentage of attendees, although not necessarily everyone, will present to the whole group.

As with 1:N meetings, the outcome of this type of meeting is that people leave more informed.

Decision Meetings

In this type of meeting, a decision needs to be reached. Examples include adopting a company health plan, deciding which product to purchase, brainstorming, developing a design, or simply deciding what the next steps are in the process. It may not be the final decision. It could even be deciding that more meetings are needed (always fun) or that the decision needs to be delayed. The outcome of the meeting is that some deliberate action has been taken, or information created, typically in response to a question.

That's it. Those are the three meeting activities. Meetings can take place with attendees seated around a table, over lunch, with activities (particularly common in training or brainstorming), or in many other ways, although, sadly, most happen with attendees sitting in a windowless room.

One meeting can intentionally incorporate more than one meeting type. For example, a team leader may take fifteen minutes to give some updates to everyone and then ask the team to make a decision.

It's important to recognize which meeting type is being employed and make sure it's the appropriate one. Many people waste time in meetings that drift or don't require everyone to be there. Conversely, sometimes decisions take place when they weren't planned for that meeting; they can get made by those who happen to be in the room, who may not include all key stakeholders. Even if all are in attendance, they may not have prepared ahead of time for a spontaneous decision, and so the decision may be all the poorer. Organizations feel that they need to make fast decisions, but that should be a conscious choice and not simply a result of, "Hey, while you're all here, let's quickly decide on . . . ." without realizing that only 70 percent of the people who should be there are actually there.

Another common problem is the purpose of a meeting morphing over time. A meeting that began for one purpose may be used for another purpose, but the people or timing of the meeting may not make sense for the circumstances. It just happened that way, because it was convenient.

Map out what communication needs to happen: Who needs to provide what information? To whom? By when? Is it a one-time meeting? Is it triggered by an event, such as after each signed contract? Is it recurring (say, weekly or monthly)? What meetings are needed to make sure the right people have the right conversations at the right times?

Also be sure to ask whether a meeting is necessary. Some things are best communicated in person, others by email, or simply by posting a note in the break room.

AGENDAS

It helps to have an agenda for each meeting, optionally with time estimates. Some companies like formal, detailed lists; other organizations are more casual. Whichever you choose, everyone should understand which meeting type(s) the meeting is and what the expected outcome is, for example, reviewing the quarterly sales numbers or deciding on the budget for the holiday party.

Without that clarity, it's easy for meetings to drift. With a clear agenda specifying topics and goals, the plan for the meeting is obvious. If the meeting is no longer useful, it can be changed to one that is useful, or it can be dropped altogether.

Be sure to get input from the whole team on the agenda. Too often, people in meetings where there is already too much on the agenda feel they don't have a place to raise their issues. Consequently, they feel disengaged. The meetings are for everyone attending, not just the organizer.

UNPLANNED TOPICS

Most of the time, companies would do better to have more formally organized meetings with clear agendas. But inspiration cannot be planned; insights aren't easily scheduled. Sometimes, there is significant value in going off on tangents or bringing up unplanned items because it suddenly seems relevant. Do it! Don't be afraid if this happens, because this is part of running a modern, evolving organization. Just be aware of when this is happening.

If you're going on useless tangents too often, it's time to revisit the meeting plan. If it happens once in a while, great. Plan an agenda that only takes fifty minutes. Now you've given yourself ten minutes to follow those tangents if they come up.

Keep in mind what that tangent is (an update? a decision?), and ask yourself whether the right people are in the room for it, but in general don't be afraid of a tangent. Some of the biggest corporate value has come from tangents. How much time should be allowed for these is up to you.

This deviation from the previous advice is an example of why business is subtle and tricky. "Rules" always have exceptions. Knowing when to bend business rules and even when to sometimes break them is the mark of a good manager. In this case, stick to your agenda, except sometimes when you shouldn't.

SIX HATS

One tool for making meetings more effective is Edward de Bono's Six Thinking Hats methodology. It breaks down communications into six categories, each represented by a hat of a different color. The idea is that all statements fall into any of six categories, and by recognizing this, the team can make sure that everyone is having the same type of discussion, as opposed to talking across different modes of thinking.

Management: Process

- Blue: Management
- White: Information
- Green: Creativity
- Yellow: Optimistic Support
- Black: Critical Review
- Red: Emotions

Blue: Management

These are meta-statements. They are about the process being used.

Examples:
- We have forty-five minutes left for this session.
- Perhaps we should each give one idea and then compare them.
- Let's vote on which idea is best.
- We should have marketing join this meeting.

White: Information

These are informational statements, facts relevant to the discussion.

Examples:
- The theater's seating capacity is 415.
- The contract needs to be signed no later than April 30th in order to hold the event in July.
- When we proposed this before, the legal team didn't approve the project, citing a contract violation.

Green: Creativity

New ideas, particularly creative, out-of-the-box thinking.

Examples:
- What if we were to partner with an energy company?

- Let's do the benefit outdoors this year.
- I know we don't have the money yet, but if we did, what would the budget look like?
- Imagine a version of the enterprise product designed for the consumer market.

Yellow: Optimistic Support

Positive, optimistic statements. Often these are statements supporting an idea by mentioning its value, benefits, or opportunities.

Examples:
- That would allow us to expand internationally with minimal investment.
- It will reduce the time to market.
- Couldn't that also reduce our costs?

Black: Critical Review

This is the opposite of yellow; it's critical analysis of the situation. It looks at negatives and risks. This is the hat worn when playing the devil's advocate.

Examples:
- People won't buy green-colored food; it's unappetizing.
- It will be hard to get the rights to those images.
- That many people will create logistical challenges.

Red: Emotions

This is the opposite of the white hat. Instead of objective facts, these statements express emotions and feelings. They can also include hunches and intuition and can be positive or negative.

Examples: (positive / negative)
- Great idea. / I don't like it.
- This feels right. / My gut says this won't work.
- Do you think you can make it work? / Are you sure you can pull it off?
- I like the color. / It's ugly.

You can begin to look at discussions as combinations of the Six Hats statements. Classic brainstorming is the process of throwing out new ideas but without criticism or discussion. That's green and yellow (new ideas and support) but not black (criticism). Negative feedback is typically black, but then it often includes yellow or green when supportive statements or ideas for improvement are offered.

Most discussions aren't so rigid; people don't formally invoke what hat they are using, but that's sometimes the problem. When one person is trying to get the relevant facts out (white), and another person simply doesn't like the idea and keeps saying as much (red), it can feel like they're talking at cross purposes. Similarly, as you're trying to come up with new ideas (green), having someone at the table who is always shooting them down (black) puts a damper on the creativity.

Some companies are very explicit in their use of the hats (right down to having people physically hold colored hats or colored note cards to signal their thinking). A team might say, "Let's just start with some white-hat discussion to make sure we all have the same facts. Then we'll do some green-hat idea generation." During a discussion, someone may chime in, "I'd like to make a blue-hat point that we have thirty minutes left in this meeting." It doesn't matter if you are that formal or not, as long as you recognize the types of hats. If you find that a discussion doesn't seem to be going anywhere, start to look at the statements being made, and see whether everyone is having the same type of conversation. If not, applying a little structure (blue hat) might help.

The important thing is to avoid having people talk at cross purposes in the discussion.

Communication Channels

Today we have multiple channels for communication. Understanding how to use each, and more importantly, making sure everyone on the team is using them the same way, matter.

It's not what you say, but how you say it. Some sources say that up to 90 percent of communication is non-verbal. While that statistic is usually stated out of context,[35] there is no doubt that your communication is more than just the words you say. Physically, there are body language, facial expression, and tone.

There's also a temporal component. When you send an email, you generally don't expect an immediate reply. On the other hand, when you're talking to someone face to face, after you speak, standing in silence for minutes waiting for the other person to respond would be socially very awkward.

Considering these dimensions can help you decide which channel to use. There's no right answer; some companies prefer email over instant messages, while others do the reverse. Some are adamant about face-to-face meetings, while other companies work virtually.

It's important that there be a common understanding among the team as to what channels are used for what purpose. You don't want

---

[35]. Mehrabian, A., & Ferris, S.R., "Inference of Attitudes from Nonverbal Communication in Two Channels," *Journal of Consulting Psychology*, 31, no. 3 (1967): 248–52. The study found that when the verbal and non-verbal channels disagree, the non-verbal channel dominates. However, the methodology of the study was that the speaker would give a single word, such as "maybe," with different intonations. It was not a full conversation. The authors did not suggest that the non-verbal always dominates in all communication.

someone waiting for an email when, unbeknownst to them, a voicemail has already been left.

The table below is meant as a guide to what each communication channel offers:

	Words	Tone	Body Language	Visuals	Speed of Response
Face-to-Face	Yes	Yes	Yes	Yes	Instant
Video Conference	Yes	Yes	Partial	Yes	Instant
Phone Call	Yes	Yes	No	No	Instant
Email	Yes	Limited*	No	Yes	Varies
Instant Message	Yes	Limited*	No	Yes	Varies
Text Message	Yes	Limited*	No	Limited	Varies
Voicemail	Yes	Yes	No	No	Slow

TABLE 2. Communication Channels
*While there is no audible tone, generally people who know each other can detect a tone in written communications.

When deciding which channel to use, consider which information needs to be conveyed and the expected response. Agreement across the team is more important than which channel you choose. Make sure everyone on the team understands what channel is to be used for what purpose and why.

The Career Toolkit

The Project Triangle

One important, but often overlooked, decision when managing any project is how to balance competing constraints. There's no shortage of methodologies,[36] but they all require that this fundamental balancing decision be made. Once decided and disseminated, the team must then select activities to suit that decision and respect the balance. The hiring triangle described earlier is based on an older constraint-management philosophy known as the "project triangle."[37]

Imagine that a customer requests of a housebuilder, "Here's an empty plot of land and money for three construction workers. Have them build me a seven-bedroom, five-bath mansion in the next sixty days." No chance. Three people simply cannot do that much construction in sixty days.

Now imagine that the customer asks the builder to do it over five years. That's doable. Alternatively, what if the customer were to say, "Here's money for twenty construction workers"? Perhaps then it could be done in sixty days.[38]

---

36. Examples include waterfall, critical path, Agile, Scrum, Six Sigma, Kanban, Lean, PERT (Program Evaluation and Review Technique), and PMI/PMBOK (Project Management Institute / Project Management Body of Knowledge). You can readily find plenty of books, articles, and training courses on them.

37. It's sometimes also referred to as the "engineering triangle."

38. There is a limit though. There's an old adage by Fred Brooks known as the "mythical man-month," described in his book of the same name, that says that simply adding more people doesn't always make a project go more quickly. At a certain point, more people start to slow down the project, because they now require additional coordination and management. A second person can work side by side with the first. Ten more people would require someone to coordinate them. In the extreme, imagine that we added 800 people to this project—at that point, there's not even room for all 800 people to work on the house at the same time. There are also some tasks that cannot go more quickly with additional people; Brooks famously quipped that nine women cannot make a baby in one month.

Management: Process

Alternatively, suppose the customer were to ask for a small two-room shack instead of a mansion. That's certainly doable by three construction workers in sixty days.

Cost. Time. Scope. Pick two. You can't constrain all three.

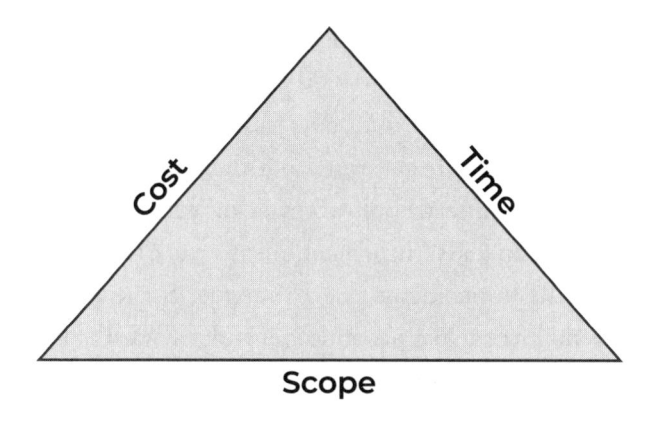

FIGURE 4. The project triangle

"Cost" is how much money can be spent. It's helpful to think of this as money spent per unit of time, such as per week or per month. Commonly, this determines how many people are working on the project—the more staff, the higher the monthly cost of the project.

"Time" is simply how much time there is to complete the project, usually specified in days, weeks, or months.

"Scope" is how big the project is, in other words, how much you're trying to achieve by the project deadline. Scope can take on a wide range of meanings. In this case, it might be how big the house is. Alternatively, maybe it's just how finished the house is. The rooms may be built, but with no wallpaper or lighting; maybe the plumbing needs to be done, but not the electrical. In manufacturing, it might be how many items need to be physically produced, while in software it's how many features go into the release.

The Career Toolkit

Inexperienced managers often try to specify all three constraints. As we saw with the house, you can specify all you want, but reality may not agree, and it's in reality where we actually do our work. Recognizing that so many people can produce only so much work over so many days prevents you from setting an unrealistic plan into motion.

Some people try to cheat, such as making salaried nine-to-five employees work from 8:00 a.m. to 8:00 p.m. That's like magically raising the cost cap, for no additional money; suddenly it's as if there were 50 percent more employees. It can work, but there are limitations. Asking accountants to work ninety hours a week can work for a few weeks, but not for months on end. Asking a machinist to work ninety hours a week can quickly result in accidents due to fatigue. Some even argue that white-collar employees, like accountants and software developers, also quickly start to make mistakes when they work long hours—in those cases, the consequences are errors and bugs, not physical injury.

The bottom line is that once the first two dimensions are constrained, the third cannot be. In more complex models, the triangle becomes a quadrilateral or some other shape with more sides, representing additional factors such as quality, risk, flexibility, and more. The principle is the same, in that you cannot specify every dimension, and the more you constrain some, the more variance is needed in the remaining dimensions.

Companies that use an agile software development practice, which can be applied to non-software projects as well, follow this principle. There is a fixed time known as a "sprint" (typically one to four weeks), during which there are a set number of people on the team, trying to achieve a number of tasks (known as "stories"). Time is fixed. Cost is fixed with the number of people. The manager may ask for fifty stories, but the understanding is that the team will do whatever it can do, and that's the reality. With time and cost fixed, what varies is scope—the number of tasks actually completed.

Process Improvement

No matter what process you choose, and what balance is decided in the project triangle, things won't be perfect. But while perfection may not be achievable, improvements are. Even in the best case, the world isn't static, and any process needs to be adjusted for those changes that occur over time. These tools will help you adjust your process as you go.

RETROSPECTIVES

Every process should include a retrospective. This is key to getting the information you need to improve. Traditionally, companies have called this a "post-mortem," a review of a project after it goes off the rails. Many companies make this a practice for all projects, whether they're a success or failure. Software firms, which have fast development cycles, now do it much more regularly, sometimes every week or two. The U.S. military version is called an "after-action report." This will work for any team, not just software companies and the military.

Retrospectives take anywhere from thirty minutes to a week, depending on how much time and effort you want to put in and how complex the project is. If you're reviewing the last two-week cycle for a team of six, an hour is probably fine; if it's a review of an eighteen-month, five hundred-person project, you might need a solid week.

For larger retrospectives, when you want to really dig into things, you'll find excellent scenarios and instructions in Norman Kerth's *Project Retrospectives: A Handbook for Team Reviews*. For smaller ones of one or two hours, it can be as simple as having a discussion and walking away with what you want to improve. To develop a simple plan for a retrospective, organize your ideas into three categories:

Do More
Things the team should do more often, whether it's starting a new process or policy or increasing the frequency at which something is done. Your goal might be, "Let's make sure we send status updates more often."

Do Less
Things the team should stop doing or reduce in frequency, such as, "Let's only test once a week and not every day, since it takes a while to set up, and not much changes from one day to the next."

Interesting
Other observations, comments, or thoughts.

Some people use the terms "start," "stop," and "continue." It doesn't matter whether you use those three categories or make four of your own. You could also use two categories or follow any other method. The key is that at the end of the review, you should have an idea of what to do differently to make things run better at your company or organization.

However you choose to implement it, there are two important things to remember when doing a retrospective:

First, try not to take on too much at once. Lots of people make New Year's resolutions, but most people know you can't wake up on January 1st and suddenly quit smoking, reduce your drinking, eat better, start going to the gym, and wake up early every day. Rather, on January 1st, tackle one change. Maybe you start by going to the gym. It's hard. You feel the call of your couch on a cold January day, and you need to force yourself to get to the gym. But once you've been going for a few weeks or months, it starts to become a habit. It's no longer a daily battle of willpower but something you do automatically. Then you can focus on the next activity, such as eating better.

When you do your first few retrospectives, you may find a number of problems. A good manager knows how to prioritize when you can't do it all. Pick one or two things to change, and work on those for a few cycles.[39] Once they become a habit, move on to the next priority.

Second, use the prime directive, created by Norman Kerth:[40]

> ***The (Retrospective) Prime Directive***
> *Regardless of what we discover, we understand and truly believe that everyone did the best job they could, given what they knew at the time, their skills and abilities, the resources available, and the situation at hand.*

Things won't always go well at work. Sometimes it will feel as though someone else is trying to make your job harder. Once we go down that path, there will be distrust and hostility within the team. Norman Kerth always recommends making sure everyone feels comfortable with that statement before starting a retrospective. If people don't feel comfortable with that, then there's a bigger underlying issue afflicting the team: mistrust.

This matters because, without trust, you can't have honest conversations, and without honest conversations, you can't understand what's really happening. If people feel they'll be attacked by their co-workers or boss for admitting a wrong decision, they won't bring it up, and the problem will be harder to address. We hire humans, not machines, because they can make judgment calls. If someone

---

[39]. Here we're talking about habits to change, like "Remember to email the team after you edit the document." Conversely, things like, "Let's move the weekly status update from Monday to Wednesday," where it doesn't require conscious habitual change on the part of each team member, can easily all be done at once.

[40]. Different from, but probably just as important as, the Starfleet Prime Directive from *Star Trek*.

repeatedly and consistently makes the wrong call, that's another issue. But if you, as a manager, jump on a person every time he makes a wrong but well-intentioned call, people will either stop making decisions or stop admitting to them when they go wrong, and you'll be in the dark.

Hanlon's Razor

There is an older version of the prime directive called "Hanlon's Razor": Never attribute to malice that which is adequately explained by stupidity.[41]

As Murphy's Law warns, bad things will happen. There may, indeed, be an evil genius out to get you. But, as another philosophical razor, Occam's Razor, tells us, most of the time there isn't, or more generally, the simplest explanation is usually the correct one. Colloquially: Shit happens.

Years ago, I oversaw collegiate dancing in New England. The national organization ran a large event that was scheduled to be in the UK that year. A college team wrote me and asked me to confirm that the event would be taking place; they wanted to buy their plane tickets but needed to confirm that the event would be taking place before committing the money. I reached out to someone more senior in the organization and got confirmation that it was going to happen and relayed the message to the college team.

Two days later, the event was canceled. It is quite possible the team bought the tickets and felt that I had lied to them. Had I? To the best of my knowledge, I'd told them the truth; I hadn't known of any risk to the event. Defensively, I could say it wasn't my fault, or that it was the other person who lied to me! But had I been lied to? The person

---

41. Earlier variations of this quote exist from other sources.

who confirmed the event to me may have been in the same position, getting her information from someone else and relaying that to me. Maybe the person at the root of the chain never lied. Perhaps the organizer himself sincerely believed that the event was going to take place, but then a fire hit the facility, and no alternatives were available. Or maybe someone in the organizer's family had a serious illness, and he couldn't spend time organizing an event. Any of a number of other things could have happened.

We shouldn't jump to conclusions. When dealing with someone, if you find a pattern, and things repeatedly don't seem to go your way, then maybe someone is being duplicitous or possibly just incompetent. Either way, it's a consistent pattern, and you should be wary of working with such a person. By default, assume stupidity, that is good intentions and bad luck, rather than malice.

If you've ever been in a tense situation with someone, then you know it's easier to escalate than de-escalate. Whether it's a schoolyard fight, a heated argument with a significant other, or a sour relationship with a co-worker, the hard part is trying to move back from confrontation. If you assume malice, you are moving toward confrontation. You can always move in that direction later. Moving away from it and de-escalating the situation, while harder, can often lead to improved communications, improved decision-making, and improved relationships. Don't take that first step toward confrontation. Don't escalate by assuming malice unless you're absolutely sure.

ROOT CAUSE ANALYSIS

Another common tool is root cause analysis (RCA). It's similar to a retrospective but usually focuses on a single issue. RCAs are commonly used in situations involving a workplace accident, design flaw, server crash, or other type of significant error.

The Career Toolkit

What applies to retrospectives applies here, too. You need to start with the prime directive and believe that everyone was well-intentioned. Otherwise, this will inhibit your ability to get all the pertinent information.

The main difference between an RCA and a retrospective is that an RCA is about a specific incident, and it gets very detailed. You will look at the timeline of events and will review each decision made along the way. The goal is to trace back and find places where different decisions or actions could have led to different outcomes, for instance, making sure legal was looped in to verify any compliance risk or having an additional monitor that would have alerted the team to slow server response time.

Wrong decisions or inaction during the timeline lead to your post-RCA action agenda. What needs to change now to make sure you don't repeat the problem? As much as I don't want my team to make mistakes, most of my jobs don't involve human safety or significant amounts of money based on a single, irreversible decision. We don't always have the time or resources to triple-check everything, because speed to market is often more important, so sometimes mistakes are made. The one thing that isn't acceptable is repeating a mistake. Once my team makes a mistake, we need to learn from it and prevent it from recurring. RCAs are how we do that.

FIVE GORILLAS

Retrospectives and RCAs are formal methods to process improvement. Equally important is creating a mindset that's open to change. One of my favorite (although no doubt apocryphal) corporate parables is the one about the five gorillas.

A scientist puts five gorillas in a room. In the center of the room are steps with bananas suspended above them. Whenever a gorilla begins to climb the steps to reach the bananas, every gorilla in the room is blasted with ice water from a firehose. Very quickly, they all learn not to touch the steps.

Management: Process

The scientist then removes one of the gorillas and replaces him with a new one. The new gorilla spots the bananas and heads toward the steps. The other gorillas try to stop him. Undeterred, the new gorilla forces his way forward. The other four gorillas then use force, beating him to teach him not to go near the bananas. Soon this new gorilla learns not to touch the steps.

Then another of the original gorillas is replaced. Again, the new gorilla heads toward the steps, and again ultimately the other gorillas beat him into staying away, including the one from the previous round, who has now learned this behavior.

One by one, each gorilla is replaced. In the final round, the new gorilla heads toward the steps. The other four gorillas race to stop him, and yet none actually knows why. None of those gorillas was around for the first stage of the experiment. None experienced or even knows about the water, yet they continue this learned behavior.

Sadly, this is how many organizations operate. What's really sad is, unlike the gorillas, we have a more sophisticated language, verbal and written, such that we can communicate our reasoning. Gorillas can only use force, but we can leave process documents or hold meetings; heck, we could even leave Post-it notes about why we should or shouldn't do something. Nevertheless, this situation arises surprisingly often.

One of the most important things you can do as a manager (or non-manager) is to ask why. There may be a good reason. Or there may have been a good reason in the past that no longer holds. Blindly doing something because that's how it's always been done isn't leading or managing; it's yielding, and that's not why you've been given responsibility.

More broadly, on my teams, I encourage everyone to ask why. Not just about process but about everything. Why this product? Why is this the plan? Why partner with that company? They can, and should, question things they don't understand.

The Career Toolkit

The person asking the question gains a better understanding of the situation; they see another part of the elephant. The person answering the question gets feedback about a potential issue, or even just about something that may not have been explained well to the team. My team members know that if I can't justify a decision, I shouldn't be making it. They have an obligation to question everything.[42]

One variant of this is the Five Whys. You ask why something is done and then keep asking why, drilling down each time until you get to the root motivation. This is a helpful technique to use during RCAs.

Why did the assembly line get shut down? Because a unit overheated. Why did it overheat? We ran out of coolant. Why did we run out of coolant? Because we forgot to order more. Why did we forget to order more? Because the person who does so is on paternity leave, and the person covering for him got very sick. Why was no one else aware that we ran out? We don't have an alert. Solution: Create a monitor to alert multiple people when the coolant level gets too low.

Whether you use the Five Whys or some other approach, doesn't matter. What is important is fostering a culture of making sure that ideas and practices are justified. Equally important is recognizing that what made sense yesterday may not hold true today. Encourage questions, because they help everyone learn and improve.

Leadership vs. Management

You've now been exposed to a chapter on leadership and two chapters on management. What's the difference? Some will argue that leadership is about vision and inspiration, while management is planning

---

42. I do know of one case where it's taken perhaps too far. In that company, anyone can question anyone. I've heard from folks there that sometimes an expert, someone who literally wrote the book, will have to spend significant time fielding questions from everyone else at the company who is empowered to question the decisions of others. Balance appropriately.

and organization. Others may define the difference as big picture versus everyday details. It could be viewed as goals and persuasion versus actions and implementation.

In some sense, the debate is pedantic. Would you follow a leader who sells you on a vision and then says, "Okay, now you go figure it out and make it happen"? Would you work for a manager who simply says, "Do this. I don't know why, that's just what they tell me we need to do"? Leaders manage, and managers lead. Be sure to do both.

Summary and Next Steps

Managing office workers means having to manage and foster the flow of information. The three precepts of management, which help you do that, are: setting goals, fostering collaboration, and supporting the team.

You're going to spend a lot of time in meetings; making them effective can have a huge impact on your career. There are three types of meetings: 1:N (broadcast), N:N (update), and decision. The motivation of a meeting and the type (standing meeting, one-off, triggered meeting) should be clearly understood so the right meetings are held for the right people. Agendas help you stay focused, but going off on tangents, to some limited extent, can be helpful. Look at the meetings you have, and ask whether they are efficient for the information flows needed.

The Six Thinking Hats framework allows you to identify the different types of conversations people may be having. The hats are: blue (management), white (information), green (new ideas), yellow (support), black (criticism), and red (emotions). They can be used formally in meetings or simply to identify people talking at cross purposes. *Six Thinking Hats*, by Edward de Bono, is an easy read that explores this topic further. Try it out at some meetings for a few weeks. It can seem cumbersome at first, but simply making sure everyone is aware and has

The Career Toolkit

a common language can allow you to identify issues of people speaking with different hats on in the future—even if you're not formally using the framework.

We have many channels of communication, such as email, text, or video chats. Each expresses words, tone, body language, and visuals differently; there are also different expectations on response time. Make sure everyone on your team has a shared understanding of when to use which channel.

There are many processes and project-management frameworks. All projects are constrained by cost, time, and scope (the project triangle). You can't constrain all three; if you fix two (say, time and people), then the third (scope) is set by those constraints. There's a whole industry dedicated to project management, including books, classes, and articles.

No matter what process you use, retrospectives are an easy way for teams to learn and continually improve, while RCAs (root cause analyses) are used for one-off incidents. There are a number of books and articles on retrospectives and RCAs; you can get a sense of how to do them with just a few hours of reading. Remember Hanlon's Razor: "Never ascribe to malice that which can be explained by mere stupidity." Don't assume the worst; take the time to understand why most people are trying to do the right thing and aren't out to get you. Consider adding retrospectives or RCAs to your team if you don't use them already.

The five gorillas parable reminds us to always ask why. If you can't justify the answer, then you need to start asking why. Consider using the Five Whys to really drill down. Most important, create a culture that encourages people to ask questions, without going overboard.

These tools, while managerial in nature, can be employed by anyone on the team. Understanding the information flow helps you understand how the organization works and where and how it can work better.

INTERPERSONAL DYNAMICS

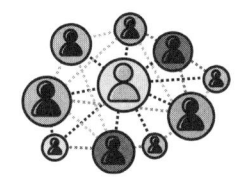

Chapter Seven
Communication

> "The single biggest problem in communication is the illusion that it has taken place."
>
> —George Bernard Shaw

Communication is a skill that is often discussed, but few people understand it well. Far too many problems in the world come from a failure to communicate.

Much communication training focuses on public speaking, for example, projecting your voice and making eye contact, or writing the pedestrian five-paragraph essay. While those are useful skills, they disguise a fundamental problem that is common in corporate communications.

Many fail in their mission to communicate because the very idea is unclear. While a staticky radio transmission can be hard to listen to, far worse is a clear radio transmission of a presenter who is incoherent. Making this especially tricky is that, most of the time, we do communicate sufficiently well so that we don't realize that the potential for a problem exists. When we aren't effective at communicating, it can sometimes be due to the critical nature of the discussion; the times we're most likely to miscommunicate are exactly the times when it's most important that we do not. Understanding the fundamentals of communicating your ideas is a critical skill at every level of an organization.

What Is Communication?

Fundamentally, communication is the act of conveying an idea from your head to someone else's head. That's it. Simple. There's no shortage of tools for doing that: talking, writing, drawing. Even playing the game "charades" is communication. So, why is it so difficult?

In the movie *Donnie Brasco*, Johnny Depp plays Donnie, an undercover FBI agent who has infiltrated the mob. In one scene, a member of his FBI team asks, "What's 'Forget about it'?" Donnie replies,

> *'Forget about it' is, like, if you agree with someone, you know, like 'Raquel Welch is one great piece of ass. Forget about it!' But then, if you disagree, like 'A Lincoln is better than a Cadillac? Forget about it!' You know? But then, it's also like if something's the greatest thing in the world, like, 'Minghia! Those peppers! Forget about it!' But it's also like saying, 'Go to hell!' too. Like, you know, like 'Hey Paulie, you got a one-inch pecker?' and Paulie says 'Forget about it!' Sometimes it just means, 'Forget about it.'*

This expression has multiple meanings, all depending on context. Two are exact opposites, so how do you know if they're agreeing or disagreeing? It should be apparent from the context, but if you don't have a sophisticated understanding of the context and the usage of the expression or term, including intonation and body language, you could easily get the wrong impression of the speaker's intention.

While most business and personal communications don't have such a range of interpretations for "Forget about it," they still lend themselves

Communication

to multiple interpretations—often with much bigger implications than those of a bar-side chat.

The obligation is always on the speaker (or writer) to make the effort to communicate the information correctly and effectively. The tools in this chapter are designed to help you do just that.

Meaning

Do you need a hero? Some of you might be thinking about Superman, but others may be thinking about food. If we're talking about food, depending on where you grew up, you may call it a "sub," a "hero," a "hoagie," a "grinder," or just a "big sandwich." Most people are either aware of this or figure out the meaning from context; your waitress isn't asking about your favorite superhero. This is a simple example of people having different contextual or mental models of a concept or term. Here "model" is used only in the simplest of ways.

A step farther are idioms. There's a Spanish expression, "El mundo es un pañuelo," which literally means, "The world is a handkerchief." Native speakers know that it means, "It's a small world." In English, "It's a small world" literally describes planetary size, but, of course, we say it to mean that people are interconnected. In this case, an expression means something else. If you know the idiom, you don't take the words literally; you have a mental model that tells you the words mean something else. Some people know the idiom, and those who don't might think you're speaking nonsensically.

At one company, we had a travel blog with different sections for family travel, adventure travel, and more. One was the all-inclusive blog. In travel, "all-inclusive" means one price that includes hotel, food, and activities. The software developers first interpreted it as one blog that included posts of all the other blogs. It was a small mistake, but a good example of how people interpret things differently without context.

Going farther, we get into distinctions in meaning that are both larger and more subtle. Most Americans agree that we must protect individual rights. The debate is about how to define those rights. In the gun-control debate, the question is: Which is more important—the right to life, as stated in the preamble of the Declaration of Independence, or the right to bear arms, as specified in the Constitution? Both sides talk about safety, but on one extreme, safety comes from very limited access to guns; on the other, it comes from a prevalence of guns.

When someone says something as generic as "It's about freedom," it can be interpreted in a wide variety of ways. Two people can argue without end, each wondering why the other person doesn't seem to understand the meaning of "freedom." If someone says, "I believe there are too many deaths, and so to protect the right to life, we must restrict guns" or "I believe that while deaths are tragic, restricting guns will erode freedoms and cost more lives in the future," we've more clearly defined the disagreement—in this case, the prioritization of conflicting rights.

While the disagreement in terms outlined above is understood by parties active in that discussion, within our corporate organizations, it's not always so clear. "We must minimize risk!" demands an executive. What risk? Risk of spending too much money? Risk of failure? Risk of missing a market opportunity? Risk of product failure in the field? These choices can be in opposition. If you're worried about cost over-runs, tighter financial controls are the answer. If the concern is about missing a first-mover market opportunity, money be damned. Get there as quickly as you can. If the risk is about the negative PR from product failures, you might take more time and spend more money to test the product or make it more robust. If risk isn't well defined, everyone could walk out of the room with different views.

It's important that your meaning be very clear when you talk. When in doubt, overcommunicate or express the idea in multiple ways. Those receiving the communication should hear a consistent message, and if they note any inconsistency or don't feel it's sufficiently defined, they should flag the issue and ask for clarification.

Models

Linguistic differences are relatively easy to spot. If someone says, "It's a small world," you either know what it means or know enough to ask. What's less clear are the mental models we carry in our heads.

I was first educated to be a physicist. Physicists are trained to model the real world in terms of forces and constraints and to make approximations. One common physics problem is calculating the speed of a car rolling down an inclined plane. We look at the angle of the plane, the force of gravity, the weight of the car, and the friction of the road. We don't care about the color, make, or model of the car, whether it's an aerodynamic race car or a 1970s box van. We don't care about wind resistance; it won't make a practical difference unless we want to be accurate to some tiny decimal place. We're trained to define a sufficient (not perfect) model and understand how the bodies in the model interact.

Contrast this with people who are trained in finance. I worked for two Harvard Business School finance professors some years back who often had a very different perspective from mine. Finance professionals are trained to look at the world in terms of cost, time, and risk. Why do stocks generally have higher returns than bonds? Because stocks are riskier. Risk, return, and time need to be in balance; a riskier item needs to provide a greater expected return than a less risky one. The longer your capital is locked up in an asset—be it a bank account, bond, or manufacturing plant—the greater the expected return needs to be to justify it. If one of these items is out of alignment with the other two, there's an arbitrage opportunity.

That point was made to me very concretely one day when I was driving us in my beat-up, eighteen-year-old car. The car, old and dented from an accident, had a blue book value of $1,000 (if I'm being generous). It had been stolen a few years ago, so I used the Club, an anti-theft device that goes on the steering wheel, in addition to locking the doors. One professor thought I was being inefficient. To him, it was so old and beat up that no one would steal it. I was wasting a little time each and every day locking and unlocking the car doors and using the Club. I thought the risk was higher and that it was worth my time. For most people, this would have simply been a theoretical discussion, but he saw a misalignment of risk and time. He offered to sell me insurance. I would pay him fifty dollars a year, and in exchange I wouldn't have to lock my doors or use the Club, thus saving me time every day. If the car were stolen, he'd pay me the value of the car. Recognizing a disagreement in risk assessment, he immediately saw how to define it monetarily. I never would have thought of that, because at the time I hadn't been trained to think that way.

Lawyers, unlike physicists, don't approximate away things like friction. Contract lawyers know that each and every word in a contract has an implication. The use of a comma can alter the meaning of a contract. Most people don't worry too much about comma placement, but lawyers (and book editors) are paid to do exactly that. They know to be very careful with words, and they know that each choice could expose you to liability. Lawyers think about how to minimize liabilities, given the constraints needed to achieve the goal.

Master networker Keith Ferrazzi, in his book *Never Eat Alone*, sees everything as a networking problem. Most of us think of using our networks when we need to find a job. Ferrazzi also recognizes the application of a personal network for hiring people, getting customers and partners, finding suppliers, figuring out what to do on your vacation, and just about everything else. In his model, the answers to all your questions lie in your network.

Communication

Visual artists, on the other hand, notice things like the choice of colors, relative placement of objects, and subject matter. When I see a painting from a few centuries ago, I see a picture. They see symbolism in who is sitting versus standing, who is close versus far, on the right or left, in the light or in the shadows. Likewise, if you show me an advertisement, I might see the product and no more, but graphic designers and other artists understand why the product was displayed as such, from a certain angle, at a certain time of day, in a certain setting.[43]

We are each trained with certain mental models that reflect how we view the world. Consider this one: Curtis Brooner was once locked in a Burger King bathroom. After taking over an hour to get him out, the manager apologized and offered him free meals for life. Brooner happened to be a regular at Burger King and took advantage of the offer. After a couple of weeks, Burger King headquarters told him it wasn't going to honor the deal. Brooner sued the company for $9,026.16, enough to buy a meal once a week until he is seventy-two. That's a seemingly small amount, especially when going up against a corporate goliath with a large legal team. One of the reasons Brooner chose to pursue such a high-risk, low-reward case was because he had grown up in the foster care system, where he didn't know whether he'd have a home or anything to eat the next day. To Brooner, the one thing someone always had was their word, and that mattered to him. In the end, Burger King settled for the full amount. While most people would have said it wasn't worth the high risk of fighting Burger King for that little money, to him it was all about the principle. Brooner values a promise more than most people would. That's his mental model.

When we see problems, challenges, and opportunities, we tend to view them through our mental models. Each of us has our own.

---

43. Analog watch advertisements typically display the time as 10:10 because it's symmetrical, doesn't obscure any elements, and looks like a smile. Before I knew this, I never realized most watch advertisements all had the same time displayed.

The Career Toolkit

Many communication problems stem from having these different models. Sometimes we're each seeing a different part of the elephant (as described in "The Blind Men and the Elephant"), not because we can't see the whole thing but because of perspective: The physicist sees a five-ton cube, the lawyer sees liability if the elephant mauls people, the financier sees discounted cash flows, the artist sees a performance art opportunity, and the networker knows someone in his network who really wants an elephant.

An effective team needs a common language. Here, language isn't just about words; it's a broader means of communication and a shared understanding. To be clear, you don't want everyone to have the same models. A room full of artists might come up with some great ideas for art but fail to think about the costs. The networker might think to walk the elephant over to the zoo and give it to them, but he wouldn't take into account that, on the way, the small-town bridge he'd have to cross couldn't support that weight.

We want a diversity of mental models to see different risks and opportunities. While you want to have mental diversity, you must also recognize that diversity in your communications can be problematic. Specifically, when communicating, you need to recognize that your words come from the context of your mental models and get interpreted in the context of your listener's mental models. For subtle or complex thoughts, it's important to provide some deeper insights into the model you're using and explain that model and how it works.

This is obviously costly in terms of time and effort, so you don't need to explain your model all the time. Most of our daily conversations have a sufficiently shared model. When you find yourself making complex decisions, or if you find yourself disagreeing, make sure you include those mental models explicitly in the discussion to help provide the context for the ideas.

Shared Understanding

Beyond having a shared mental model is the need for a shared understanding. Earlier we learned the tale of The Blind Men and the Elephant, where each person was touching a different part of the animal, and so each only grasped part of the picture. In real life, that does happen on a large team.[44] They may all see the whole elephant but view it differently such that an engineer may see the problem differently from the way an accountant does, because of how they've been trained to think. Conflicts in understanding like this can be hiding in plain sight. In a Rorschach test, two people see different "scenes" while viewing the same image. This happens very frequently in the workplace.

Sometimes it's obvious, such as when engineering says, "We can build it," and procurement says, "We can buy it," and then a classic buy-versus-build debate ensues. Other times, everyone thinks the answer is obvious, but the obvious answer is different for each party. "Make sure the users can see a chart showing usage by month." Sounds clear enough. But in a rideshare company, "users" could mean the people hiring cars, or the drivers of the cars, or administrators who manage their company's corporate rideshare account. They are all users but with very different needs. Two people on the project can both hear "users" and assume a different subset of "users," resulting in the wrong functionality being built.

One of my favorite *Saturday Night Live* sketches has Ed Asner working at a nuclear reactor. The skit opens at his retirement party, and as he is leaving, he says, "You can't put too much water in the nuclear reactor." Moments later, someone opens the water spigot. When his co-worker questions him, the first man's tone suggests, "You can't possibly ever make the mistake of putting too much water into the water in it [so add more water]." The second man repeats Ed Asner's line in a way to

---

44. "Large" is relative. I once consulted for a company of fifteen people where I heard at least five different explanations of what the company did.

be interpreted as, "Take care not to ever put in too much water, as that would be bad [so limit how much water is added]." The rest of the skit involves a growing debate about interpretation and ends with Ed Asner happily retired on the beach looking off in the distance at a mushroom cloud. One statement, two interpretations. Forget about it.

I can't tell you how many times I've seen two people walk out of a meeting in complete agreement, although, unbeknownst to them, with a completely different understanding of what they're agreeing on. There's no hard-and-fast rule to prevent this, but there are a few things that can be done to minimize risk.

PROVIDE A SUMMARY

After a decision has been made, it helps to summarize it, especially in writing. Sending an email around after the meeting both provides a record (in case people forget) and literally gets everyone on the same page.

AVOID PRONOUNS

Beware of pronouns: *he, she, they, it, this, that*. Such words lend themselves to misinterpretation, especially by someone not totally focused during a meeting and not paying close attention. You might use pronouns during the conversation for the sake of brevity, but when it comes to summarizing a decision, don't say, "their meeting." Say, "the operation team's weekly status meeting." Don't say, "She'll get the data." Say, "Carol will get the data." Be explicit.

REPEAT IT BACK

When giving directions to someone, have them repeat it back, in their own words.

These three steps won't absolutely prevent all misunderstandings, but they will go a long way toward reducing them.

Communication

Thinking Modes

A different type of mental model is a mode of thinking. This can come in many forms. Many people are familiar with the concepts of left- and right-brained people. In this thinking model, left-brained people are more quantitative and methodical, whereas right-brained people are more creative and artistic.

Have you ever had someone give a presentation with so many numbers and formulas that you just tuned them out because it got too complex? Maybe you saw a talk that had a great vision but seemed to be short on details? Perhaps someone proposed a plan that had laudable goals but was so abstract that the audience just didn't connect with it?

In both the sections "Assessment Tools" and "A Different Type of Diversity," we discussed different models, or more commonly, different "personality types." As noted in those sections, it wasn't about competency but rather preferences—preferences in how you like to think about problems.

I'm very much a numbers guy. If you want to convince me, at some point I need to see numbers to give me a sense of what is involved and how they all add up. Whether it's people, money, time, risk factors, or other units, numbers help me understand scope and scale. You may have met "big picture" people who don't do well with minutiae—they leave that to others—but that can envision new ideas and can speak about them passionately. Contrast that personality with someone who always makes you feel relaxed and welcome. They may not be good with numbers or visions, but they know how to connect with you and make you feel appreciated or heard or respected.

There are many such "personalities," and no type is better than another. Some people have a primary mode of thinking, while others can operate in multiple modes, meaning they can naturally engage in different thinking modes, just as there are decathletes who can excel

The Career Toolkit

across multiple sports. Like those of us who aren't a natural decathlete but train up to become one, we can also train ourselves to be sufficient, or even great, working in other mental modes.

As with other types of mental models, what's important is to recognize your own preferences and thinking modes and then realize that others may be different. Ideally, you recognize the modes of your audience and can adapt your message to their particular styles.

That works well with people you know, such as co-workers. The general concept isn't new. Many people already know things about their co-workers. When asking your boss for project funding, you might know that it's always best to get him to buy into the grand vision before providing the numbers, or maybe he doesn't care about the vision but says, "Just give me the general idea, and then tell me how long and how much." You would pitch the idea differently to your boss in each case.

You won't always know whom you're speaking to, personality-wise. Some people are better at reading others and can adapt quickly. When you walk into someone's office, what do you see? Is everything neatly organized and perfectly positioned? Are there photos of the person with different people they're close to? Are there lots of desk toys strewn about? What type of questions do they ask? A single data point or two may not be accurate, so don't read too much into any one signal, but over time you might start to get a sense of whom you're talking to. Some companies use personality assessment tools explicitly for this reason: so that people on a team begin to understand themselves and their colleagues better, helping them communicate better as a result.

In other cases, you may be speaking to a large, mentally diverse audience. In such cases, you need to take a broad approach with your messaging. If you look at a State of the Union Address given by most presidents, such as the ones given by former presidents Obama, Bush, and Clinton, they tend to hit multiple notes. They will lay out a vision,

Communication

connect it with a personal story, provide a plan, and have supporting numbers. If a politician were to speak about college grants, she might say:

I want to share with you the story of a young girl named Jill. She grew up with a mother who worked three jobs. Jill would go with her mom to work each night at eight p.m. and do her homework while her mother mopped floors. Each night, Jill would fall asleep at the office after her schoolwork was done to be carried home and tucked into bed by her mother. Thanks to our college grant program, that young girl was able to afford college and then went on to medical school. She's now a doctor treating children with cancer.	Personal Connection
I want every student in America who has Jill's story to have Jill's ending. That's why I'm proposing the College Grants for All program so that every student who wants to go to college can afford college. We can have a country where everyone can get the education they want, because education for all means prosperity for all.	Vision
While this may seem ambitious, it is achievable. First, we find the three most cost-efficient colleges in each state and expand those programs to take more students. Second, we provide a fast-track process to apply for student grants. Third, we require a minimum GPA to ensure that such grants are being provided to those who are worthy of them.	Plan
Such a program pays for itself over time. I'm asking for thirty billion dollars to start. Studies show that college graduates earn 31 percent more than high-school graduates. With the increased productivity and tax revenue, the program pays for itself in fifteen years.	Numbers

Some people might hear that and think, "It's the right thing to do" and not focus on the cost. Others may say, "I only care about programs that won't raise my taxes." Still others may hear the story of Jill and relate to her because someone they know couldn't afford to go to college. Because politicians need a message that will resonate across a wide set of people, they promote their ideas in ways to be received through the many different lenses. It won't always be so formally divided, but their overall comments will hit people with different styles.

No matter how you choose to define thinking modes (the four above[45] or a completely different set), you need to recognize that people are mentally diverse. As such, being able to adjust your communication to your audience's modes makes it all the easier for them to receive your message.

Public Speaking

While most of this chapter has been about the mental models of communication, it's important to address public speaking, because it is so fundamental to our jobs. You've no doubt had to speak publicly and have had your teachers talk about basic public speaking techniques—rehearsing, projecting, making eye contact. There's no need to repeat it here. What I do want to impress upon you is that you're engaging in public speaking far more often than you think.

Narrowly viewed, public speaking is standing in front of a group of people. Typically, there's a speech, sometimes not so well rehearsed: You stand up, give your talk, and sit down.

It turns out you're actually doing public speaking weekly, if not daily! When you're talking in a meeting, it's a form of public speaking. It may not be rehearsed, and you often aren't standing, but you're likely engaging in the "persuasive argument" public speaking mode. Fundamentally, you

---

45. These are taken from the Herrmann Brain Dominance Instrument.

Communication

have a point to deliver to an audience (your teammates). You're going to make a cohesive argument, project enough so everyone can hear you, make eye contact, vary your tone, and speak with a degree of confidence and conviction. The only differences between this and a prepared speech are that you're sitting down (not standing), it's brief (maybe only a few sentences), and you probably didn't practice what you were going to say.

You can debate whether or not this should be classified as public speaking, but that's beside the point. The reality is that the skills you use when speaking on a stage are also used here. Conversely, the skills you apply during discussions at meetings will apply during your more formal public speaking engagements.

Even interviewing is a form of public speaking. You're sitting down, and it's one on one; in some cases it's more conversational in style, but it's still public speaking. You're trying to get some points across to an audience, namely that you're the best candidate for the job and that they should compensate you well. Making eye contact, varying your tone, and speaking with confidence all apply.

Arguably, it's even more like public speaking than a meeting. While the utterances during a meeting tend to be spontaneous, most of your interview answers are not. You know many of the questions they're going to ask: Why are you the right candidate? Why did you leave your last job? Tell me about a time you failed. Like a speech, you should have practiced answers—practiced but not over-rehearsed down to the word—for dozens of questions so that when you're asked, you know exactly how to answer them.

Parts of networking are public speaking. The conversation itself should be natural, one-on-one spontaneous conversation. However, parts of it will briefly cross into public speaking. If you're asked, "What does your company do?" you'll jump into your elevator pitch about the company. It may only be a thirty- or sixty-second monologue, but it's briefly a moment of public speaking (with perhaps an audience of one), before going back to natural conversation.

I raise these points because most people fear public speaking. The truth is, you're doing it without realizing it, and you're probably better than you think. Recognize that public speaking skills will help you even when not at the podium. Likewise, when you do need to stand in front of an audience, it helps to realize that you've been doing it for most of your life, just without the podium or audience.

If you do want to get better at public speaking, there are plenty of organizations that can help. Toastmasters is a worldwide organization that helps people improve their public speaking skills. Your manager and HR departments can help, as can friends and co-workers. You can also learn by watching other speakers and taking a moment to ask yourself, "What was it they did well? How can I incorporate that habit into my speaking?"

Most public speaking issues are related to a lack of confidence. I was a terrible public speaker when I was younger and joined the high-school debate club to help me improve. What helped me even more though was being part of the ballroom dance team. A ballroom dance competition is not unlike public speaking for many people: You're in front of a large crowd, being judged (literally), and really hoping you don't embarrass yourself, at least when you first start out and are still insecure. No words are spoken, but you're very much on stage. Gaining confidence as a ballroom dancer helped me gain confidence as a public speaker. For you, it may be acting, singing, or sports. What matters is that you have some experience where others are watching, letting you gain the confidence that, even if you stumble, it will be fine.

Going forward, you'll begin to see public speaking all around you, and you'll find everyday opportunities to develop and improve this skill. The more you do it, the more confident you'll become.

Crafting Your Image

Before leaving this chapter, I want to expand your thinking about communication. We often think of communication as oral or written, or even body language. In truth, it's much broader. We've all learned that "actions speak louder than words," and your actions have been communicating about you for years.

When people are asked what superpower they want, most people give standard answers like flying or time travel. One of the best powers I've heard is the ability to see yourself as others see you. This is far more powerful than it might seem.

Many years ago, I was at a company for an onsite interview as a technical architect. Over lunch, I was in the dining area talking with some of the employees about building a corporate culture. A woman joined us and listened in for about ten minutes. At one point, not knowing who I was or what role I was interviewing for, she asked, "Are you a businessperson, or do you have any technical background?" I replied, "Well, I have a computer science degree from MIT," and that seemed to instantly end her questioning, although that wasn't my intent.

She had listened to a conversation about culture and hiring, had seen that I was formally dressed, and viewed me as a "businessperson" because I was talking about subjects that "businesspeople" discuss. When I mentioned my MIT computer science degree, I instantly gained credibility as a technical person. Each one of those actions (conversation topic, appearance, degree) gave her some perception of me.

One reason I focused on the skills in this book for myself was because a few years into my career, I discovered that I never had to prove myself technically, but my business acumen was always in doubt. No one ever asked, "Will he be able to keep up with the math?" because my MIT degrees signaled that I could. What people weren't as quick to believe

The Career Toolkit

was that I understood discounted cash flows, corporate culture, and leadership. It wasn't obvious from my résumé; I didn't have any degrees or job titles commonly associated with that knowledge or those skills. This is one reason so many people go to business school—when you come out, it gives you credibility in a number of business-related subjects. People will assume you are knowledgeable about business.

When we lived in small tribes fifty thousand years ago, individuals knew everyone in their group, and each day there weren't a lot of new people, nor was there new information. Today, we meet new people on a nearly daily basis, and we need to make quick assessments of them. It could be everything from "Will he rob me?" to "Do I give this person my lunch order?"

To make decisions efficiently, we follow behavioral scripts; we make assumptions based on circumstances: where we are, what the person looks like, and the like. The guy in a mask in a dark alley is probably going to rob me, and the stranger in a restaurant who is walking toward my table in a white shirt and black pants holding a pad is probably going to ask for my lunch order. The man in the expensive three-piece suit is probably an executive at the company, while the guy in overalls with grease stains likely works on the factory floor. We're not always right, but these shortcuts help our brains focus on more critical information.

When people meet you for an interview (and remember, you're always interviewing), they will begin to make judgments about you. Your schools, your degrees, your previous companies, and your job titles all say something about you, as do your clothing, your style of speech, the words you choose, and your body language. Your image also includes anything that is publicly known about you or on the Internet. Right or wrong, people judge you on your handshake. You may not be aware of every signal you send, and you may or may not want a particular signal to be sent, but it's always happening. We are constantly broadcasting information.

Communication

Unfortunately, we can't know exactly how other people perceive us—at least we can't directly look inside other people's heads. But we can begin to get a sense of it in two ways. First, we can ask for feedback from friends and co-workers. We can ask how they view us, what their first impressions and overall impressions are. Dorie Clark, author of *Reinventing You*, recommends simply asking people you know, "What three words would you use to describe me?" Annual reviews are another form of feedback. Second, we can also see how people treat us. I realized I broadcast technical competency when people would make comments like, "This is some complex stuff, but you went to MIT, so you should be able to pick it up with no problem." They're telling me what they think of me. What people do and don't do around you, what they say and don't say, all provide clues as to how you're perceived.

In your goals, you will have certain roles you target. People have a perception of what skills are needed for those roles. You need to understand what is expected and then not only have the skills but also convey to others that you have them. Founder of Blueprint Talent Group, Chris Resto, likes to say, "Perception is reality." It's not simply what you say in the interview but a number of things, many of which happen long before you set foot in the office. When your career plan targets a future role, if your image doesn't align with what people expect for that role, then you need to put "change your image" into your career plan. It may or may not mean changing who you are, but it definitely means changing how people see you.

Take care of what your image is. Don't lie or deceive people. But also recognize that who you are is not necessarily whom you are seen as. Align your image to your goal. While the examples in this section were for an individual, this concept also applies to your products and your organization.

Summary and Next Steps

We all perceive the world differently. Our mental models, from formal or informal training, allow us to see different risks and opportunities. A different type of mental model will cause different people to focus more or less on aspects like quantitative reasoning, holistic pictures, process, or interpersonal relationships. The onus is on the presenter to convert his thinking into a format more aligned to the models of the listeners. Listening to other people and how they approach problems and communicate ideas can help you begin to expand your own experience with those mental models.

Public speaking is something you do daily, although it doesn't always look like public speaking. The skills you already have will make you a stronger public speaker. Even if you never step in front of a podium, public speaking skills will help you in meetings, interviews, and networking. Toastmasters is a great organization that can help; sports, dance, or other performance activities will also help your public speaking, even if you never say a word when doing them.

You have an image, whether you intentionally created it or not. Work to understand your image by getting feedback from others. Think about whether this image aligns with the goals in your career plan, and if not, work to change that image.

Chapter Eight

Networking

> "The currency of real networking is not greed but generosity."
>
> —**Keith Ferrazzi**

Networking is one of the most talked about but least taught skills. Think about it: You've heard countless people tout the importance of being good at networking, but have you ever had a single class teaching you how to do it? Consequently, it's one of the least understood skills and one that most people do poorly.

Many people think, "I need a new job, time to network." Networking is a philosophy more than an activity. As such, it is a regular habit that you can build up using the tools in this chapter so that your network is always at the ready. Whether it's for a job search, to help navigate your company, or to provide you with non-work opportunities and experiences, building and maintaining a strong network will help you in all aspects of your life.

Networking is about relationships. The techniques discussed here will help foster those relationships but should never be considered the relationship itself. A relationship is a connection between two people,

The Career Toolkit

with all that it entails. The tools presented below help you meet people, stay in contact with them, and build a relationship, but it is the relationship itself that is the purpose of networking, not meetings or favors in and of themselves. As you read this chapter, don't think, "That's how I get . . ." but rather "This helps to build that connection." While these techniques can be used in a less genuine, more manipulative way, I want to strongly emphasize that a sincere relationship should be the goal.

What Is Networking?

TRUST

Former Harvard Business School professor George Chacko once told me, "Business is about trust." When you walk into a store and buy a Coke, there is trust. You trust what you'll be getting. You know exactly what it will taste like. You also trust that it's safe to drink. We take these things for granted, but throughout most of human history, there were no guarantees about either.

Generally, when you buy a product, you are trusting that it's a good value for the money, compared to the alternatives—the food will taste good, or playing with the toy will be fun. We use cues such as brand names ("They've always produced durable goods that don't easily break"), expert advice ("Siskel and Ebert give it two thumbs up"), or recommendations from trusted sources ("My brother-in-law swears by this"), but fundamentally we're taking the trust in one entity and applying it to another. In essence, we're using a chain of trust.

When one company partners with another, it is doing so because it believes the overall quality, price, support, and reliability are more valuable than with a different partner or no partner at all. When a job offer is given, it's because the company trusts that this person meets the qualifications and is the best candidate from the available pool.

We may be wrong. Sometimes we don't like the movie, we return the blender that broke after a week, or we fire a recent hire who didn't work out. In each case, that trust took a hit. Nevertheless, we continue to employ trust because it helps us make efficient decisions. Trust is the centerpiece of networking. When we use our network, we are trusting in the relationship.

Trust takes time to earn, but it can be lost in an instant. Recognize that it will take time to build a relationship with someone, and throughout the entire relationship you must be sincere. If your only goal is to get something from the other person, that's not sincere, and it will show. If you are merely going through the motions when you meet people and apply the techniques in this book, it will be recognized as insincere and will work against you.

If you're not ready to build a relationship with someone, that's okay. You don't have to; you can still conduct commerce and engage in other interactions with them. But if you want to foster a relationship with someone, be sincere in getting to know and care about that person, and create a two-way relationship. Anything less, and you're wasting their time and yours.

TRUST IN HIRING

Trust is especially important in hiring, where many of us most commonly use our networks. Your friendships and romantic relationships are built by spending a number of hours together. On a first date, the two are on their best behavior. Even on a fifth date, people may not let their guard down; they're still trying to make sure their date sees their best qualities. Interviews are no different—but it rarely gets to a fifth date before they commit to hiring you.

A typical interview process involves filtering résumés, a few rounds of interviews, and maybe a skills assessment. Just as going to a dinner and a movie isn't the same as running a household and raising kids together, the interview process is significantly different from actually working at a company. We use the interview (or date) as a proxy for future actions. As such, no one expects the interview to be a perfect tool.

This is where trust comes in. We look for clues in the trust network. If someone went to a top-twenty school, we trust that they are likely above average in intelligence.[46] If they worked at certain well-known companies with rigorous hiring standards, it's a sign they've been vetted by others. If they have worked in a similar role and been successful, it's a sign that they can handle the work required of this role.

This signaling isn't perfect. We know that legacy students, who may not be as qualified, get into top schools, that some people know how to work a system to survive at a company despite being in over their heads, and that a good interviewee with a fuzzy ethical line can make a prior job appear to be more than it really was. To provide a better signal, we use personal trust.

When a candidate is referred to the company, the referrer is vouching for her. That can mean something basic, for instance, the candidate has a record of showing up to work on time or has demonstrated a thorough knowledge of bookkeeping. It could also mean something much more impressive: that the candidate is very seasoned and could lead a team through a dynamic transition or generate millions of dollars in new business.

While trust can be used in all cases, it doesn't always hold the same weight. If a candidate for a line position at a fast-food restaurant held a job at another fast-food restaurant for eighteen months, we can generally infer from the résumé alone that the candidate was reliable and showed up on time. Contrast this with a company that is seeking a candidate who can take a demoralized marketing team and, in six months, turn

---

46. I always remind people that schools have floors but not ceilings. While it's rare—though not impossible—to find dumb people at top schools, we can find plenty of smart people at schools all over the college rankings.

them around and rebrand a product line. Unfortunately, this is much harder to tell from prior experience or a résumé. Consequently, a positive signal from the network about a candidate's abilities carries much more weight for this role. The network in this case can provide a more critical signal than an interview or résumé could.

TRUST IN RELATIONSHIPS

Generally, trust is the basis of human relationships. When I start my talks on networking, I often begin with the question, "Who here can lend me $10,000?" Unless there's a personal friend in the audience, there are no hands in the air. Assume you have the money to spare, and someone you met five minutes ago asks you to borrow money. Would you lend it to them? Why not? (Take a moment to consider your answer.)

Is there anyone you'd lend it to? (Again, assuming you have it to spare.)

The answer typically is that you might lend this amount of money to a few close friends or family members. Why would you lend to them, but not other people?

It's because you know them, which is a proxy for saying that you trust them. If you were to give so much money to a stranger on the street, you'd reasonably suspect that you might never see him again. Even if he sincerely wanted to repay you, there's a chance he's going to lose it, invest it unwisely, or experience something else that will prevent him from returning the money.

A friend you've known for twenty years is different. You know she's responsible and won't blow it buying magic beans. You know she keeps her commitments. You also trust that she values the friendship more than the $10,000. So, she wouldn't want to ruin the relationship just to keep the money. By the same logic, there may be longtime friends or family members to whom you specifically would not lend the money, because you know the previous statements do not hold.

The Career Toolkit

Networking is about creating relationships; those relationships can later provide you with value. It's rarely direct financial value; they won't literally be lending you $10,000. It might be introducing you to someone important or getting you sold-out concert tickets. It could be giving you information you need that isn't widely available, or simply showing up when you need help. Each of these things is valuable in its own way.

Creating and maintaining the relationship is 95 percent of networking, and it's what we'll mostly be focusing on in this chapter. However, I want to address the second part, the "value," before we go on. Not all relationships are about networking, and, sadly, not all networking attempts are focused on building relationships. When we date someone, we very intentionally to try form a relationship; however, no one would be so banal as to suggest the relationship's purpose is to gain value *from* the other person. We gain value from being *with* the other person. That is a relationship without networking. Likewise, familial relationships and friendships are formed purely for the sake of the relationships. Your friends and family are in your network and may help by opening doors for you or providing other value, but you choose to have a relationship with them because the relationship itself is the value, not what you can get from them.

When engaging in business networking, we often select people because of who they are. As we'll discuss below, you shouldn't base relationships solely on what you'll get. Still, for most people, their professional network isn't necessarily composed of people they would hang out with on their weekends. You have a relationship with your co-workers, but you may not consider all of them friends, and that's okay.

Friends and family are in your network. Likewise, people in your network can, and often do, become friends, and sometimes even family. But I want to draw a distinction, even if imperfect, to clarify that these relationships are different from friendships.

Networking

What does it mean to create relationships? It means exactly the same for us as adults as it does for children in kindergarten. Play nice, share, be respectful, and help others. I think of networking as karmic: Don't keep score, but the more you give, the more you get.

When in doubt, give. When I meet someone, one way I try to get to know them is to understand their needs. What can I do to help this person? And to the extent that I can, I do.

What do I mean by help? If I just met them, and they need to borrow that $10,000, we probably haven't built the relationship well enough for me to provide it. If they forgot their wallet, and we're standing by the coffee cart at a conference, I'll buy them a cup of coffee.

Again, it's rarely so directly financial, but I want to emphasize that the value you give may change over time. It could be suggesting companies for them to look at. It could be providing an introduction to someone or giving advice about a situation or product. It's usually nothing immediate, so don't worry if you don't immediately see a need to help. It's about building a relationship, and relationships, like Rome, aren't built in a day.

The level of trust should grow over time. If I just met you, and I know you're looking for a job, I might pass your name along to a friend who is hiring. What I'm saying is, "Hey, friend, I'm asking you to invest sixty seconds in looking at this résumé." On the other hand, if you want to meet a CEO of a multi-billion-dollar corporation to pitch your service, I'd have to say, "Hey, Mr. Really Busy CEO Whom Everyone Wants to Meet, spend an hour of your very valuable time meeting with this person." My contacts are relying on me as a gatekeeper. I've introduced friends to that CEO when I've known the friends well and known that the services could be of value. If I were to do it for every random vendor, the CEO would no longer trust my judgment. The person I just met wouldn't get that introduction, at least not initially. Only once I knew him better and saw a better fit would I "spend" my currency (trust) with the CEO to make the introduction.

You absolutely should not keep a log of every favor you've done and then call someone and say, "On March 25th, I introduced you to Jackie Shen, so now I need you to introduce me to Marty Grossman." On the other hand, we all know that when someone does a really big favor for us, we owe them. If you need a big favor, it helps to have first given a big favor. The little stuff, though, should be given out freely. And small stuff, over time, adds up. Don't keep track; don't say, "I did three favors for you, and you only did two for me." If it's a true relationship, it will even out over time.[47]

Ultimately, it is the trust built up over time in a relationship that allows us to make use of the relationship for help. If someone trusts you, that will give her the confidence to help you or to pass along that trust to someone else.

The Wrong Way to Network

Poor networkers are very common. I've been to many events where people try to "work the room." They go from person to person, spending two to five minutes with each person, making sure they provide their name, job, and company. They get the same information from the other person, exchange business cards, and move on to the next person. You feel like you're on an assembly line.

The modern equivalent is the person who simply adds connections on LinkedIn or other social media. Doing so gives you a very large address book, and there may be some value in having that, but I would

---

47. Occasionally, you may come across someone who is a user. You'll notice there isn't a balance. In such cases, question whether this is someone with whom you really want to have a relationship.

Networking

not call this true networking.[48] Saying that some stranger who's one of your "connections" on LinkedIn is in your network is like saying the person who swiped right on you on Tinder is your significant other. To which of these 20,000 connections would you lend $10,000 or make an introduction to a CEO?

The absolute worst are the people who disguise their needs as networking. I often get recruiters who write, "I'd like to network with you to fill this role." What they're really saying is, "Ninety-five percent of my job—the hardest part, in fact—consists of finding someone qualified for this role; I'd like you to do that for me so I can get paid for your effort. So that it doesn't feel like you're doing the work for me, I'm going to call it 'networking' and, hey, maybe if I can make money off of you in the future, we can 'network' again."

What's the same in all cases is that people aren't trying to build a relationship. They are trying to build a large address book or get someone to help them with an immediate need. I'm not saying they won't consider building a relationship with you in the future, but they want to take value before building the relationship. They want the $10,000 today, and the trust in the future. This is not networking.

The other common mistake is to network when you need something. I've met many people who say, "I need a new job. Time to start networking." The right time to start networking was two years ago. Harvey Mackay wisely quipped, "Dig your well before you're thirsty" in his book of the same title. When you need that $10,000, you get it from a longtime friend, not someone you met the night before. When you need a warm introduction to a well-placed, busy executive at a company, it's going to come from someone who knows you well and will put his own relationship credit on the line for you, not someone you met yesterday.

---

48. My cousin happens to be one of the most connected people on LinkedIn and likely has a different view of networking. I love him just the same.

Stop Trying to Sell Me That You're Networking

Enterprise salespeople often confuse their job of selling with the work of building relationships. Business is about trust, and for me to spend tens of thousands of dollars of my budget on your product, not to mention the time invested in setting it up, I need to trust that the product meets my needs. A good enterprise salesperson recognizes that in order to get a sale, they need to build some degree of trust. The more I trust them, the more I trust what they tell me about the product meeting my needs. That can be done through a relationship or through other means. For instance, if I see your presentations and customer references, I may choose to buy your product, even if personally I don't care to have a relationship with you.

Many, however, confuse this with relationship building. Executives get multiple emails and calls a day from salespeople who say they want to get to know us. They want to take us to lunch or understand our needs. That's not networking; that's helping them sell to us. I'm not saying they aren't open to having a relationship with us, but they are reaching out very specifically to sell us something now or in the future. The goal isn't the relationship but the sale. I don't fault salespeople for having a sale as their goal—that's their job—but it's insulting when they pretend it isn't. A relationship isn't about asking, "How can I get . . . ?"

Salespeople, like the recruiters mentioned earlier, justify such spam emails as, "Well, you never know. Maybe you are in the market for . . . ." They're buying (or creating) a mailing list, emailing everyone on it, and making each person waste time and mental energy seeing and deleting their email, because it can help them close a sale. They are saying, "Hi, stranger. My need to sell justifies taking some time from each and every one of you to deal with my spam." This is the opposite of how to build a relationship; you're taking value from the other person (a small amount of time) before any relationship even begins.

If you're in sales and need to sell, go sell. If your company believes that cold calling or email blasting is the right approach, do what you have to do. Just don't pretend you're trying to build a relationship. That's insulting to the people you contact. You may wind up building a relationship, or you may not, but you're reaching out to sell. Be honest with yourself and your recipients.

Who Is in Your Network?

To begin networking, we need to consider which people should be in our networks and where we can find them. The answers are: Nearly everyone, and all around you.

You can meet people in business settings, such as your office, conferences, and industry events. You can also meet people at social activities, such as going to a bar with your friends, or attending an alumni event. You can meet people through non-professional organizations like hobby groups or at places of worship. Anyone can be in your network, and you can meet them anywhere.

Even an interview can be a chance to extend your network. If we met at an event, and I spent five minutes telling you how amazing I am and listing all my talents and accomplishments, you'd think I was arrogant—but not so in an interview. Expounding on your accomplishments and skills is exactly what you're supposed to do, but not in a bragging way of course. No one faults you during an interview for talking about your accomplishments. Non-interview situations where you get to drone on about your successes are extremely rare. To be clear, when you walk

The Career Toolkit

out of an interview, you likely haven't built a relationship with the other person, but you've taken a step toward building one and have helped sell the other person that you're someone she should know. Even an interview that doesn't lead to a job can be one that leads to a relationship. I've kept in touch with both candidates and hiring managers I've met along the way. Remember: Jobs are short; careers are long.

Obviously, respect the culture of the environment that you're in. Don't go to a religious ceremony and then try to exchange business cards with everyone you meet there. Likewise, respect that if you're at an event with someone, the other person may not have the time to talk extensively with you, because they need to talk with other people as well.

One of the most important concepts when building your network is that of gateway connections; these are people who have limited overlap with the rest of your network. I was in a college fraternity, and we had about ten people per class. So, with the three classes ahead of me and three behind me, there were roughly seventy people in my fraternity during my college years. Most are in my network. If I were to pick any one of those seventy people, odds are pretty good that they know most of the seventy people who were in the fraternity with me. We also know many of the same fraternity alumni. There's a good chance that we both know some other people from our college, outside of the fraternity. In short, we have a high degree of correlation in our networks, or at least this part of it. If any one of them were to disappear from my network, it wouldn't impact my network much, because I could likely reach the people in their network through other connections. You have similar patterns with people from college, your jobs (assuming your co-workers know many of your other co-workers), and other affinity groups.

On the other hand, a few years back I got to know a minister. As an engineer, I know many other engineers—hundreds of them. But I know very few clergy. He, on the other hand, knows scores of clergy, because he went to divinity school, trained with them, worked with them, and met them at events in his field. He and I have a very low degree of correlation between our networks, and his being in my network greatly expands my network into that field, as I do for him.

In that sense, he adds much more diversity to my network than one of my college fraternity brothers does. To be clear, I didn't explicitly target building a relationship with him for his network. But in a measurable way, his potential value to my network in terms of additional connections is higher than that of someone with a high degree of correlation to me. Note that this is different from their value as people or the value I place on the relationship I have with each. These gateway connections provide tremendous value to your network.

The larger takeaway is that it's not just what the person in your network brings to the table himself, but rather what his entire network brings. The rookie mistake is to think, "I'm a doctor, so I just need to know other people in health care." In fact, people throughout your network can be helpful in a variety of personal and professional ways to you and your family.

Likewise, I often encounter people who are looking for work who respond to my offer to help with, "Oh, you're not in my field, so you can't help me." This attitude presumes that people are only connected to others within their field. If the person you need to talk to isn't someone you know, someone in your network may know her, even if they have no professional connection. For example, your friend from the neighborhood association who does pharmaceutical marketing may have gone to high school with the VP of procurement at the company you want to reach and may be able to make the introduction, even though professionally they have no direct relationship.

This is actually what makes tools like LinkedIn extremely useful. In the past, if you wanted to reach that VP of procurement, you needed to go through your network and ask the people you thought were most likely to know her. This friend from the neighborhood who has no professional link to her might never have crossed your mind. Some online social networks allow you to find someone and see how you're connected, which can make the whole discovery process much more efficient.

The flip side is to ask who shouldn't be in your network. Where you draw the line is up to you. For me, everyone in my network is someone I trust to some degree. It might be someone I've worked closely with for years. It might just be someone I've only met briefly but felt a connection to. My rule is that I can say something positive about everyone in my network, and everyone in my network is someone who will respond to a request from me. I'm not saying they'll fulfill any request I make, but at least they will open an email and will get back to me.

I don't add someone I briefly met once. I don't add strangers who connect to me online. I don't add people who saw me give a talk or read something I wrote. I will try to respond to them, and I will probably try to help them, depending on the nature of the request. But I won't consider them part of my network, nor will I formally add them to my online social networks. I don't know them well enough to trust them and give them access to the rest of my network. You let friends into your home, but not a random person you just met on the street. Think of your network like your home; only let in people whom you trust won't harm it.

I've also dropped a handful of people. They've typically engaged in unprofessional or unethical behavior. If I don't feel comfortable helping them or introducing them to others, they shouldn't be in my network.

The Right Way to Network

Now that we know who should and shouldn't be in our network, how do we actually build the network?

Networking

First and foremost, you need to get out there. You're never going to meet anyone by sitting at home.[49] Get out to events. The most obvious events are industry events, conferences, training, and workshops. There, you'll meet lots of people in the same field or industry as you. As noted earlier, you should also consider events outside your field where you'll meet other people and, equally important, you'll get exposed to new ideas.

But one conversation does not a relationship make. If you went on one date, would you consider this person your significant other? If you met someone once, is that person a good friend? In those situations, the relationship develops over time, usually over repeated interactions. This is true for your networking relationships as well.

As you finish a conversation, you should try to find a way to stay in touch. I like to get a business card, but it could also be as simple as finding someone online or exchanging information electronically.

After the event, I do two things.[50] First, I send a follow-up message, usually an email, but it can depend on the situation. In that message, I reference when and where we met, since that person may have been to multiple events and met multiple people over the last few days. I will likely bring up something unique to our conversation, and it will be a way to remind him of who I am or what we talked about. If he was meeting a lot of people, I might even throw in a helpful descriptor, such as "I was the guy in the green tie." If there's a specific follow-up, I'll mention it. If not, I might leave it open-ended, such as, "Let's catch up the next time you're in town" or "Please keep in touch." Here's an example:

---

49. Take this metaphorically. I have been involved with activities and gotten to know, only online, a number of people whom I trust and have added to my network, but they are much less common than people I've met in real life.

50. Realistically, I try to do these two things. I can't say I've always been perfect at doing them.

The Career Toolkit

> Sandy,
>
> It was great meeting you last night at the Techie Youth Fundraiser. I really enjoyed hearing about your trip to Africa a few months back. You said that your company was looking to retain an ad agency. As I mentioned, I used to work at BigAdAgency, so I'm happy to meet over coffee and see if I can answer any questions you might have about what to look for in an agency.
>
> —Sam

> Hi Devon,
>
> We met last week at your son's soccer match. (I'm Alex's dad, the guy wearing the yellow windbreaker.) You mentioned your company has been growing, and I'm actually starting to look for new opportunities. I looked on your website and saw some open accounting roles. Do you have a few minutes in the coming week for a quick call so I can get some background before I apply?
>
> —Chris

This reminds the other person of who you are and provides context. If you don't immediately build a relationship, and often you won't, should you need to reconnect months later, you now have a record to remind you (and the other person) of when and where you met and what you talked about.

The second thing I do is take notes. Harvey Mackay created a list, the Mackay 66: the 66 things you should know about each of your

Networking

customers.[51] I'm not saying you need to know all 66, but you should work toward learning as much as you can, and since you can't remember it all, write it down.

Personally, I take notes on many people I meet. I don't necessarily do it with people I think I'll get to know well, such as new co-workers I'm going to see daily. But for someone I meet at an event and may not see for a while, I need to take notes. I just keep the notes in a simple text file. You can use a CRM or fancier tool, your phone's address book, or even a physical notebook if you prefer pen and paper. It doesn't matter how as long as it works for you.

What are the 66 items? It starts with name, job, and contact information. There's background, such as where your new connection grew up or went to school. There's personal information, such as hobbies, religion, interests, political views. There's family information about the spouse and kids (names, ages, interests), and there's health information, such as allergies or food preferences, and information about business and needs. Obviously, you shouldn't interrogate someone, but during a conversation, someone might say, "My wife and I just went to Paris for our twentieth honeymoon." Now you know he's married and roughly for how long.

Why include things like kids and allergies? Because they help you relate to the other person. You don't take someone who is in Alcoholics Anonymous out for drinks. Of course, they may not say they're in Alcoholics Anonymous, but you might notice that at events they stick to club soda. So, whereas you might normally suggest meeting for a drink, maybe do coffee or lunch instead. I often send food gift baskets to people as a thank-you. After one big project, I sent them to my whole team but made sure to customize them for each person. To the married guy who

---

51. You can find a full list at http://cicorp.com/sharkware/Mackay66.htm.

201

spent a lot of late nights working, I sent a wine and cheese gift basket to him and his wife, thanking him for his hard work and also her for putting up with his long hours. I provided the basket so they could have a romantic evening together. If she thinks I'm a bad boss, he's eventually going to think I'm a bad boss as well; if she thinks well of me, it can only help. To another employee who is a vegetarian who doesn't drink, I sent a vegan gift basket, which he very much appreciated. Imagine if I had sent him a wine gift basket with prosciutto; after putting in weeks of long hours, his "thank-you" would have been something he doesn't want. That would have been a slap in the face.

Knowing hobbies, personal history, and interests is also a great way to find things in common. Maybe it turns out we're both avid fans of classical music. Even if we don't have anything in common, it helps me know how to relate to my new connection.

It may be that there's an obvious next step to take with someone you meet. More often, there is not, so you need to keep in touch. But how exactly do you do that?

One way to keep in touch is to find reasons to reconnect. Want to see the ballet next weekend? Why not see who in your network might enjoy going with you? How about a talk on proposed tax legislation? Who among your network might be interested in joining you in that? To do this, you need to know what's of interest to the people in your network.

It doesn't have to be an activity; it could just be a "thinking of you" outreach. Are you the proud alum of a college with a great football team? "Hey, Dana, I just saw that Auburn made the playoffs, and it made me think of you." Did you see something that might interest your connection? "Leslie, I know your high-school-age daughter plays the clarinet; I'm sending a link to an article I just read about college scholarships for musicians." Of course, you need to know something about the person to be able to do this.

Social media has made this much easier. It reminds us of birthdays, promotions, work anniversaries, and so much more. Everyone I'm connected to on Facebook is guaranteed to hear from me at least once a year on their birthday. And, of course, you can also look at someone's social media posts to see what they've been up to.

If you want to get back in touch with someone you haven't spoken to in a while, it's pretty easy to find an excuse. You always have health, wealth, and family. (See "Health, Wealth, and Family.")

Just remember, networking isn't about what's in it for you, keeping score, or manipulating people. Build a relationship with others because you want a relationship with them, not because of what they can do for you. It just so happens that competent, nice people tend to help each other. Above all, be sincere, and focus on the relationship for the sake of the relationship. Even in a business relationship where it's clear that you might not have a personal relationship if not for the overlap in your work, you should still be sincere. Both parties may realize it's a business-only relationship, and that's fine, as long as everyone is sincere in their intentions.

Health, Wealth, and Family

In his book *Never Eat Alone*, Keith Ferrazzi advises his readers that there are three things every person cares about: health, wealth, and family.

We start many conversations with "How are you?" Though few people actually mean it, we should. Certainly, if someone is in the hospital or faces a serious health issue, we care very much about his state. We all care about friends and family who face such issues. Health is universal.

The Career Toolkit

Most of us have a career, and unless you have enough money in the bank to retire, you care about advancing it. So does everybody else. This could mean helping someone get a job or executing in their current job, such as hiring staff, finding customers and suppliers, or providing general information like industry trends or new tools. I can count on one hand the number of people who didn't appreciate an offer of help when job hunting.

"Let me show you pictures of my kids" is every parent's refrain, and everyone else's nightmare conversation starter. People care about their family—their spouses, parents, siblings, and kids. Whatever else may be true of another person, there is likely someone in her life she cares about, be they a family member or someone who is like family.

We're all different. Salespeople care about finding and closing clients, health care practitioners are all about helping patients, and scientists care about new discoveries. But nearly everyone, no matter who they are or what they do, cares about health, wealth, and family. If you know nothing about someone's interests, you can safely assume they care about these three things.

How to Talk to Strangers

For most people, the hardest part is breaking the ice; it's walking right up to a stranger and saying, "Hello." It's still hard for me, and I've been doing it for years. It's helpful to remember a few things. First, this isn't junior high school, so even if you come off as awkward, the social penalties we had as tweens no longer apply. Second, you'll probably never see most of these people again.

Often, the key to networking is getting there early or staying late, because most networking at an event happens at the beginning or end. If you're there right from the start, it's very easy to talk to the second person who shows up.

Networking

One technique that some people use is to do something to stand out. Women have an edge here, because their clothing usually allows for more variety. An interesting brooch or scarf can be professional but also gives people something to comment on. I met one person who would walk around with a gimmicky blinking pen in her pocket. That made it easier for people to approach her and ask, "Where'd you get the blinking pen?" It was a conversation starter.

Ultimately, you just need to walk up to someone and say, "Hello." After the exchange of names and a handshake, you can safely go with "What do you do?" or "Where do you work?" But that does tend to get very repetitive. A more interesting conversation usually flows from your shared interests or experience, which you can surmise from the event. Some examples include: "What did you think of the keynote speaker?" or "What's been the most interesting talk you've seen at this conference?"

I like to ask people's thoughts and opinions. They often have a different perspective or insight from mine, so I'm likely to learn something or at least see it a new way. "What do you think will be the biggest changes in our industry this year?" "Have you been to any other events you'd recommend for people in this field?" If you're young, ask people for career advice: "As someone who has only been working in this field for seven years, I'd be interested to hear any suggestions from someone more experienced, such as yourself." Again, be sincere. If you don't really care about their opinion, don't waste their time.

What makes the conversation a positive one for me? It usually comes down to looking for one of two things: something we have in common or something I can learn from the other person. Whenever I'm stuck in a conversation with someone I find boring, I try to create focus, despite the boredom. I think, "This person must know something really interesting—have some knowledge, experience, or perspective that's different from mine—and my job is to find it." Digging through a

The Career Toolkit

haystack quickly gets boring, but if you're searching for a needle, it helps you stay focused while you dig.[52]

Here's the big secret: Ninety-nine percent of us feel just as awkward and scared as you do at these events. People are often standing by themselves or looking at their cell phones because they're too nervous to approach someone else. Most of the time, if you're walking up to someone who is standing by himself and introduce yourself, you're doing him a favor, since he was probably feeling awkward and unsure about how to approach anyone else.

Sometimes, by the time you get to an event, everyone has formed off into little groups. Breaking into them is hard. You don't want to butt into someone else's private conversation, but you also don't want to stand by yourself. Unfortunately, there's no easy way to do this when you're the outsider. If, however, you find yourself in a group of a few people talking and see a lone person standing near you, I strongly encourage you to invite her to join your discussion. Again, 99 percent of the time, people will appreciate it, and they will be thankful to you in particular for saving them from an awkward situation. Remember, networking can be thought of as giving before receiving; you just gave this person a reprieve from social awkwardness.

If you are by yourself, you could also stand near an entrance, the bathroom,[53] or the food and drinks. People will definitely be going to those areas, often alone, and you have a better chance of catching someone who is now also by himself.

Don't worry if you don't follow all of this or aren't perfect at it. I'm not either. I don't know anyone who is. The whole point of this book isn't to become perfect, just to get better. (Remember, you're not outrunning the bear, just the other camper.)

---

52. This technique also works with very boring dates.

53. Important tip: It's usually better to catch someone on the way back from the bathroom, although be prepared for slightly wet handshakes.

Networking

One common question I get is how to exit a conversation. This is far easier. You can excuse yourself because you "want to catch <name> while she's here" or "need to talk to <name> about something." Just be sure to go to that person so that it doesn't feel like you're trying to get rid of the person you've been speaking with. You can also excuse yourself to go to the bathroom. Personally, I like to have a glass that's only half full. If I ever need to end a conversation, I can speed up my consumption and then excuse myself in order to get something more to drink. You can, of course, also choose to be direct and say you want to make sure to meet a few more people while you're there.

The key is how you leave. When excusing yourself, regardless of the reason, be sure to thank the other person for her time or the conversation, and shake hands. What's important is that you acknowledge, through words or body language, the time you spent together. If it's someone you want to build a relationship with, you can end your discussion by asking for their business card and then offering your own.

Asking for a business card is always an effective way to end a conversation. "I really appreciate getting your perspective. Do you have a card?" After the exchange of cards, you can thank the other person for her time and move on. An exchange of cards is typically done at either the start or at end of a conversation, so if you didn't exchange cards immediately, asking for someone's card is a signal that you're going to move on—but in a positive way, because the relationship is just beginning.

Sometimes you're stuck with someone who seems to talk with no end in sight. You can't get a word in edgewise. In these situations, you're going to have to end abruptly, but when doing so, you're going to need body language as well as words. At whatever point seems most appropriate, take a small step forward, or shift your body weight forward, shake the other person's hand, and say, "Thank-you." Follow this with some appreciation and excuse, such as, "Thank you for such

The Career Toolkit

an informative discussion. I need to make sure I catch Harper before it gets too late."

It takes practice, but these techniques do work. Over time, it will get easier. For some of us, myself included, it may get easier, but it's never truly easy.

How Are You?

Most people hate it. We do it because it's a social norm. It's such a social norm that we do it on autopilot. "Hi, how are you?" "I'm doing well; how are you?" "I'm fine . . . ." Okay, now we can begin the conversation. We're so automated in this that most people will say, "I'm fine" even if they've just fled a burning house.

It doesn't have to be this way. If the question doesn't have meaning to you, then don't ask it. If you're at a networking event, you can just skip it and go right to other questions like those mentioned earlier in the chapter. If someone asks, "How are you?" use it as more than a placeholder by saying something more than, "I'm fine." Rather, reply, "I'm doing well; we just finished budgeting for the next year, and I'm so glad to have that behind me" or, "Doing great and really looking forward to applying some of the concepts in the talk we just heard" or "A little tired, we just launched a new marketing initiative, so there've been some extra hours at the office to get everyone ramped up." This is an opportunity to help direct the conversation, perhaps to help craft your image as discussed in Chapter 7, Communication, or discuss something of interest to you. Make the most of it.

It can throw some people off a little, since they were expecting some two-word reply, but if they're actually paying attention to the conversation, they'll go with it. The question is open-ended, so use it to direct the conversation where you want it to go. What turns people off is if you go off on a monologue about what's happening in your life. Keep your reply to a single sentence, and let them ask follow-up questions if they want to know more.

If you still prefer to start with "How are you?" which I do, then actually mean it. Ask it hoping that the answer will be more than "I'm fine." If they give you an answer more than "Fine," it tells you something about them. If you sincerely want to build a relationship with this person, then you want to know how they really are and what's happening in their job or their life.

Together, we can put an end to pointless chatter.

Advanced Techniques

Networking doesn't only happen at professional events. Networking is about building relationships, and that can happen anywhere. Business events are natural places for it to happen, but it could also be at hobby-group gatherings, religious activities, talking to other people at your kid's soccer game, volunteer work . . . anywhere. And of course, following the principle of gateway connections, these new relationships might bring significant variation to your network.

If you want to get really advanced, get involved as a group organizer, or join committees. Olivia Fox Cabane, author of the best-selling book *The Charisma Myth,* points out that the two best committees for building your network are the membership committee and the awards committee. You'll build relationships on any committee, but positions on those two committees in particular involve meeting other people. On the membership committee, your job is to find new members and make them feel welcome. Members of an award committee vet people and ultimately give them an award—who doesn't want to be told they

The Career Toolkit

deserve an award?[54] In both cases, your job provides a reason for you to reach out and get to know other people.

Better yet, host your own events. Many years ago, I joined a private social group. I didn't expect much to come from it but figured I'd try going to one event and see what types of people I'd meet. Not much happened at first, but a few people said they were traveling to my city in two weeks. I proposed getting drinks on a Saturday night and expected maybe I'd get ten people to show. We quickly had 250 people coming. Where do you even find a place for 250 people in New York City? Thankfully, a smart club owner was on the list and saw that I didn't have a venue, so he proposed his club. He opened it up early for a private event just for us. I had never met any of these people before, but to them, I was a guy who could organize a private party at a club in NYC for 250 people. Everyone wanted to meet me.[55]

That was lucky; it won't always be so easy. But you can and should organize events. It's great to do professional events. You can also do social, non-work events.

Keith Ferrazzi recommends throwing dinner parties. He points out that they don't need to be fancy, gourmet meals on your best china; they can simply be paper plates and buffet style. I used to co-host dinner parties with a friend who didn't cook, so our events were potluck—everyone brought something to the table.[56]

Living in Manhattan, my own apartment wasn't well suited to dinner parties. Who said you need to sit or even eat dinner? Olivia Fox Cabane and I used to throw wine and cheese parties. You buy $50 worth

---

54. It also applies to the speaker's committee, whose job it is to say, "You're so impressive we'd love to have you speak to our group."

55. It turned out to be a number of very nice people, many of whom are my friends to this day.

56. If you do potluck, remember to coordinate dishes so you don't wind up at a dinner with three salads and seven desserts.

Networking

of cheese and crackers, cups, and a few bottles of wine; most people bring something to a house party, so everyone brings a bottle of wine, and you're done. Less than $100 and two hours of your time.

Throwing events allows me to accomplish a few things. Most important, I have fun. It also helps me stay in people's mind. You probably have friends you haven't thought about in a while. My friends in the city are reminded of me every few months when they get an invitation to one of my parties. The events also give me a reason to reach out to people. If there's someone I've just met, this gives me a reason to reach out and invite them to my next event. Additionally, it allows me to introduce two people to each other.

This last point is a great technique from a networking perspective. Imagine two strangers who will one day have a great relationship. How appreciative will they be that you introduced them? In the extreme case, introducing someone to their future spouse gets you a lifetime of appreciation.

From an effort-reward standpoint, it's hard to beat the introduction of two people in your network to each other. It takes only a few moments to make an introduction, but the rewards can be huge. Imagine connecting someone looking for a job with someone hiring. One connection gets a job. (Who doesn't appreciate help finding a great job?) The other connection gets a new hire. (Who doesn't appreciate filling a role with someone he can feel confident about?) Both sides greatly appreciate what took you very little effort. Whether it's jobs, sales, partnerships, or personal relationships, you can quickly and easily positively impact two people at once simply by being the mutually trusted party who makes the introduction.[57]

---

57. It should also be noted that if you introduce someone who is a problem to the other person (for example, is unreliable), that reflects back on you. Again, trust comes into play; you must trust that the person you are recommending will work out.

Most people do a mediocre job at introducing people. With a little bit of effort, you can make them much more powerful. When doing an email introduction, I'll first check with each party to see whether they're open to being introduced to the other, and I'll tell them why I'm making the introduction. I won't give the other party's name—just some general background, such as "A junior in political science is looking for an internship." This does two things. First, it ensures I'm not wasting people's time or getting someone's hopes up with the introduction. Second, because they said yes, it commits them to engaging with the introduction.

Once I have the go-ahead to make the introduction, I don't simply provide names and emails and say, "Go talk to each other." Rather, I provide a little relevant background on each person and why one person would be of interest to the other. Then I propose specific next steps, such as who should reach out to whom, to prevent the dropped-ball scenario. In general, the person with the greater or more urgent need (or the more junior) should take the next step.

> Ben,
>
> Clara has been running the new CleanWaterForAll non-profit, providing clean drinking water solutions to developing nations. They work primarily in Africa but have done some work in Asia. She's based in NYC but gets to SF regularly. As a non-profit, they're always looking for cost-effective solutions—and additional PR never hurts.
>
> Clara,
>
> Ben is the VP of Partnerships at NewSolarEnergyStartup, which has developed a low-cost rugged solar generator. They are

looking to get some case studies and publicity, so there might be a way for them to do a pilot with your organization.

Ben, why don't you send Clara some more information on what you're looking to do.

—Mark

If it were an in-person event, the introduction would be pretty similar: I would provide the relevant background and common opportunity. The main differences might be the wording, and I wouldn't necessarily propose the next step. They would have a conversation on the spot and determine next steps for themselves.

That "next step" often gets overlooked in email introductions. People aren't always sure who should reach out next. I make it explicit by obligating one party to reach out.

I Don't Have Anything to Offer

One common refrain among my students (and junior employees) is, "I'm just a student [or entry-level employee]. I have nothing to offer my network, so no one will want to invest their time in me." This is wrong for a multitude of reasons.

First and foremost, networking is about relationships, and relationships take time. As we learned earlier, the wrong way to build a network is to do so when you need something now. People will want a relationship with you, if for no other reason than they see long-term value from that relationship.

Second, you have far more to offer than you think. Your network itself has value you didn't realize. Your family, your friends, and the co-workers from your last internship are all part of your network and may be valuable to someone.

In fact, college students, and recent college graduates in particular, have amazing access to a resource they take for granted every day—other college students. Go to a college campus, and you can't throw a rock without hitting a past or future intern.[58] Businesses tend to hire interns (and seniors looking for full-time work), but they don't really know how to find them. Sure, companies know they live on college campuses, but how to reach them, get the word out about the job, and identify the most promising students on campus is rather opaque.

You can help with that. You know lots of students. You know which ones to tell about a particular internship, and anyway, the company only needs to hire one or two interns. If someone at the company knows you and trusts you, then sending along a student's résumé even helps them identify the most promising candidates. College students take all of this for granted, because they see students every day. But to the average person in the corporate world, students are distant and hard to find.

I was once teaching a module at a class in the fall, after our students had come back from their internships. One student, having heard about the consulting I did, came up to me and said, "We probably could have used someone like you at my company this summer." I asked him whether he felt comfortable making an introduction. Although we had just met, he had enough trust in me—from seeing me talk or knowing that this college program trusted me to be an instructor—that he was open to making the introduction. I wound up with a six-month contract, all because a college student opened a door for me.

You have value. We all have some knowledge or some connections in our network that someone else doesn't have. Don't sell yourself short; people will want to build a relationship with you.

---

58. Don't actually throw rocks to test this out. Colleges frown upon this, so just take my word for it.

Business Cards

I'm still a fan of the old-fashioned business card. Yes, you can keep track of people with online address books and can find most contact information easily, but I still like using cards for two reasons. First, when coming back from an event with business cards, I effectively have "notes" about people I met. Second, there's some serendipity when, by chance, someone comes across it in their desk drawer two years later, and it reminds them to reconnect with me.

Some 99 percent of the people I know, including salespeople, tend to keep their business cards sitting in a box on their desk and rarely give them out. Business cards can be purchased for about four cents apiece, so the question is: "Is it worth risking four cents to potentially foster a connection?" The answer is always yes; it's a small price for a potentially huge future payoff. It only takes one connection to get you your next job (maybe with a huge raise). Isn't it worth buying a bunch of 4 cent lottery tickets for a chance to win that prize?

You need business cards most when you're not in your office. I always have them on me by keeping some in my wallet. Other people use a purse or a cardholder.

To really ensure that I always have business cards on me, I also keep them in multiple places that I'll have with me outside of the office. In addition to my wallet, I keep a few in every sports coat and suit jacket. And I have some in every outer coat and jacket. And more in my laptop bag. And a big pile in my suitcase. If I'm at an event and run out of cards in my wallet, odds are I'll have one of those extra stashes with me. Remember to replenish cards each time you get back home. I keep a stack by my door to do so as soon as I get home.

The Career Toolkit

> I do often, although not always, transfer the information from the card elsewhere. Remember the Mackay 66, the 66 things you should know about someone? What's on the card answers some of those questions, and I know that sooner or later I'll lose the card.
>
> I also try to hand out a card a day on average. At some events, I give out a lot of cards in a few hours, and other times I may not hand one out for a week or more. One thing I do know is that cards in my pocket or on my desk do me no good, so it's a reminder to always be giving them out.
>
> Many people today prefer going paperless. That's perfectly fine. I like cards, because they remind other people of me when they later find them in a pocket or wallet. And remember, if you're ever stuck in a conversation, just presenting a card is a signal to end the conversation. It's a graceful way to exit.

Summary and Next Steps

Networking can seem daunting at first, especially if you're introverted like me, but in reality it's what you've been doing naturally with friends and co-workers for years. Networking is about building relationships, and relationships are built on trust. When you ask someone for something, their willingness to help is based on their trust in you.

Simply collecting business cards or social media connections is not networking. Don't mask your desire to sell or get something as networking. Invest in building a relationship. Meeting for coffee is a low-cost way to meet up.

Start by attending events—no one ever built a network sitting on his couch. Community calendars or meetup groups and other community events are good places to start. Asking others where they go to build their networks will help you find places, and you will potentially have someone to go with to those events. Go early or stay late, because that's

Networking

when most of the networking happens. Some people like to have a rule, such as "I need to talk to three new people at every event." You can start small by just talking to one new person per event. Remember to get a business card.

Your network can include anyone. Don't simply focus on people in your field; the value someone brings isn't simply what they know, but also who is in their network. Gateway connections, that is, people with whom you have little overlap in your networks, can add significant value.

Relationships will take time, far more than the initial meeting. Find ways to get together or just reconnect. Learning about the other person will help you find areas of common interest. The Mackay 66 is an extensive list of things to know about someone, but remember that everyone cares about health, wealth, and family. Even reaching out on holidays or just sending someone an article they might like is a good way to stay in touch.

Talking to strangers is hard for all of us. Efforts you make to reach out to someone at an event are usually welcome. There's something interesting about everyone, and your job is to find it; one easy way to start is to ask about where you are or what you've both learned from the event you're attending. "How are you?" should be sincere, and if you're asked, give more than a two-word answer. Asking for a business card is a good way to signal the end of a conversation. Always be sure to thank people for their time, and show interest in them. Sending a follow-up email helps remind them of you and gives both of you a reference back to when, where, and how you met.

Being on membership and awards committees lets you do outreach, which is a great way to build your network. Organizing events helps bring people to you and lets you introduce people in your network to each other. Introducing two people is the most time-efficient way to help others in your network.

Even as a student or junior employee, remember that you bring value to someone's network. Relationships are not about what you can do for someone today. A person in your network is always valuable to someone.

Consider carrying business cards; they cost pennies but can lead to a valuable relationship. If you do use them, keep some in jackets, bags, and suitcases so you always have some on you at all times. Try to hand out at least one a week, and work your way up to one a day.

Chapter Nine

Negotiation

> "Let us never negotiate out of fear.
> But let us never fear to negotiate."
>
> —John F. Kennedy

What if I were to tell you that with one day's effort, I could get you $30,000? It sounds too good to be true, but if it were true, you'd do it in a heartbeat. It is true for many people—they just don't know about it.

Imagine that at age thirty-five you get a job offer. Instead of accepting immediately, you negotiate your salary and get $1,000 more a year. You never take another job, never get promoted, and your only other raises are annual cost-of-living adjustments. That one little negotiation just got you $1,000 more per year for the next thirty years of your career. That's $30,000.

If you think that's not realistic, you're right. You won't just have one job for thirty years; you'll have multiple jobs, each with an offer, and you can negotiate each one. You also may buy or sell a house or a car more than once, and you'll make more or save more money on those transactions. And those are simply the direct cash negotiations. It's not just salespeople who negotiate. Everyone negotiates at some point, even if they don't realize it. Each time you do so, you successfully move your career forward. If you could get better at negotiating in just one day, it would pay off in tens of thousands of dollars or more over your lifetime. And you can.

If you think it's unrealistic because you can't get better in a day, or can't magically get $1,000 more in your salary, read on. You can, and you will.[59]

What Is Negotiating?

Negotiating is an activity where two (or more) parties with overlapping interests try to make a deal. It is not commanding, intimidating, directing, or controlling. There are two independent parties who are interested in making an exchange, be it money, goods, services, or other types of commitments. For instance, one country agrees not to invade another.

Commonly, it's two people who want to trade. If someone wants to buy your car, but you don't want to sell it, there's nothing to negotiate. If one party wants to buy, and the other wants to sell, there is a negotiation to be had. This is an overly simple example, but it helps illustrate some fundamentals.

Then the question is, "Are there overlapping positions?" If the seller wants to get at least $10,000 for the car, and the buyer doesn't want to pay more than $6,000, they're not going to reach an agreement.

On the other hand, if the seller wants at least $7,000 for the car, and the buyer is willing to pay up to $9,000, then there is a range of solutions acceptable to both. The only question is, "Where in the range do they wind up?" We'll come back to this question shortly.

---

59. This doesn't apply to union jobs or other roles with fixed pay scales.

Negotiation

One fundamental point to remember is that negotiations are multi-party endeavors. It's important to remember that you cannot control the other side. I'll say this again: You can do whatever you want, but you can't control what the other party does. You can't make them like your offer or want what you think is reasonable. They will act however they choose to act.

Analogies are often made between negotiations and jazz or improv comedy. Unlike a play, improv is not scripted. The fundamental rule of improv is "Yes, and . . . ." If I'm doing a scene with you, and you ask, "Why are you holding a chicken?" I can't say, "No I'm not." I now have to act as though I'm holding a chicken. I can be a chicken farmer or a chicken thief, or I can say I'm holding a rubber chicken, or I can have a chicken in one hand and the keys to my sports car in the other hand, but one way or another I'm holding a chicken. I can't control what you're going to say, nor can I say, "You're wrong, I'm not holding a chicken." I can only accept it and react to it.

Some people object to this analogy and say that jazz musicians and improv folks aren't out to get you the way someone is in a negotiation. If we're on stage together, you're not trying to put one over on me. We all have the same goal: to put on a good show. The thinking is that negotiations are more adversarial. That's incorrect; in negotiations, both sides actually have the same goal of reaching an agreement—it's just that you may want different versions of it.

Chinese baseball player Sadaharu Oh, who played Nippon Professional Baseball in Japan, holds the world lifetime home run record. He was once asked how he viewed hitting. He commented, "I look at the opposing pitcher as my partner who, with every pitch, is serving up an opportunity for me to hit a home run." That may seem strange, since the pitcher would definitely prefer that Sadaharu not hit home runs. But by viewing the situation this way, Sadaharu was more open to the possibility of seeing good pitches. The other party may seem like the

221

opposition, but two people genuinely negotiating in good faith really are partners, and if you see them as such, you may be able to uncover more opportunities.

Keep this in mind not just when negotiating things like salary, but also when in heated disagreements with co-workers or vendors. You can't control what they say or do; you can only control how you respond. And while they may seem adversarial, viewed a certain way, you are, indeed, partners.

Zero-Sum Negotiations

The car-sale example is the most linear type of negotiation, known as "zero sum." It's called that because there is a fixed amount of value, and more for you means less for me. In other words, whatever is gained by one side is lost by the other. In the car negotiation mentioned earlier, the buyer has $9,000 in her pocket. The only question is, "Does all $9,000 wind up in the seller's pocket, or does $7,000 go into the seller's pocket, and $2,000 into the buyer's pocket, or some combination thereof?" In the end, no more than $9,000 (and one car) is split between the two of them. Every extra dollar the seller gets is one dollar fewer for the buyer, and vice versa.

Most people think of negotiations this way. In reality, most negotiations are not so linear. They are not single-issue, zero-sum cases. These multi-issue negotiations are known as "integrative negotiations." While they sound more complex, as we'll see, they allow for better negotiating outcomes because the different parties may perceive value differently.

Consider a company that is looking to build a factory in a town. The company has asked the town to provide land and tax breaks. Those both have real dollar costs, and those alone are zero-sum—the factory can pay full price for the land and get no tax breaks, or it can get both the land

and tax breaks, resulting in fewer assets and less revenue for the town, or some middle ground of partial breaks.

The town, however, has interests beyond just money. One interest is job creation. Town officials might be willing to provide tax breaks, but only if a certain number of jobs are created by the company. The town may also be concerned about noise or industrial waste.

There may also be additional, indirect costs. The factory may need heavy trucks, which means a bridge in town will need to be reinforced. Someone will need to pay for that. Perhaps the factory jobs will require special training. Who will pay for that? The factory owners or the town (say, via the community college)?

The ideal spot for the factory, in terms of land and roads, might be too close to a residential area, in which case it's less a matter of money than it is of being a nuisance to the neighbors. One option is to find a less desirable plot of land, away from people. Another might be to provide sound-dampening walls around the factory, or other types of mitigation.

Everything has a cost or benefit—land and sound-dampening walls aren't free, and new jobs bring in more taxes for the town. However, each cost or benefit may not be equally valuable to all parties. This is key. For example, an empty dirt plot on the outskirts of town, away from people, may be of little value to the town, but being near a highway and away from a residential neighborhood makes it quite valuable to the company.

These multi-issue negotiations often have non-linear trade-offs, where the value is perceived differently by each side. This is a good thing; it's what allows negotiations to happen and provides for better solutions. Each party can trade away to the other what it values less, in exchange for what it values more. This process is known as a "Mutual Gains Approach" (MGA) to negotiating. Not everyone will gain the same amount, of course. In the case of the factory, the low-value property on the outskirts of town, where no one wants to live, is valuable to the company as a factory site.

Positions vs. Interests

When negotiating, it's critically important to distinguish between positions and interests. Suppose homeowner Taylor demands that the next-door neighbor, Sasha, put up a wooden fence. Sasha doesn't want a fence. This is a problematic negotiation; a wooden fence is binary—you either have a fence or you don't. You can imagine the two of them going back and forth, shouting at each other:

"You need to put up a fence!"

"I am not going to build a fence!"

The key is to ask why Taylor wants a fence and why Sasha doesn't want one. Sasha has a dog who keeps digging up Taylor's backyard. Taylor is naturally unhappy about that and wants to keep Sasha's dog out of the yard. Sasha bought the house partially because every day she can sit outside, look across Taylor's backyard, and see a beautiful sunset. The fence/no-fence decision means either Taylor loses a nice yard, or Sasha loses a nice sunset view.

Taylor doesn't really care about the fence. What Taylor really cares about is not having Sasha's dog in the yard. You can probably already imagine some potential solutions. Sasha could get a leash for the dog, build a dog run, install an invisible pet fence, put up a mesh fence Sasha can see through, or build a fence with a gate that Sasha can open at sunset while the dog is on a leash.

The mistake Taylor initially made was staking out a position: "Build a wooden fence." Positions are often yes/no, and if the position is not amenable to one side, it doesn't work. Then the discussion devolves into shouting yes and no. When interests are used as the basis for a negotiation, they allow each party to come up with one or more solutions that may meet the interests of all sides. Good negotiators know to discuss interests, not positions.

When it comes to negotiating money, every dollar figure is a "position," so to speak. The sum of $115,500 isn't really different from $115,499, but it is a position nonetheless, and large differentials in monetary positions, like $110,000 versus $115,500, do matter. On the other hand, during a salary negotiation, the money itself is not always the end goal but rather what the money buys, for instance, moving expenses, professional dues, or tuition reimbursement. The company may be able to provide that specific item directly, possibly at a lower cost because of some pre-existing arrangement it has. Obviously, the candidate will still want some monetary compensation, but not all money is simply money for money's sake. Even money can be traded off for other options rather than viewed as zero-sum.

Ultimately, when negotiating, you need to find a solution that reaches common ground. The more you satisfy the other party's interests, the more appealing the option is for them. Obviously, and more importantly, you want to meet your own interests, too. The key is that each side evaluates its interests independently. One dollar is one dollar to each side, but other solutions may have more or less value to each side. Ideally, you'll convince the other side that what you want meets their interests, and ultimately you'll gain more value than you'll give up.

Stages of Negotiation

With these fundamental concepts in mind, let's look at how a negotiation works. Most people think of negotiations as two people at a bazaar proposing prices, where the seller starts high, the buyer starts low, and they eventually meet in the middle. In the case of the factory coming to town, the company sits down with the mayor and hammers out an agreement in a meeting. That would be analogous to thinking American

The Career Toolkit

football is simply a bunch of people throwing the ball on a field. That might be the most visible part, but what most people don't see is the off-field work. It begins with a team figuring out what type of players it needs (offense, defense, and special teams), understanding the budget, drafting and trading the right players, coming up with plays, and then training. During the game, the players may be on the field, but the coaching staff is making real-time adjustments that affect who is playing and what plays they are running. Then, after the game, the coaches watch the tapes, learn, and revise. Negotiations are similarly much more than just discussions while sitting across a table.

SET YOUR GOALS

The first step of any negotiation is figuring out what you want. What are your goals? Why are you coming to the negotiating table? What do you hope to achieve?

You might have your dream goal, which is some ideal outcome, but you also have some likely outcome(s) and your bottom line. Start by considering your ideal case. What is it you really want? Then consider your bottom line, known as "BATNA"—Best Alternative To a Negotiated Agreement, as described in the classic negotiation book *Getting to Yes* by Roger Fisher, William Ury, and Bruce Patton. What if you don't like the terms the other side is offering? At what point do you walk away? This is what your BATNA tells you.

In the case of the used car, your BATNA tells you, "Although I want the convertible, my limit is $9,000, and I know I can find another car for that price. It might not be as nice, but it would be good enough to get me to work." The cheaper car is your best alternative to negotiating for the convertible.

You could have more than one BATNA for a complex deal. In the case of the town, there may be a trade-off between jobs created and a land discount. The town might say, "If the factory doesn't guarantee at least one hundred jobs, it's not worth giving them the land." Another BATNA might be, "If the factory doesn't guarantee at least fifty jobs, with no more than a 50 percent discount on land price, it's not in our interest."[60]

Knowing your BATNA prevents you from making a deal that leaves you worse off than if there were no deal. It doesn't mean that if the first proposal from the other side is worse than your BATNA, you walk away; it means there are more discussions to be had. But if, during the negotiations, you're not able to find a deal at least as good as your BATNA, then you should not agree to any deal offered.

RESEARCH AND PLANNING

Once you have your goals, you need to plan. Just as a champion debater spends much of her time preparing for the debate, so, too, does a good negotiator spend most of her time preparing. The first thing you need to do is to research and analyze the situation. Like a debater, you don't simply find information that helps you, you also find what hurts you. Where are you strong, and where are you weak? Also look at the situation from the other side. A debater practices against opposing arguments so she is prepared and not caught off guard. This is true for any sport; you come in with multiple types of plays and, if possible, think about how the other side will act. You need to do the same for a negotiation and think about all of the questions from the perspective of any and all other parties in the negotiation.

Why are you in your current circumstances? Why are any of your solutions helpful to the other parties? Are there other alternatives that could be helpful or explicitly not helpful—perhaps deal-breakers?

---

60. Astute readers might realize there's a frontier of possibilities in this case of job-discount combinations below which it's not worthwhile, for example, ninety-nine jobs and a 1 percent discount, ninety-eight jobs and a 2 percent discount, and so on. Of course, that assumes there's a linear trade-off between the two. The frontier of BATNA options won't always be linear.

The Career Toolkit

Why are your negotiating partners in their current circumstances? What do you think they are looking for? What would be valuable to them? What's more valuable? Less valuable? What might be unacceptable? What might their BATNA be?

What are your interests and their interests? What positions might come out of those positions on either side? What facts and arguments best support those interests and positions?

What might be your opening offer? What might theirs be?

Learn, review, practice. Unlike a formal debate, you don't need to practice what you might say (unless you think that would help you), but you do need to know the topic well enough from all sides so that as you're going back and forth in discussions, you can respond to their points and counterpoints.

Sometimes the answers may be obvious, such as, "We need widgets for our product, and they manufacture widgets." Sometimes you may not be able to answer questions about the other party. For long, complex negotiations, you can spend hours and days planning. For simple ones, it may just be minutes. A professional actor prepares before a scene, an athlete before a game; any professional negotiating should do the same. Even a limited amount of preparation—an hour or so to consider these possibilities—can lead to improved outcomes.

One important note to keep in mind, expressed as a central theme of Lawrence Susskind's *Good for You, Great for Me*, is to recognize that there are likely two aspects to your plan. We traditionally think of negotiations as dividing the pie between two or more parties. Professor Susskind reminds us to also consider ways to enlarge the pie, allowing more pie to be divided between the parties. The key is that you still want as much of the pie as you can get, but the path may first mean enlarging the pie for everyone and then grabbing as large a piece as you can. During a negotiation, you may shift back and forth between value creation (enlarging the pie) and value claiming (getting as big a piece as you can for yourself); recognize which of your actions supports which of those activities.

OPENING OFFER

Typically, one party will make an opening offer. There are two opposing factors when making the first offer.

The first is that you may reveal information. Consider the car example, where the buyer is willing to pay up to $9,000, and the seller wants at least $7,000. If the seller asks, "How about $8,000?" the buyer immediately knows $8,000 is acceptable and will never suggest a higher price. An opening offer in a case like this can reveal too much information. This is why, in the classic bazaar haggle, the opening offers seem insultingly high or low, because they want to start but don't want to reveal what is actually acceptable. Everyone experienced in the bazaar haggle culture knows that initial offers are not realistic.

The second is the concept of anchoring. Consider a piece of art from an unknown artist. Unlike a car, where you can find comparable value by looking at similar cars and prices, there's less information about what the true price should be. Maybe it's worth $5,000, maybe it's worth $15,000. If the seller says, "Well, for a painting of this quality, I suppose I could sell it for $14,000." Now suddenly the buyer thinks, "Oh gosh, I guess this is on the more expensive side of the price range." With no other contrary information, part of your brain, even if you're conscious of this, is anchored to the high price, and so you then try negotiating down from there.

On the other hand, if the artist doesn't have a sense of market pricing, and a collector comes in and says, "Hmm, for this piece, I would pay $6,000," the artist may think, "Oh, perhaps I was being too optimistic thinking I could get over $10,000 for this painting. Well, let's see if I can do better than $6,000." Now you've anchored to the low price and have to negotiate up.

The Career Toolkit

So, what to do? The cases above were both zero-sum, single-issue negotiations. In such a case where the value is hard to ascertain, make the first offer to anchor the position. If you're going to be able to ascertain the value, meaning you can find blue book values for cars and can have your mechanic look over the car to evaluate its condition, let the other party go first to gather information. You can always counter with a different value assessment, which would be the blue book value of the car. This is different from simply giving a different number because you want the price to be lower or higher. In such a case, it's not "you" giving the other number but the third party, such as the blue book, which helps to counter the anchor.

In cases of multi-issue negotiations, it's less straightforward. When you make an offer, you need to decide which categories you want to anchor in, and which you may leave open. Or you decide for what categories you want to leave room to concede. It's all based on your prior research of what is important to you and what is important to them. The thinking about revealing information and anchoring still applies, but now to each issue in the negotiation.

Don't feel bad if your offer is rejected. In fact, if your first offer is accepted, you probably weren't aggressive enough—or you may be missing key information. Jim Camp, author of *Start with No*, welcomes "No" because it is followed with "Why?" and you begin to understand the needs of your negotiating partner.

Some negotiators like to explore before making an offer. "Are you more sensitive to price, or is guaranteed on-time delivery of the monthly shipments more important to you?" Asking this question allows you to explore their needs. If the other side doesn't want to give an answer, or if they don't know which they prefer, then you can put it to the test by offering multiple positions and seeing how they respond. "Would you prefer $5.00 per unit and delivery no later than the fourth of each month or $5.25 per unit and guaranteed delivery by noon on the first of each month?" These negotiators may prefer one or the other, or they may be indifferent. Negotiation researchers Neil Rackham and John Carlisle note that above-average negotiators seek information 21.3 percent of the time, compared to only 9.6 percent of the time for average negotiators.[61]

If you do make an opening offer, remember the advice of Richard Shell in *Bargaining for Advantage*: Give the biggest (or smallest) opening offer you can make with a straight face.[62]

AT THE TABLE

The heart of negotiations involves exploring interests and making offers and counteroffers. You can propose positions or ask exploratory questions like, "Would you rather . . . ?" While negotiating, keep a few things in mind:

First, it's a rookie mistake to go issue by issue. In each case, on a single issue, both sides will try to maximize their gain (their share of the pie). It often becomes a zero-sum game per issue, and that limits options. Instead, explore multiple issues at once, which allows for trade-offs. Consider a store trying to maximize profits. It might offer free shipping—a clear loss—for large-enough orders because the profits from the items offset the loss from shipping. When negotiating multiple issues in parallel, not only might you not do well on one issue, you might even take a loss on an issue—that is, take a position that costs you—because you'll more than gain it back on other issues. If a store were to "negotiate" each item individually, it would never offer free shipping.

In general, your planning tells you which issues are more important to you, and which are less important. Trade off less important issues for

---

61. John Carlisle, "From Negotiation to a System of Profitable Collaboration," self-published, December, 2013. Accessed from http://in2in.org/od/thought/2013-12-ThoughtPiece-Carlisle.pdf December 23, 2019.

62. Here, culture very much matters. In some cases, as noted, you need to make a seemingly outrageous opening offer; in others, the expectation may be to start with something realistic.

The Career Toolkit

more important ones. If you were able to determine which issues were more or less important to your negotiating partner, either through your research or from seeing how your partner reacts to proposals, then you have an even better idea of what trades might be acceptable to the other side of the table.

Second, remember that you can't control the other side, but you can influence them. When making any offer, think about why this helps them, or why it's appropriate; for instance, "This is the standard rate for such a service." A proposal by itself can seem arbitrary, especially as proposals and counterproposals are going back and forth. By providing a justification for the proposal—why it makes sense or why it helps them—it's much more likely to be considered. Although again, remember that you can can't control the other side's thinking; they may view your proposal differently from how you do.

Third, don't get wed to any position. Much like spelunkers exploring a cave, sometimes you might take a wrong turn and need to backtrack before finding better progress down another path. If you're getting stuck on a position, it's okay to backtrack. It might seem as though you're giving up some progress, but sometimes you need to go backward to go forward.

Fourth, don't get caught in the heat of the moment. Most negotiations aren't time sensitive. Even if there is a deadline, it's typically days or weeks ahead, not minutes or hours. If you find yourself getting emotional (annoyed, angry, tired), you can take a break for a few minutes or ask to resume discussions the next day. Likewise, it's okay to say, "I don't know." If you get an offer that you can't evaluate on the spot, you can ask to take some time to consider it. That may mean literally stepping away from the table to talk to your teammates, or it could mean ending the session to go back to the office to get more input from others who aren't present. If someone demands that you make a decision on the spot, be very careful; it likely means they are concerned about what you may discover with time to evaluate it.

Fifth, remember again that you'll shift back and forth between value creation and value claiming. This is natural. It's a mistake to simply think of doing all the value creation up front and then trying to divide the pie afterward.

CLOSING THE DEAL

After one or more rounds of negotiations, it's finally time to draft the agreement. Everyone seems happy with the terms. Congratulations—but your job isn't over yet. No matter how good a contract is, something is going to go wrong. You can plan for most of it, but you won't always get it right. If it were always clear, courts would settle contract disputes in a matter of minutes, not months.

To the extent possible, you want to create deals that are "self-enforcing." If your contract is based on the number of cars that drive on a road, make sure you agree on how to count. Will one party do it? Both parties? Can you audit the other's numbers? Will it be a third party? Government data? What if there's a disagreement between counts?

If a condition is not met, what exactly happens? If you're supposed to deliver one hundred widgets, what happens if you deliver ninety-nine? Is the whole contract void? Is there a penalty? Much of this comes from practice, and the standards and remediation processes will vary by industry. If you don't know what they are for your industry, it's a good time to tap people in your network who do.

Finally, consider a post-negotiation deal. After you have a deal in place, preferably signed, consider negotiating further. This is an advanced technique, and to be honest, when I suggest it, most people look at me as though my head isn't screwed on straight, but there's no downside. Most people, especially after a long negotiation, think, "We're done. Why would we do it again?" There may be another deal out there that's better for both parties. This won't work with zero-sum deals (or with job offers), but it can work with multi-dimensional ones. You have a deal already, so the worst case is you can't do better; your BATNA is now your signed, existing deal, with which both sides are happy. But maybe you can do better. Since both parties already know a deal exists, you can suggest some more creative options because you know that if none of them works, you still have a deal.

Unethical Negotiating

Unfortunately, a lot of bad negotiating behaviors plague business dealings. It's important to be aware of them in case you encounter them.

One of the most common approaches is known as "hard bargaining," in which the other party simply wants what's best for themselves and doesn't care about what works for you, or maybe the other party even wants you to lose, just as a matter of principle. These are people who don't believe in conceding or who will play games that will suck your time and energy. They're playing a war of attrition. You get tired and just want to go home, so you start to make concessions. They either refuse to make concessions or, after being pressed, make much smaller concessions.[63]

Hard bargaining tends to focus on positions, not interests. When negotiating with hard bargainers, try to explore their interests. If they refuse to divulge any information (and many hard bargainers will refuse, seeing it as a sign of weakness), give them options in the form of "Would you rather . . . ?" to understand what those interests might be.

---

63. Similar to the considerations in the section "The Myth of the Alpha Male," don't confuse stereotypical hard-bargaining tactics, such as shouting or slamming the table, with actual hard bargaining, anchoring, and little effort to compromise. Some hard bargainers are quiet, and some loud people focus on reaching a win-win agreement.

If they still refuse, or if it's just taking too much time and energy, remember your BATNA. You can always walk away.

Another technique is the "back room." In the classic underhanded car salesman trope, you spend an hour bargaining over every little detail—price, car color, floor mats, power steering, undercoating, and more, then you finally reach a deal. You shake hands, and he says, "I'll just get this signed by my manager." He steps out to see his manager, and when he comes back there's a forlorn look in his eyes. "I'm so sorry, my manager says that to get everything we agreed to, I have to up the price five hundred dollars." Some people simply cave. They feel so emotionally invested in the negotiation that they don't want to start from scratch and simply agree to the new terms.

This is an unethical trick. One of two cases is true. Option one, he's lying. There is no manager demanding more money, and he just wants to trick you into paying more. Option two, there is a manager whose approval he needs, in which case he didn't negotiate in good faith. After you sincerely negotiated, now you find out you have to do a second negotiation? Either way, this is not someone you should deal with.

When you sit across the table from someone, the assumption is that they have authority to negotiate the deal. This isn't always true; sometimes a party needs approval from a higher-up, but in such a case that should be disclosed up front with a disclaimer like "I'll ultimately need my board to approve any deal we reach." Anything else is inappropriate.

Another common issue is lying. Sometimes it's a blatant lie. The other party might tell you, "Under no circumstances can we consider letting you use that land," but, in fact, that land might be available. Sometimes the distinction is a little more gray: "This is a very generous offer," a CEO once told me, but it wasn't. He may have thought it was, or maybe he just thought it was better than average. One very common tactic among founders who are raising money for their companies is to say, "The deal is closing in seventy-two hours, so you need to commit by then."

The gray areas are the ones that most people would let slide. Note that you can almost always use variants for any of them without raising ethical concerns or lying. "Unfortunately, the land isn't on the table right now." You don't have to say why. "If you want to be in the deal, I need to hear back from you within seventy-two hours." Most lies can be avoided if you spend a little time to think consciously about what you're saying. Remember, you're not obligated to give a reason or an answer to every question the other side asks. While we generally encourage negotiators to share their interests (not positions), sometimes doing so shares too much information. If pressed, you can politely say you can't get into more detail.

Finally, beware of what can't be in the contract. Famously, when Ray Kroc, CEO of McDonald's, bought out the interests of the founding McDonald brothers, he offered them cash and a small royalty but claimed he couldn't put the royalty in the contract, so it would have to be a handshake deal. The McDonald brothers never saw a penny from royalties. If it's not written down, there's a chance it will not happen. Even if the other party is sincere in their intentions, outside events such as recessions, project cancellations, and layoffs can prevent them from fulfilling a handshake promise. When someone says, "Trust me," I say, "I absolutely do. But if you get hit by a bus tomorrow, it's the person who takes over who I don't know well enough to trust. Let's write it down."

You can't put everything in a contract. If you have a long-term relationship, that might engender some trust. If your new boss promises that you'll be put on a project as a condition of your joining the company, she may not be able to put that into the job-offer letter. At the very least, try to get an email expressing the expectations, so

> that if she's fired the day you start, you have something to show your next boss about promises made.

Types of Negotiations

Bargaining for Advantage and other authoritative sources model different types of negotiations falling across two dimensions: the value of the transaction and the value of the relationship. The value of the transaction is simply the monetary value (or equivalent) of the item(s) being negotiated. Are you buying a used textbook or a fleet of planes? The value of the relationship is the long-term relationship between the two parties. At one extreme, you have a strictly transactional relationship with someone you may never see again, and on the other it's a family member, friend, business partner, or co-worker with whom you are transacting. The relative weighting along these two dimensions impacts your negotiation strategy.

TRANSACTION: LOW / RELATIONSHIP: LOW
When the value of both is low, the optimal strategy is to avoid conflict. Consider two strangers getting to a parking spot at the same time, when there are other spots half an aisle down. The time it takes to fight over the spot is less than the time it takes to drive slightly farther and walk from there. In these cases, just do whatever it takes to resolve the issue quickly.

TRANSACTION: LOW / RELATIONSHIP: HIGH
When the transaction value is low, but the relationship is high, value the relationship. Suppose you'd like to go to Japan for a vacation, but your spouse very much wants to go to France. Going to France is still not a bad choice, and keeping your spouse happy is definitely a good choice. Given the importance of the relationship, is it worth the fight?

The Career Toolkit

Early in my career, I hired an employee through a recruiter. There was a structured payment plan so that after sixty days of employment, I would owe the recruiter about $14,000. The employee was good but very quickly had personality conflicts with of few of the earlier hires. It was a personality mismatch, and I wasn't experienced enough to know how to fix it. It soon became clear that the situation wasn't going to work, and the employee quit on day sixty-two. By contract, I was on the hook for $14,000 and called the recruiter to tell him I'd honor it. He had already known me a few years and knew that, over my career, he was likely to place me personally—or place candidates with me—many times over. He recognized that everyone had made a good faith effort, but the placement wasn't a good fit, and so chose not to hold me to the contract. He gave up the $14,000 because the relationship was much more valuable. That was not just a nice thing for him to do, it was financially the right call. Whenever I needed a recruiter, he was my first call. He valued the relationship and a good experience for all more than trying to make short-term money on any one placement.

TRANSACTION: HIGH / RELATIONSHIP: LOW

When the transaction value is high, but the relationship is low, press to maximize value. Consider the case of buying a used car from a stranger. You're never going to see this person again, so you have no incentive for them to walk away liking you. Don't be rude or unethical, but otherwise get all the value you can; in this case, push for the lowest price you can get.

I'll contrast the last example with another recruiter I used. Recruiters are paid 25 percent of the base salary—the higher the base salary, the more the recruiter makes. After about three weeks, I realized the recruiter wasn't good and was wasting too much of my time sending scores of unqualified résumés. So, I was going to stop working with him. But one of the many, many résumés he sent over was someone qualified.

I completed the process with that one qualified candidate and was ready to make him an offer. It was February of 2000, right before the dot-com crash, and back then I was paying $60,000 for junior software engineers. The recruiter told me the candidate was making $40,000 and wanted to stay lateral with the move. The candidate had taken the last job within the last year. The recruiter was clearly unaware of market demand and salaries. Should I pay the candidate what he was really worth? Or should I take the savings?

I did both. I didn't care about my relationship with the recruiter, so I hired the candidate for $40,000. The recruiter's fee was therefore based on a percentage of only $40,000. I maximized my value of the transaction.

After about a month, giving time to make sure the candidate was as competent as I thought when we interviewed him, I sat him down and gave him a raise to $60,000. Why? With my employees, I care more about the long-term relationship than the money. Maybe I could have saved money, but likely sooner or later he would have realized he was underpaid, and then I'd either have to give him a raise or lose him and have to replace him at the market rate. By giving him the raise, I got a very motivated employee (Can you imagine getting a 50 percent raise after a month?), and he knew he had a manager who looked out for his interests. That's more than worth the temporary savings I could have had.

TRANSACTION: HIGH / RELATIONSHIP: HIGH

When both are high, you need to keep both dimensions in mind. A daughter who is buying a house from her parents falls into this category. Normally, when buying an item as expensive as a house, you want to maximize your value, but here you have a very close, long-term relationship with the other party that you don't want to jeopardize. You need to find a balance between the two.

This happens with complex, high-value business partnerships. Consider the case of the Boeing 737 Max grounding. The grounded flights cost the airlines tens of millions of dollars. That lost revenue needs to come from either the airlines or Boeing. In the coming decades, the airlines will potentially spend billions of dollars on more Boeing planes and services; Boeing needs to make sure the airlines are happy and will continue to buy from Boeing and not a competitor. They need to balance the short-term costs, potentially subsidizing the cost of grounding, with the long-term relationship (future sales).

The concept of a relationship like this is formally described in game theory as "multi-round." A restaurant that charges premium prices can serve low-quality food to maximize its profits, but customers will realize the poor quality of the food and stop coming back. The restaurant wins the first round but effectively loses the rest, because no one will come back for additional rounds. You may have a multi-round relationship with a vendor when you regularly come together to continue a contract, as with unions and employers, or you may have a continuous relationship with a friend or co-worker you see regularly.

Of course, negotiations don't all fit neatly into the four categories. A moderately valued item with a moderately valued relationship falls right in the middle. You have to decide where a situation falls along both axes and choose your strategy appropriately.

It's All a Negotiation

Most of the examples we've looked at are easily recognizable negotiations: a job offer, buying a house, an agreement with a supplier. But negotiations happen far more frequently. There are the minor, everyday ones that are so simple that we don't even register them, such as deciding what you and your spouse should watch on TV or making weekend plans. Both these cases have different parties with different interests.

Of course, these are generally low / high negotiations, so we rightly don't put much effort into them.

More important, but equally hard to notice, are discussions at work where you make trade-offs. Different groups with competing proposals may look to find a compromise solution. Your manager asking you to put in some long hours, but promising to send you to a conference or giving you extra vacation time, is a negotiation. Agreeing to do a project you don't really want to do in exchange for later being put on another project you value more is a negotiation. We might not formally sit at a table and go back and forth with proposals, but negotiations happen all the time.

It turns out that most things in life can be negotiated. "No refunds" can often mean "maybe" if you try. For example, in a retail store, if you point out that you're a good customer, they might make an exception or perhaps give you store credit. Stores don't normally negotiate prices, but if you're buying a lot, you can ask the manager for a discount. It might not always work, but it does some of the time. And that's a negotiation. Remember, not all negotiations are successful.

Finally, while we have discussed two-party negotiations, negotiations are often not only multi-issue but multi-party. Consider the building of a dam. There are the energy company; the landowner; the local town; the potential workers at the dam (some workers won't be from the local town); the suppliers, including the local concrete company that will do a lot of business as a result of the new construction; environmental groups; politicians; regulators; people who use the river; and more. The guidelines above apply, but the situation gets complex. The good news is that these situations often have more opportunities for complex but beneficial solutions.

How to Negotiate Your Job Offer

One of the most common types of negotiations (and the one I'm asked about most often) is negotiating a job offer. This section is a crash course on how to do that. It's important to recognize that there is more to your compensation than money. Yes, salary is important, and generally the more you get the better, but it's not the only thing. Other compensation components include bonus, equity, benefits, vacation, location, training, and title.

Not all companies will allow all of these details to be negotiated, but you can try. How open a company is to negotiating a component usually has to do with what line items the budget is divided into and the authority of the hiring manager over that line item. A company's budget is often allocated for specific purposes. Salary and benefits may have different internal budgets from travel and training. A hiring manager's hands may be tied by corporate policy. For example, corporate policy is to pay all salespeople a base salary of $50,000, but the manager may have discretion over other budgets, such as one to send employees to training seminars. Smaller companies usually have more flexibility than larger companies.

ROLE

This seems moot, since presumably you're discussing compensation for a job you applied to, but don't discount this. An entry-level job or a job at a large company with fixed roles may not have much room. At smaller companies, or if you're at a higher level, you can negotiate your responsibilities. For example, years ago, I wanted to gain more experience as a business owner responsible for a P&L (profit and loss statement), so I negotiated that the CTO role would include being GM (general manager) of a business line. The nature of the role is the most valuable thing you're getting, with the possible exception of money, since it will impact your happiness at the company as well as your career growth.

BONUS

Bonuses are fairly common. It could be a little as 5 percent, while in other jobs (think Wall Street), it could be more than 100 percent of your base salary. You can try to negotiate not only the size of the bonus but also the frequency and the triggers. A bonus given annually is worthless if you wind up leaving a job in November. If you get your bonus quarterly, then when you leave in November, you'll have gotten three-quarters of your bonus for the year. You can also try to negotiate the triggers—the bonus may be based on some number, such as sales, hires, or pageviews. Keep in mind that sometimes the bonus pool is budgeted separately from the salary pool. So, even if the salary is fixed, there may be more flexibility with the bonus. In some cases, the bonus policy, like salary, may also be set at the corporate level, so there may not be flexibility.

EQUITY

If you work for a startup, you may be offered stock options. At a larger company, there may be stock options or equity grants. While companies often have salary bands, they are less likely to have strict equity bands, or they may be more flexible about deviating from the bands. I've had undergraduate students who had little leverage when asking for more money on their summer jobs get more equity—all it took was asking. Note that usually only quantity can be negotiated; the other equity terms are typically set company-wide.

BENEFITS

Benefits like health care and your 401k tend to be fixed, so there's usually not much wiggle room. But the sky's the limit with other benefits. Getting you a work computer for home? That will cost them $1,500, and if it makes you more productive at home, it would seem to pay for itself. Company car? Some places offer it. Are you tall? Maybe getting them to commit to paying for the extra-legroom seats on flights is meaningful to you.

The Career Toolkit

Again, while there is a direct cash value here, this example comes from a travel budget and not a salary budget. Can you align the benefits to their needs, such as the home computer helping you be more productive?

VACATION

Vacation is another possibility. At some companies, it's fixed; at others, there may be flexibility. For my friend who volunteers at the National Scout Jamboree every summer, being able to take time off is important to him. Maybe the company will provide extra vacation time for that, or maybe it's unpaid time off, but the company is okay with it. Maybe they have an office in a city where you have family, and just being able to work from the other office or work remotely is of value to you.

LOCATION

For some companies, the location is a single choice. At large companies, being able to choose which city or which office in the city you work at may be important to you. While a vacation has direct financial cost, working from home one day a week usually has little or no direct cost to the company, so the barrier tends to be the concern of setting a policy (or exception) and the impact if everyone else tries to do it, too.

TRAINING

Training typically aligns well with company needs. My father was chief of medicine at hospitals and, as such, had to stay abreast of changes in the medical field. He used to have in his contract that they would send him to two conferences a year; he would get to pick at least one of the two. The hospital knew he needed to go, so giving him the option to choose didn't cost them much, and it allowed him to combine the trips with a family vacation. Typically, we'd have a few days as a family and a few days where we'd be vacationing, and he would be at the conference during the day and then see us at night. The hotel room for

Negotiation

those nights was covered by the hospital, since they needed to send him anyway. Whether it's tuition reimbursement for classes, sending you to training courses, offering online programs, paying for certifications, or just giving you a book budget, it's easy to make a case for the value to the company; whether they agree is another story. Also, the training budget is sometimes separate from the salary budget. So, imagine if they were to offer you up to $3,000 a year in reimbursement for an approved class you planned to take anyway. That's like getting a $3,000 bonus. And if the class you take is a negotiation class, you'll do even better next time.

TITLE

Your job title may be important to you, and it may or may not be on the table. On the one hand, titles cost nothing; on the other, companies need consistency in titles. The larger the company, the less flexibility. At a smaller company, saying, "I'm good with the salary, but I'd like the title 'senior staff accountant' and not just 'staff accountant'" may be possible.

START DATE

This may seem minor, but it can matter. Many companies these days need someone who can start yesterday, but you might want to get in a vacation before starting another long job. If the job market is decent, and they want you, pushing it back a few weeks probably won't make a difference, since they're hiring you for the long term, not for next month. There might not be flexibility if there's a major event or deadline or if there's a training program, and the schedule can't be changed. It's not uncommon to say, "It sounds like you're really pressed to get someone in the office. I can start next week, but I need two weeks off next month, since I have a vacation already planned," which may use vacation days or may just be unpaid.

SALARY

Salary is always viewed as zero-sum. Every dollar a company gives you is one fewer dollar in its budget. Also remember that what you want to be paid is not relevant to the other party—except in so much as they want you to accept the job. What you think you should be paid isn't a strong argument to the other side.

The best approach here is to look for data supporting your position. I had a subordinate who was due for a raise, but instead of just giving it to her, I wanted her to negotiate for it. I knew I was going to give it to her either way, but I thought this would be a good chance for her to practice negotiating and have a positive outcome. Her argument went as follows: "I'm making $90,000, but according to [a salary website], the average salary for my job in our city is $95,000. I think I'm above average, and so I want $100,000." She got the raise.

A friend of mine got a job out of college and was told, "All new college hires in this role make fifty thousand." She pointed out that she had worked for a number of years before going to college, and so compared to the other new college graduates, she had more work experience; she got $55,000. In both cases, the employee justified why that number was fair.

OTHER

The above are typical, but anything is possible. There could be a signing bonus or an allowance for work clothes or tools. You could ask that someone specific at the company be your mentor. A university that is trying to solicit a well-respected professor may help find a job for the spouse. There could be a relocation budget or time off for house hunting if they need you to start right away. Another common tactic is to say, "I can start at this salary, but can we do a salary review in six months?" Of course, you have to trust that your new manager has the power and willingness to boost you if you do prove worthy. You also have to trust that what you think qualifies for a raise is what your manager thinks qualifies for a raise.

Generally, you'll want to use one of two strategies. The first is to appeal to some standard. The second is to differentiate yourself from a standard in a way that justifies paying you more. In some cases, as with the first salary example above, you can do both.

Remember, of course, that in each case, you shouldn't simply ask for what you want. You need to justify it. Think about the company's needs, and align your ask to what they want.

Another thing to consider: Know whom you're negotiating with, or rather what flexibility that person has. At big corporations, titles and salaries may be set by the HR department, and the hiring manager may not have any authority to change them. In other cases, hiring managers may not see how to get you what you want—this is where understanding different budgets can matter. In smaller companies, the manager may have much more flexibility.

Of course, you also need to know their BATNA. If you're a new college graduate, there are a hundred other new college graduates with your grades who want your job, and the company knows it. Their BATNA is to say, "No negotiations. Take it, or we'll take the next student." It's different if you're a rare commodity, thanks to some combination of skills, experience, location, and timing. More senior hires have more leeway to negotiate, meaning the $1,000 more a year you get at age thirty-five could be supplemented by the $10,000 more a year you get negotiating at age forty-five.

For those who jumped to this section first and found it helpful, I'm glad. I'd encourage you to read the other chapters in the book, too. If this helps you get $30,000 more in your career, imagine what the other skill lessons in this book could do for you. The other chapters may not seem as directly of value, compared to negotiating your compensation, but each of the skills in this book can help you be more successful and earn more. Not a bad return for an hour of reading per chapter.

Summary and Next Steps

A negotiation is two (or more) parties with overlapping interests who want to make a deal. Negotiators should focus on interests, not positions.

While we often think of negotiations as single-issue, zero-sum processes, most negotiations are not so linear. Multi-issue, or integrative, negotiations allow one party to trade something of lower value in exchange for something of higher value. Negotiations are surprisingly common, not just when you're sitting across the table from someone. Most things in life can be negotiated.

A negotiation begins by setting your goals, including your BATNA (Best Alternative to a Negotiated Agreement). Research helps you understand your needs and options as well as those of your negotiating partner. Even a little research goes a long way.

For a given issue, you should make an opening offer if the value cannot be ascertained, allowing you to anchor. If the value can be ascertained, let the other party propose the first offer. Either way, don't negotiate one issue at a time; discuss multiple issues at once to allow for trade-offs. Expect to move back and forth between value creation (making the pie bigger) and value capture (getting a big piece for yourself). Ask, "Would you rather . . . ?" to help uncover preferences.

When you create a deal, take into account how it will be measured and enforced. Reality is messy, so make sure the deal addresses variance. Optionally, consider a post-negotiation deal.

Hard bargainers will be very demanding and make few, if any, concessions. They play a game of attrition. Beware of unethical negotiators who lie. You can avoid lying by using different phrasing.

Similarly, beware of those who negotiate in bad faith by misrepresenting their negotiating authority.

When negotiating, consider the value of the transaction versus the value of the relationship, and balance accordingly.

When negotiating your job offer, consider not just salary but also many other forms of compensation, including bonus, travel, training, title, and anything else that's important to you.

Negotiations, like leadership, sports, or public speaking, require practice. You can only learn so much from books.

This chapter looked at the basics of negotiations and generally at two-party examples. In reality, negotiating in the corporate world is a multi-party endeavor and involves a number of issues. The examples here were kept simple for illustrative purposes; expect to face more complex situations in the workplace.

If you're in college, you can take a negotiation class, or join (or start) a negotiation club, where you can practice with negotiation simulations. Researchers in the field have developed thousands of role-play exercises where you and your negotiating partners are each given one side and need to reach a deal. If you aren't in school, you can take a negotiation class, either at a university or through a negotiation training service like the famed Harvard Negotiation Project.

You can also gain experience by helping your friends. Even if you're not the one at the table, when your friend is negotiating, you can still participate and gain experience. Remember, most of the work isn't done at the table. It's the research, preparation, and thinking through the interests and supporting arguments that are the keys to success.

One of the hardest skills is learning to ask for what you want. Many people have difficulty asking for the raise or the opportunity. It's often due to fear of rejection. Learning to have the courage to ask is key, and that comes from practice. As the old saying goes, nothing ventured, nothing gained.

Chapter Ten

Ethics

> "The only thing necessary for the triumph of evil is for good men to do nothing."
>
> —**Edmund Burke**

Ethics in business is too often given only lip service. It is not a part of most core curricula and not emphasized in companies. The companies that do talk about ethics typically do so only for compliance.

Doctors have taken the Hippocratic Oath, or its modern equivalent, for centuries. Medicine requires it because doctors have power over the lives of others. Contrast that with officers of a corporation, who have, by law, a fiduciary responsibility to make money for shareholders. Beyond that, there are no formal legal requirements regarding morality or ethics for other employees, subordinates, or shareholders, nor obligations to the community (local or global) other than staying within the bounds of the law. Yet, companies and their employees have the power to significantly impact others within the company, as well as customers, communities, and the environment. Consider that the Great Recession, created by

The Career Toolkit

the financial industry, apparently caused over 10,000 suicides,[64] not to mention the countless cases of environmental damage, harassment, and consumer harm that companies have caused over the past century or more.

Far too often in my career, I have seen individuals and companies engage in inappropriate activities. Again and again, when it has happened, people, myself included, haven't spoken up enough. You do not always need to be a change agent for good, but when you stand by and do nothing as lines get crossed, you are consenting to the misconduct. We as a society need to do better.

One of the reasons people don't speak up is because they are caught unprepared. If we witness a hit-and-run accident, we call 911 without hesitation, because a stranger has clearly committed a crime, and we know that a rapid response is important to help the victim. If we uncover a co-worker misusing a small amount of money for personal use, our reaction is more muddled: It's not a stranger, it may feel like a victimless crime (or it may be in a gray area), and we don't have to make a snap decision. Both are uncommon circumstances, but society has trained us to take action in the case of a hit-and-run. Not so for office quandaries. Similarly, we've been trained to leave a building immediately when we hear a fire alarm, but when we hear cries of help down the street, reactions are slower and more varied as people consider their options.

This chapter can help train you. I don't give you the answers here but rather help you become more familiar with some questions you will face so that you can know how to react when you inevitably face them. And I'm certain you will.

Disclaimer: All advice here is given as my personal opinion. I am neither an ethicist nor a lawyer. Nothing in this book is legal advice,

---

64. Dallas, Mary Elizabeth, "Recession linked to more than 10,000 suicides," CBSnews.com, accessed December 24, 2019, https://www.cbsnews.com/news/recession-linked-to-more-than-10000-suicides-in-north-america-europe/.

and you should check with a lawyer as to the validity and legality of the advice given, which may be constrained or subject to laws in your jurisdiction as well as any legal agreements you may have entered into. Ultimately, you are responsible for your actions and their consequences.

Ethics in the Workplace

Business ethics is a broad and complex topic. This chapter touches upon some of the more common ethical questions you will inevitably face in your career.

There are the blatant examples of lawbreaking: theft, harassment (sexual and otherwise), and outright lies and deception. Harmful products, cover-ups, and outright corruption are included on this list. In such obvious cases, most people know what to do, or they at least know where the lines are (even if they don't always choose to enforce them).

It's not always so clear. Perhaps there's a company policy limiting expenditures on food or hotels, but an executive regularly exceeds this limit. The expenses may be approved, but the approver is sometimes in a more junior position than the executive. Is this a double standard? Is it theft? What if the executive is combining work and personal expenses? Was that trip really in the best interest of the company or just well timed to coincide with some otherwise personal travel? More than once, I've heard people say, "We'll just say there was a client with us" so that different expense rules apply.

There are more subtle questions. Suppose that, as a manager, you have been given a list of your subordinates who will be laid off this month. Most would agree that the list is confidential and that you shouldn't tell anyone until it is formally announced. What if an employee is about to make a major decision, such as buying a house. Do you have an obligation to let that person know? Probably not. Again, it's confidential corporate information, although it may personally be hard to stand by as

The Career Toolkit

an employee gets into a difficult financial situation. What if the employee asks about future plans, like being on a project or attending a conference? Now you're the one in a difficult position. If you're at a company that may be downsizing in the next quarter, and no one formally told you, but you are reading the corporate tea leaves, do you have any obligation to give your team a heads up? Would it be right or wrong to do so?

What if you know the company has stopped paying a supplier? I worked at one company where the CEO simply chose not to pay contractors. One sued successfully but then learned that judgment enforcement wasn't so easy, and the other just decided it wasn't worth it. Would it have been right for me to keep working for that company?[65] Did it matter that I was the one who brought the supplier in?

If you were intentionally or unintentionally misled about available opportunities before joining a company, is that ethical? Every startup CEO I've ever met talks about the great opportunities in the company's future. I have no doubt most of those CEOs believe what they say. I have also known employees who felt misled, even outright lied to, once they started at those companies and saw a different picture. In some cases, the "great opportunities" could be attributed to the CEO's optimism; in others, the CEO sold a vision as amazing as winning the lottery jackpot but intentionally left out the disclaimer that it was also only as likely as winning the lottery jackpot. At what point is this behavior unethical? Is it ethical for a CEO to suggest that something is likely when they think it's a long shot? Is it ethical for you to work for such a company or for you to help recruit and hire for such a company? What about pitching that future to investors? Is there a different standard when talking to investors[66] than for employees?

---

65. I stayed briefly, thinking that from the inside I could help get the payment processed. When it became clear that I couldn't, I left.

66. Investors often have to be "accredited investors" who meet certain minimum standards; blue sky laws about transparency also apply to fundraising but not to recruiting.

Ethics

Catholic priests have been part of an organization that has been covering up unethical scandals for years. It's not just a few bad apples but systemic abuse and cover-ups by the church. Is it right, then, for a moral priest to stay in the priesthood? Unlike most jobs, such priests can't easily change employers. Can they reasonably stay as long as they themselves are moral and do more good working from the inside, helping parishioners? What if a police department had rampant corruption, like the New York Police Department in the 1960s, or systemic racism? Is it better for an officer to resign in protest or try to change it from the inside? Can an officer be ethical simply by not being racist himself but not opposing racism in the department? What if it's a small town, and he doesn't have many other employment options? Where is the red line? At what point does he think that staying on the job does more harm than good?

MIT accepted money from Jeffrey Epstein, a convicted sex offender. Was it right for MIT to do so? What about the money MIT received from the Koch brothers, who regularly fund anti-science campaigns in direct opposition to the mission of the school, or MIT's engagement with the Saudi government?

What about your organization? Does it need to draw a red line? Where? Do you believe you shouldn't work with any company that does something you disagree with? What if those practices are common in the other company's country? What obligation does an organization have to investigate the behavior of its partners? Is there a statute of limitations? If not, then should IBM still be ostracized for working with the Nazis nearly a hundred years ago? Should other companies be penalized for discrimination they committed in the 1950s?

There are also questions about corporate policy. Are you comfortable working at a company that builds weapons? What if, instead of a gun, it's a tool to track people, ostensibly criminals? (There's an old saying,

"One man's terrorist is another man's freedom fighter.") What if it's sold to a government of another country whose policies you don't agree with? What if your government uses it in a way you don't agree with? What if it's something as mundane as hammers, but they are being sold to the government for a project you disagree with? In 2019, Wayfair workers walked off their jobs to protest the company's sales to U.S. immigration detention centers. What would you do?

In the past few years, we've seen major companies grapple with decisions about working in, or with, certain countries when the employees of such companies disagreed with those policies. In large corporations with many units, do workers fully understand all the goals associated with what they're working on? And how their work may impact other units with different goals?

We've seen technology get weaponized. Social media is used for undue political influence. Is that right or wrong? Does it make a difference if the influencer is a rich corporation versus a foreign government? "Deep fake" technology, allowing the creation of realistic-looking fake videos, can erode public trust and undermine video technology used in criminal investigations. Printable 3-D guns can undermine safety regulations. What obligations, if any, do the inventors, manufacturers, and distributors of such technologies have to society?

These questions are taken from today's headlines, but in any given year, you can find countless other examples. These are not isolated events, but activities that occur all too frequently.

Where do you personally need to draw the line? One day, you will have to answer at least some of these questions. Don't wait until you face them; think about them ahead of time, and discuss them with people you respect. When you do inevitably face them, it will likely be in a complex situation, and there will be pressure not to make waves. Asking these questions ahead of time can help you be prepared for what will likely be a difficult situation.

Ethics

One good place to start is to consider one of the tenets of the modern Hippocratic Oath: First, do no harm. If what you're doing does cause harm—to other people, their physical or mental well-being, national security, or even the environment—ask yourself whether that's something you should be doing. In today's world, that's not such an easy question to answer. Consider portable ultrasounds that now make pregnancy sonograms available to people in rural communities. Unfortunately, in some societies that value male children over female children, such technology has also been used for selective abortion by gender. You won't always be able to understand every consequence in today's complex world, and the right balance isn't always clear, but by beginning to think about such issues, you can avoid some obvious mistakes.

Large companies have plans in place, and even practice drills. These plans include activities like evacuation (fires), PR crisis response (product recalls), and IT continuity (server crashes resulting in failover to backups). That way, when a problem occurs, there's a clear process, and people aren't trying to develop out a plan of action while under intense pressure. Companies should consider having some ethical guidelines as well, so they don't tackle complex issues on the fly.

Why Not Roll the Dice?

If you take morality out of the picture, every company should cheat. The American regulatory system incentivizes such behavior.

At best, regulatory agencies like the Securities and Exchange Commission, Consumer Financial Protection Bureau, Environmental Protection Agency, and others in the United States are woefully underfunded. The SEC's budget request for 2018 was $1.6 billion; Morgan Stanley alone earned over $40 billion in revenue in 2018. The regulatory

The Career Toolkit

agencies simply don't have the resources to investigate most problems, and so they can only focus on the biggest ones.

Even when they find a violation, most often, the company simply pays a fine. Consider when a British regulator discovered that Goldman Sachs had committed over 220 million transaction reporting errors over a ten-year period. As a result, the Financial Conduct Authority fined Goldman Sachs £34 million ($45 million).[67] That penalty came out to only $4.5 million a year, or about 0.01 percent of the investment bank's revenue: that's one one-hundredth of one percent of its revenue in 2018. It works out to just over twenty cents per mistake.

Goldman Sachs could have hired more people to review the transactions, but even if the people hired had a supernatural ability to only look at incorrect transactions, it likely would have cost more than twenty cents per transaction to catch and fix every reporting error. Given that calculus, why would they ever bother to double-check? In the best-case scenario, they don't get caught, and they save money; in the worst-case scenario, they get caught, and it still costs less than performing the correct behavior. It may have been cheaper than $45 million to build some system to automate checking, but the probability of getting caught, multiplied by the actual fine, makes it economical not to try. They were incentivized to avoid looking for problems, and this assumes it was an honest mistake. It probably was, and it's not clear they gained any financial benefit from it, other than the savings from compliance. But what if there was a financial upside—some extra revenue from not complying? That's even more reason to roll the dice and not comply. In the movie *Fight Club*, Ed Norton's character explains,

---

[67]. Jones, Huw, "Goldman Sachs Fined $45 Million by UK Watchdog for Reporting Failures," Reuters.com, (March 28, 2019), accessed December 24, 2019, https://www.reuters.com/article/us-goldman-sachs-regulator-fine/goldman-sachs-fined-45-million-by-uk-watchdog-for-reporting-failures-idUSKCN1R913Z.

Ethics

A new car built by my company leaves somewhere traveling at 60 mph. The rear differential locks up. The car crashes and burns with everyone trapped inside. Now, should we initiate a recall? Take the number of vehicles in the field, A, multiply by the probable rate of failure, B, multiply by the average out-of-court settlement, C. A times B times C equals X. If X is less than the cost of a recall, we don't do one.

Ethics aside, this is sound business logic. If they do a recall, it could mean more costs, bad PR, fewer sales, and angry shareholders. Keeping their mouths shut simply means looking at actuarial costs, which is something every large company is trained to do.

Michael Milken was indicted on ninety-eight counts of conspiracy, insider trading, and related charges. He served a total of twenty-two months in a minimum-security prison and paid over $1.1 billion in fines and restitution, but he is still worth many billions of dollars from his business practices. Do you know anyone who would be willing to serve twenty-two months in minimum security to be a billionaire? Would you trust that person with your money? How about with your family's safety?

The reality is, financially speaking, companies and individuals are incentivized to do the bare minimum and at times even to take the risk of avoiding compliance. The risk of being caught isn't a strong disincentive. Current penalties and fines are simply not deterrents.

There are two main countervailing forces. The first is bad PR, which can impact sales or lead to a forced resignation. As with fines, the odds of being caught and the price paid are often not strong enough, compared to the financial benefits of crossing the line or ignoring a potential problem. For major brand names that are lightning rods for attention—for instance, Disney, Starbucks, Walmart, or Amazon—they can be, but most companies are much smaller, and their scandals quickly get displaced in the news cycle.

The last line of defense is the ethics of the people who work in those corporations. Let me be clear: This means you. When your one-year-old child puts a toy in her mouth, do you trust that the company followed child safety guidelines? When you get on a ride at the county fair, do you feel confident that proper setup guidelines were followed? When you download software, do you trust that it's not taking your personal data?

Remember, if you take ethics out of it, malicious behavior is logical and encouraged by our systems. Someone may cross a line by your standards because their ethics drew a different line than yours—in such cases, they're not inherently bad, they just saw it differently. Leaving public and personal interests up to such arbitrary decision-making is not in the interest of society. The reason the U.S. has so many regulations is because, at some point, someone drew the line differently, and after a problem occurred, society needed to be explicit about where the line should be drawn.

Every time you see someone cut a corner at your company, and nothing happens, ask yourself those questions again. Ask whether there are possibly people at those other companies—the ones whose products you and your loved ones use—who are letting it slide when there's a mistake or malfeasance because they draw the line differently or because the odds of being caught and the potential penalty pale in comparison to the profit or opportunity when taking the chance of crossing a line. Wouldn't you want someone in that company to stand up and say, "This is wrong"? In your company, that person is you.

How Do We Stop It?

Given the incentives, it may seem like a Herculean task to fight unethical behavior. It can be done, but it takes some effort and grit. To borrow from a famous nineteenth-century quotation, continued vigilance is the price of an ethical organization.

Ethics

A serial killer doesn't just wake up one day and think, "I want to kill a lot of people." It typically stems from an emotional disorder that rears itself in other ways prior to murder. The killer may first display arrogance or a lack of empathy toward others. Likewise, no one just suddenly decides to start sexually harassing women. Rather, there is a long-standing view of privilege compared to those of women. Before demanding sex from a subordinate, the transgressor typically will have made comments or taken other actions, giving clues about their thinking.[68] Likewise, theft and other transgressions are often accompanied by other actions or statements that indicate the true values of the perpetrator.

Whether you spot the violation or just see a warning sign, there are three things you should do.

SPEAK UP

It is critically important to act early when opposing those who have ethical lapses, but we generally don't. Too often, we let the off-color joke go; it may be awkward and seem easier just to avoid it. "He knows what he did," the thinking goes. Maybe he does, and maybe he even sees that you weren't comfortable, but all too often the takeaway is simply not to make such comments around you again.

The broken windows theory[69] suggests that when smaller transgressions are allowed, it encourages larger ones. We see this behavior often:

---

68. This is different from a one-off failure. Someone may commit murder in the heat of the moment, or even plan it ahead of time as revenge, but such actions are in response to a specific individual under specific circumstances, unlike with a mass murderer. Likewise, someone facing bankruptcy may suddenly embezzle out of fear of losing his home and family; this is different from someone who doesn't respect his clients and regularly steals from them. Those are the exceptions, not the rule.

69. The broken windows theory was developed by James Q. Wilson and George L. Kelling and popularized by former New York City Police Commissioner William Bratton. It states that broken windows left unrepaired signal that no one cares about the area, so further transgressions will have no repercussions. Thus, when small crimes like vandalism are ignored by police and society, criminals will be emboldened to commit larger crimes.

from individuals who constantly push boundaries to nation states that literally push boundaries.

When you encounter such behavior, don't wait. Speak up. This behavior can take the form of lying; hostility; bullying; sexual harassment; racism; manifesting a phobia; lack of respect for others; taking advantage of employees, contractors, suppliers, or customers; lack of respect for the law; lack of respect for privacy; or anything else that doesn't feel right to you.

First and foremost, when you speak up, you stand up to the bad actor. It begins to set boundaries they realize they cannot cross. You can't necessarily change their thinking, but you can limit their actions. As with most bullies, a little opposition goes a long way.

Second, and perhaps more important, speaking up signals to others that this behavior is inappropriate and that it's okay to speak up. Have you ever been in a meeting and wanted to ask a question but were hesitant to ask, only to find out later that many other people had the same question? We've all experienced that, and successful people know to ask a question, even a seemingly dumb one, because surely someone else wants to know, too. This principle holds here with ethical transgressions, and it's even more important that you speak up about the bad behavior. If you're not sure whether others share your view, you can safely assume in these situations that most of the time they do.

If you're still hesitant, approach people one-on-one after the incident, and ask for their thinking, or share your view with them privately to get them to open up. Once you discover that it wasn't just you thinking this way, you can have more confidence to raise the issue. Better yet, raise it as a group.

Staying silent doesn't simply imply consent. Far worse, it allows bad actors to control the dialog, unchecked. In the 1930s, and again at the beginning of the twenty-first century, we see widespread such groups pushing rumors, falsehoods, and other lies to promote their own agendas.

Ethics

The silence is all the more deafening when it's coming from our leaders who, more than anyone, should be speaking up. Do not yield the truth!

In the words of Nobel Prize-winning poet Czesław Miłosz, "In a room where people unanimously maintain a conspiracy of silence, one word of truth sounds like a pistol shot." Speak up. Your voice will amplify the voices of those around you.

KEEP RECORDS

The next thing you should do is keep a record.[70] I give this advice to all the women I know who have dealt with some type of harassment, although it applies to any type of unethical behavior. Even if you're not going to speak up, keep a record of all incidents. When you complain after two years of problems, the pushback you'll inevitably get will challenge you on the specifics—dates, where these things occurred, details of the incidents, and accuracy—because someone will ask whether you are sure you remember accurately after all this time. When something happens, that same day, go and write down all the details you can remember: who was there, where you were, and what was said or done. (Write down direct quotes if you can.) In the next day or two, get it notarized. If you can't get to a notary, you can email yourself notes.[71] Since the received email is immutable, that may also serve as a record.

The truth is, you might not remember all the details months later. The other party or the company may claim sour grapes, that you're doing this because you didn't get a promotion or had some other motivation. If you've been gathering documentation for months, you will make a stronger case. The odds that this is sour grapes from a recent incident are

---

70. There may be state laws or stipulations in your contract about keeping copies of corporate information, as well as laws regarding recordings (audio or video) of other people. Check with a lawyer before doing so.

71. Use your personal email, since you should assume you no longer have access to work email, but be careful about following rules regarding corporate information.

The Career Toolkit

lower, because you've been recording the problem for months, possibly prior to any missed promotion. The claim that you're not remembering correctly is also mitigated, because you recorded the details that night, as proven by the notary stamp (or email) only a day or two later.

I know some women who have used an audio or video recording of an incident. The right to record depends on the consent rules of your jurisdiction and your employment agreement. If you can get a witness (for example, someone standing nearby who overhears), that helps, too.

I can't say what legal weight this carries in your jurisdiction. I can say that you're likely better off with more evidence than less. Most companies would probably be more scared of a stack of notarized documents dating back months than simply a "he said, she said" claim.

Even if you never need to use this record, make it anyway. In the future, when the transgressor, who no doubt continued the practice, eventually has someone stand up to him or her, your evidence can help. Even if it's not admissible in court, it adds weight to the victims' claims and tells them they're not alone.

SHINE LIGHT

Supreme Court Justice Louis D. Brandeis famously said, "Publicity is justly commended as a remedy for social and industrial diseases. Sunlight is said to be the best of disinfectants." Companies know this and all too often hide from it.

Far too often, the case isn't black and white—there's no smoking gun—and the company decides to settle. They work hard to keep it quiet. A wronged party, perhaps an employee, customer, or other injured party, often needs the financial compensation. The company, not admitting wrongdoing, wants confidentiality. The company's money buys that confidentiality.

This generally serves two purposes. First, by keeping the financial amount private, it helps the company in future lawsuits, because future claimants don't know how much they could possibly get. Second, the company fears that even without an admission of guilt, they look bad, and so the details of the claim need to be kept confidential.

That second motivation injures us all. We see this commonly with sexual harassment. We find it isn't a one-off act but a pattern. Each claimant, however, is kept silent. The details remain hidden. This protects the company or transgressor at the cost of the employees or the public. The company simply calculates the cost of settlements as part of the cost of retaining the transgressor, and the transgressor continues to cross the line knowing he is protected by the company. It's not until the transgression becomes public that the outrage becomes too great a burden for the company to bear, not the cost of settlements.

Far too many people, post-incident, don't want to name names for fear of being sued. Other times, they need the settlement, and it comes with a confidentiality restriction in the form of a non-disclosure agreement.

I've learned to name names. I've walked away from large severance agreements and meaningful sums of money because I'd rather be able to reference the bad behavior of those parties in the future. I'm lucky enough to be in a position where I can do that; not everyone is. I don't go out of my way. I'm not going to post past incidents online just because I can. But I also want to be able to speak up when people ask. When certain names have come my way in public, such as on a mailing list or in a conversation with multiple people, I've simply said I had an issue with that person (or company), and if someone wants more information I can provide it privately.

I'm not perfect. There are things I did when I was younger that I'm embarrassed about. I wish someone had corrected my actions then. I'm willing to take the consequences and be judged for them. We're all human; we all make bad judgments sometimes. What we'll find is that while many of us have been imperfect, we're mostly good people, and most of our mistakes are forgivable; we won't be damned by our friends for being less than ideal. The people who commit egregious acts rely on the discretion of others to continue to get away with them.

I realize the three steps above are not easy. Earlier in my career, when money was tight and I needed my job, it was harder to take the chance and speak up. Now that a paycheck isn't as important, it's easier for me to walk away over ethical concerns. I hope you can do better than me, but I also understand why you may feel the same hesitation that I did. History is trending toward people more openly calling out bad behavior, and society becoming less tolerant of it. Even if you're not perfect, that's okay. What matters is to keep trying.

Summary and Next Steps

You will encounter ethical issues. It's just a question of which ones and how often. Just as you might prepare for an interview by thinking about potential questions and answers ahead of time, so, too, can you prepare for the ethical questions you will encounter. Books or even web searches can lead you to a number of topics. Importantly, don't try to tackle these alone. Get input from other people with other perspectives, since these issues can have many layers and aren't so black and white. A good place to start stems from the philosophy of "First, do no harm."

The nature of our legal and regulatory system encourages unethical behavior. In some cases, the profit and other benefits far outweigh the chance of being caught and suffering legal penalties. When there is insufficient legal recourse, our best defense is bad PR for the offending company and, most importantly, having people like you speaking up when something is wrong. Put yourself in the shoes of whomever is being hurt. What if the other party were someone you cared about? If you see a line being crossed, ask yourself how many other people are crossing lines

Ethics

elsewhere and hurting those you care about without your knowing. It is incumbent upon all of us to stop it.

When you encounter bad behavior, speak up, which will encourage others to do so. Keep records (within the bounds of the law and your contract). Shine a light, because shadows are the tool of the aggressor.

None of this is easy. It's all the more reason to talk through these issues with others so that when you do face them, you don't need to do it alone.

Epilogue

This book has provided you with an introduction to a number of essential skills that will help you in your career. Each is a tool that can be applied to many different situations both at work and in your personal life.

Reading this book has already made you more aware of opportunities to apply them. Doing so, along with feedback and reflection, strengthens these skills and makes you more effective.

These are by no means the only tools you'll need for your career. Be sure to continue to grow your toolkit throughout your career.

Summary

The firm skills we've covered are rarely taught in most formal education. Those who are curious as to why can read Appendix A: Why Isn't This Taught? This book steps into the gap and has provided you with a good foundation on which to develop these skills.

A number of topics were covered, so don't expect to remember them all immediately, let alone promptly master them. Included at the end of each chapter, rather than here at the end of the book, is a summary and next steps for each topic. A good review would be to take fifteen minutes and reread each chapter summary to refresh your memory.

The Career Toolkit

The process of creating a career plan determines your goals and defines a path to get you there. Working effectively maximizes your success in each role along the way. Interviewing will make you a stronger candidate for each job you target and will help you hire better candidates, thus creating a better team environment in which you work.

The concepts discussed in leadership and management provide you with a framework for being impactful in the roles you take. Remember that leadership and management are actions and mindsets. Don't wait until you have some specific title before applying those lessons.

The skills in interpersonal dynamics will help you be more effective when interacting with others. Sometimes they will be concrete, like in an upcoming negotiation, while at other times they will be continuous, such as in building relationships with people in your network.

The companion app to this book provides quotes and tips from the book as well as from other sources to help reinforce these topics. You can use it as a "tip of the day" reminder or to quickly refresh the information on a given topic, such as networking or negotiation. When learning a new language, you need to use the words so you don't soon forget them. Similarly, this app will reinforce the lessons.

Remember, of course, that these skills build upon each other. A basketball player may practice throwing drills, passing drills, and more, but on the court, it is the application of the right skills at the right times that creates success. That will take practice.

Next Steps

The knowledge in this book by itself won't make you an expert. I've taught you how to put on your shoes and outrun the bear, not how to become a world-class runner. Every one of these skills requires actual practice and application. With daily application of what's in this book alone, you will be able to outrun most people.

Epilogue

Having a desired future is not the same as having a plan to get there. You may have had some idea about negotiating or interviewing, but you didn't realize you engaged in those actions regularly, and not just during formal sessions. You probably didn't consider that your work as a follower would help you become a better leader. The newfound awareness will help. By identifying how you employ these skills on a daily basis, you can now actively work to improve them. What you do, even in a seemingly junior role, gives you the tools you need to succeed in any future role.

You can now decide which skills to invest your energy in. You may want to delve into a topic from this book more deeply. I wrote about crafting your public image, but with just a few pages, I could only make you aware. There was not time or space to provide you detailed strategies for cultivating it. Whole books have been written on that topic and pretty much every other topic covered. I recommend exploring other, more specialized books as well to deepen your knowledge in areas that are of particular interest you.

There are many ways to explore a topic. In addition to books, the most common of those include online content, classes, corporate training, and coaching. The website for this book will also provide additional tools and resources.

Whatever you choose, I strongly recommend doing it with others. Unlike undergraduate classes, top business schools often teach these topics not simply through books and lectures but also through engagement with other students. Learning these skills along with other people is always stronger than learning them on your own, because hearing the perspectives of other people helps deepen your understanding. Find a mentor to help guide you. Create a peer group like the study groups you had in school, and help each other understand the topics by discussing them and working together to apply them in your daily lives. A peer group that is invested in the same activity also helps hold you accountable to your own development.

The Career Toolkit

If you found this book helpful, let me know. If you didn't find it helpful, let me know that, too, since I regularly teach the content and am always open to revising or updating it. All feedback, good and bad, is welcome.

I sincerely hope this book has helped. Best of luck as you journey forward in your career.

Appendix A:
Why Isn't This Taught?

Education evolved organically from its past rather than being designed for the future. Millennia ago, children learned career and life skills from their parents. Hunting, gathering, and tribal relationships were passed down from parent to child.

Hundreds of years ago, children continued to learn primarily from parents; formal schooling was uncommon. Books have only been widely accessible for the last one hundred to two hundred years. Instead, fathers handed down their craft to their sons, and mothers taught their daughters how to raise a family.

During the mid-nineteenth to the mid-twentieth century, we had a rise in primary education, particularly in the U.S. and Europe. Reading, writing, and math were necessary for the modern workforce. College and professional disciplines remained privileges primarily for the wealthy.

In the United States, the number of people completing four years of college grew from around 4.6 percent of the population in 1940 to roughly 35 percent in 2018,[72] and the number of those with a high-school education grew from 25 percent of the population to over 90 percent

---

72. Statista, "Percentage of the U.S. Population Who Have Completed Four Years of College or More from 1940 to 2018, by Gender," Statista.com, accessed December 24, 2019, https://www.statista.com/statistics/184272/educational-attainment-of-college-diploma-or-higher-by-gender/.

The Career Toolkit

during the same period.[73] We have a more educated population than at any time in history.

At the same time, the skills we need today have broadened more than ever before. Your grandparents and great grandparents, who worked during the Industrial Age, often focused on a narrow skill set. Those on an assembly line had a very specific task they repeated over and over. Farming, mining, food preparation, and similar tasks required only narrow sets of skills. Those in professions such as accounting or secretarial work were primarily assigned tasks by their managers.

The number of white-collar workers grew from about 18 percent of the workforce to about 60 percent during the twentieth century,[74] but over the same period, the very nature of their jobs changed. The traditional manager who tells subordinates what to do is gone, as are lifetime employment and corporate training for new hires. Today you're on your own—find your own job (every five years or so), figure out how things work, and get things done. Your manager doesn't have time to explain it all to you—just figure it out![75]

Despite the changes in the demands of these jobs, the educational system has not adjusted much. The methods of teaching may have changed (books yielded to e-books, individual work gave way to more group projects, individualized learning became more common), but the

---

73. U.S. Census Bureau, "Levels of Education: Percentage of the Population Completing High School Bachelor's or Higher," Census.gov, accessed December 24, 2019, https://www.census.gov/library/visualizations/2017/comm/education-bachelors.html.

74. Cenedella, Marc, "Great News! We've Become a White-Collar Nation," Businessinsider.com, accessed December 24, 2019, https://www.businessinsider.com/great-news-weve-become-a-white-collar-nation-2010-1.

75. In Chapter 1, Career Plan, we mentioned that managers have a responsibility to develop the people who work for them; unfortunately, not all actually do accept that responsibility. Even if they do, it's usually only teaching you just what you need to get your immediate job done, not how to chart your career.

Appendix A: Why Isn't This Taught?

content being taught isn't that different. Primary and secondary education are still mostly focused on reading, writing, math, science, history, civics, and foreign languages.[76]

Which one of those classes taught you how to run a meeting or how to negotiate? In college, you focused your studies on a major such as political science or chemistry. Did any of those classes teach you networking or interviewing? You may have studied management or taken classes on a specific subject, such as leadership or negotiations, but for the most part, the skills we cover in this book are not formally taught in most high-school or college programs. Surprisingly, many universities have identified these skills as necessary for success, but they assume you'll learn by osmosis. Everyone tells you how important these skills are, but rarely are they formally taught.

In 2013, the Association of American Colleges and Universities (AAC&U) conducted a national survey of business and non-profit leaders. More important than the actual major were these essential workplace skills:

> *Nearly all those surveyed (93 percent) say that "a demonstrated capacity to think critically, communicate clearly, and solve complex problems is more important than [a candidate's] undergraduate major."*
>
> *More than nine in ten of those surveyed say it is important that those they hire demonstrate ethical judgment and integrity, intercultural skills, and the capacity for continued new learning.*
>
> *More than 75 percent of employers say they want more emphasis on five key areas including: critical thinking, complex*

---

[76]. Important topics all, but not sufficient for today's modern world.

problem-solving, written and oral communication, and applied knowledge in real-world settings.[77]

When I first started hiring in 2000, I was interviewing software engineers from top universities. Generally speaking, they all could give me the right technical answers, things they learned in class or from a book, but when it came to more practical questions, I could see them caught off guard. Not only did they not know the answers, they seemed to have never thought about them before. I began to look for training materials and found none. This is a systemic problem, because our education system was designed to teach the skills needed for the command-and-control business world of the twentieth century, not the chart-your-own-career-path dynamic offices of the twenty-first century.

Our education system is beginning to change, but it will take time, and that change will only benefit future generations. Our educational system is structured to complete education by around age twenty-five, as contrasted with continual formal education throughout our careers. Most people will never get any additional formal education[78] after a bachelor's or master's degree.

---

77. Association of American Colleges & Universities, "It Takes More Than a Major: Employer Priorities for College Learning and Student Success: Overview and Key Findings," Aacu.org, accessed December 26, 2019, https://www.aacu.org/leap/presidentstrust/compact/2013SurveySummary.

78. "Formal" means intensive semester-long classes or certificate programs, as contrasted with brief training seminars.

Appendix B:
Career Questions

These are some common questions to help you focus your career aspirations. To the extent possible, look ahead five, ten, and twenty years. If you can only come up with answers looking a few years into the future, or even just for today, that's okay.

Don't feel overwhelmed by all the questions. Pick the ones you care about, and feel free to skip the rest. Many people can only answer some of them.

Most people have careers that take twists and turns in unexpected directions, so don't be surprised if your answers change over time. That's perfectly normal. This is simply a guide to help you, and you can change it as often as you like.

PERSONAL NEEDS

This is the most important category. What is important to you? When you're at the end of your life, and you look back, what do you want to see? Some people like to write their own obituary to define what they hope to achieve in life. If that's too morbid, consider writing an article about your retirement or the introduction someone will give you when you receive a lifetime achievement award. Just think about looking back from a perspective far in the future that encompasses not only your career but all aspects of your life, including your family and your non-professional interests.

What are my goals in life?
When you look back, what would make you feel accomplished and fulfilled?

What would make me happy?
Is your dream to own a beach home? To help others? Do you want to retire early? Be known as a leader in your field? What are some things you want to achieve because doing so brings happiness?

What is the purpose of my job?
For some people, the job is simply an income; it provides for their family, travel, hobbies, or whatever really matters to them. For others, their job is their passion, even their identity. What do your career and your job mean to you?

What do I like doing?
Is there something you enjoy? Maybe it's seeing justice served or working with numbers. Do you like to sleep in late? Do you prefer a job that keeps you outdoors?

What don't I like doing?
Do you hate having a fixed schedule? Do you dislike being chained to a desk? Do you prefer working with others or being solitary? Do you want to avoid talking to customers? Do you never want to look at a spreadsheet again?

JOB REQUIREMENTS
Focus on any future job itself, whether it's two or twenty years from now. What does that job look like? If you're not sure, ask other people about their jobs. Does something sound exciting? Boring? Horrifying?

You don't need to define it exactly, but it helps to have a sense of what you may like, or at least what you want to avoid doing.

How many hours a week do I want to work?
While straightforward, remember that this will change over time. At age twenty-five, a first-year law student may not mind the thought of hundred-hour weeks, but at age forty-five, a law firm partner with a family may find long hours away from home depressing.

How much travel do I want?
This is another preference that is very likely to change over time. A young consultant may love the glamorous lifestyle of being a road warrior. Later in life though, four days a week on the road may be less appealing.

Consider the type of travel. Doing a six-month project in Miami may be fun. Doing a two-year project in a small city may not be as appealing. Going to the same city for months on end can allow you to develop friends and a personal life. Traveling ad hoc to different cities without a regular schedule can be exciting or draining, depending on what you enjoy.

Do I want to manage people? Be managed? Be independent?
Do you want to manage others someday, or do you prefer being an individual contributor? Maybe you want to be your own boss and not have to report to anyone.

How flexible does my career path need to be?
Some people have known what they want to be since they were young. I've met a number of people who went to graduate school because they didn't know what they wanted to do and wanted to delay that decision. Those who aren't certain may want to choose jobs that can more easily allow growth in many different directions.

The Career Toolkit

What skills do I want to leverage? To avoid?
Do you want a role that involves public speaking, or do you never want to stand before an audience? Do you love making spreadsheets? Are you detail-oriented? Do you like being creative?

What type of corporate or industry culture do I want?
Do you prefer companies with well-defined processes and the comfort of the familiar, or would you thrive on uncertainty and enjoy the variability of ad hoc projects? Do you like to dress up for work, or do you prefer to wear T-shirts in the office? Is a collaborative team important, or do you thrive on competition?

What trends can impact my career?
What trends exist in the industries you're interested in? What trends exist in general? For example, the retirement of the baby boomer population translates to greater demand for elder care. The Internet tends to disintermediate industries that have lots of middlemen. Artificial intelligence will radically change the nature of some jobs. How might these trends impact a role or industry you're interested in today or in the future?

LIFESTYLE OPTIONS
Your career is an integral part, but only one component, of your life. Your non-career needs will provide opportunities and constraints on the jobs you want.

Do I want a family? If so, when?
If you're twenty-two and single, you may not be able to fully control this, but you can recognize that if you want kids by the time you're twenty-six, taking a job where you work on an oil rig for three months at a time may not give you the dating opportunities you need to meet someone and start a family.

Appendix B: Career Questions

What are the expectations of employees in this industry or this role for people in their twenties, thirties, and forties? If you take time off for a family, how will that impact your job or career?

What family obligations will I have?

Will you and your partner both have jobs? Will one take care of the house and/or kids, or will those responsibilities be split between you both? Do you need to be able to drive the kids to soccer practice twice a week? Is there a family member you need to support?

Where do I want to live, and what industries are supported there?

If you've always dreamt of living in Wyoming, and you want to be an oceanographer, you've got a problem. If you want to rise to the top of the financial world, there are about ten cities worldwide to choose from (but you may not speak the native language in most of them). Do you want to be in a city or suburb? What does that mean for your commute (and your time at home)?

What lifestyle do I want?

Do you want a nine-to-five job where nights and weekends are free? Do you want to set your own hours? Are you a workaholic who wants to be rewarded for your dedication? Are you not a morning person, and prefer to show up at the office at 10 a.m.? Is working from home important to you?

How much flexibility do I need?

Do you have any outside interests that may conflict with your work? A friend of mine was a dedicated scoutmaster. He required that any job he took let him take time off for the annual National Scout Jamboree, and he was willing to do that as unpaid personal time, but he needed a company's commitment that he could take the time off. My father made it to every school play, even the ones in the middle of the day, but that required getting out of the office.[79]

FINANCIAL NEEDS

Money isn't the most important thing in life, but it is significant. While you can't predict things perfectly, estimating your likely future expenses is helpful. Is one house enough, or do you want a vacation home? If you're going to help pay for your children's college education, there's a big difference between having one child and four.

How much money do I want to earn?

It seems like a simple question, but it's the one most people struggle to answer. How much do you need to pay for the basic expenses of living the way you want to live? For example, do you want a small two-bedroom apartment outside Sioux City or a luxury condo with an ocean view in South Beach? How much will support your lifestyle? Do you like eating out a lot? Traveling three times a year?

For the jobs you are considering, what do they tend to pay? What is your preferred entry-level compensation? Mid-level? Senior? How prevalent are roles at those levels? The top actors earn tens of millions of dollars a year, but most actors struggle to get by. That's an extreme example, but recognize that the issue is not just the salary at a particular level but also how many jobs at that level are available.

Do you want to give money to charity throughout your life? In your will? Most people could find a way to give $100 annually, but do you want to make larger contributions? How often? Do you want enough money that you can work only four days a week and then spend one day a week volunteering at a charity?

---

79. Even when, being a very shy student, I would have no lines, he still came. Thanks, Dad! It meant a lot.

Appendix B: Career Questions

IMPACT
Careers shouldn't be just about financial rewards and personal success. Many people want to have an impact on their companies, their communities, their industry, and the world at large. These things can be achieved as part of, or external to, your career.

What type of impact do I want to have in my field?
Is this a job to pay the bills? Are you trying to become a recognized leader in your field? Do you want to win a Nobel Prize? Get into your industry's hall of fame? Do you want to disrupt your field?

What type of impact do I want to have in general?
What impact do you want to have on the world at large? Support your local community? Have a global impact? Support a cause?

ETHICS
Some questions are obvious: Are you comfortable building weapons? Could you provide a criminal defense for someone you knew was guilty? As the world gets more complex, the questions become murkier. If you run an online community, where is the line between freedom of expression and hate speech? Is it acceptable to partner with certain companies? Or boycott certain companies? If the technology helps to stop bad people, what are the implications if the government is immoral, and the "bad people" it stops are people fighting for basic human rights?

What are the ethical considerations of the role?
Some jobs face direct issues, such as an obstetrician or gynecologist who does not support abortion rights. If you want to be such a doctor and don't want to attend to women who choose to exercise their right to an abortion, you need to have a plan—refer them to other doctors, or tell them up front that this is your policy.

What about if you're a creative director at an ad agency, and your company lands a client that does something you don't support? The client might be, for instance, the NRA, and you might favor gun control. Are you okay working on that project? What if it's the only client the agency has, and there are no other options at the agency?

What are the ethical considerations of the industry?

You may have thoughts about an industry as a whole. Someone who is concerned about global warming may simply oppose any job at an oil or coal company, even if that company has a renewables program. Likewise, a materials science researcher may not feel comfortable working for an aerospace company, even a civilian one, knowing that such R&D may eventually be used for weapons. Some people won't work at a company that makes cigarettes or at a top Wall Street firm because many companies in both of those industries have a history of concerning behavior.

What are my limits?

If you encounter unethical behavior among co-workers or with corporate policy, what are the lines that would make you feel compelled to leave if they were crossed?

About the Author

Mark A. Herschberg

From tracking criminals and terrorists on the dark web to creating marketplaces and new authentication systems, Mark has spent his career launching and developing new ventures at startups and Fortune 500s and in academia. He helped to start the Undergraduate Practice Opportunities Program, dubbed MIT's "career success accelerator," where he teaches annually. At MIT, he received a B.S. in physics, a B.S. in electrical engineering & computer science, and a M.Eng. in electrical engineering & computer science, focusing on cryptography. At Harvard Business School, Mark helped create a platform used to teach finance at prominent business schools. He also works with many non-profits, including Techie Youth and Plant A Million Corals. He was one of the top-ranked ballroom dancers in the country and now lives in New York City, where he is known for his social gatherings, including his annual Halloween party, as well as his diverse cufflink collection.

Index

Note: Page numbers with "n" indicate footnotes.

A

A. B. See mantra, 46
Abilities, as a component of job roles, 78–82
Accountant career decision tree, 26
Adjourning stage, in team formation, 129, 130
Affirmative goal, 108
After-action report, 153
Age diversity, 86
Agendas, meeting, 143
Agile software development, 152
Airport test, 95–96
Alderfer, Clayton P., 126
Alignment, and cultural fit, 97–98
"Alpha male" myth, 117–118
Alumni mentors, 35
Analogies, in negotiation, 221–222
Analysis, interview questions about, 92–93
Anchoring, in negotiation, 229
Annual reviews, 43–44, 183
Assessment tools, 16–18
Assignments, for interviews, 94
At the table stage, in negotiations, 231–233

B

Back room technique, of negotiation, 235
Bargaining for Advantage (Shell), 231, 237
BASIS (Business and Attitude Style Information System), 16
Benefits, negotiating in job offers, 243–244
Best Alternative to a Negotiated Agreement (BATNA), 226–227, 247
Big Five personality traits, 16
Biologist career decision tree, 27
Black: Critical Review category (Six Thinking Hats), 146
Blue: Management category (Six Thinking Hats), 145
Boeing, 240
Bonus, negotiating in job offers, 243
Brainstorming, 147
Brandeis, Louis D., 264
Brandon, Rick, 60–63
Bratton, William, 261n
Broken windows theory, 261–262
Brooks, Fred, 150n
Brooner, Curtis, 171
Burger King, 171
Business and Attitude Style Information System (BASIS), 16
Business cards, 207, 215–216, 217

C

Cabane, Olivia Fox, 209–210
Camp, Jim, 230
Candidates, interview
  constancy of interviewing, 74–75
  showing initiative, 71–72
  submitting résumés, 67–71
Career decision tree, 26–28
Career path, linear, 21
Career plan, 11–48
  adjusting, 43–45
  assessment tools, 16–18
  career decision tree, 26–28
  changing options, 22–24
  constant options, 24–25
  creating, 20–34
  depth vs. breadth, 32–34
  development of, 20–22
  importance of career goals, 11–13
  inputs to, 13–15
  planning ahead, 28–32
  profession vs. industry, 26
  refining, 34–45
Careers. *See also* Career plan; Interviewing; Working effectively
  importance of goals, 11–13
  questions to ask yourself, 277–284
Carlisle, John, 231
The Cathedral and the Bazaar (Raymond), 86n
Chacko, George, 186
Change, Machiavelli on, 115–116
The Charisma Myth (Cabane), 209–210
Chief technology officer (CTO), 80
Circadian rhythm, 128, 128n
Clark, Dorie, 183
Closing the deal stage, in negotiations, 233–234
Coach, as a management role, 123
Coca-Cola, 51–52
Cold outreach, 72
Collaboration, fostering, 136–137

286

Index

Commitment, to your career, 38–40
Committees, 209–210
Communication, 165–184
  and alignment, 97–98
  channels, 148–149
  for collaboration, 137
  crafting your image, 181–183
  exiting conversations, 207–208
  follow-up messages, for networking, 199–200
  good communication as leadership attribute, 112
  interview questions about, 90–91
  meaning in, 167–169
  for meetings, 143
  models, 169–172
  public speaking, 178–180
  shared understanding, 173–174
  talking to strangers, 204–208
  thinking modes, 175–178
Compensation, delayed, 18–20
Competence, as a leadership attribute, 111
Confidentiality agreements, 71n, 265
Conflict, on your team, 88, 88n
Consumer Financial Protection Bureau, 257
Contracts, 236–237
Conversations, exiting, 207–208
Core functions, of businesses, 51–52
Corporate ladder, 15–16, 18–20
Corporations
  ethics and corporate policy, 255–256
  politics in, 60–63
  startups compared with large, 40–42
  watching for signals, 59–60
  working effectively in, 58–63
Cost
  as component of hiring triangle, 83–84, 99
  as component of project triangle, 151–152, 162
Critical thinking skills, interview questions about, 92–93
Cross-department knowledge sharing, 53
Cultural fit
  evaluating, 98–99
  importance of, 96–99
  interview questions about, 88–89, 93–94
Culture, negotiating and, 231n
Customers, learning about your, 54

D

DARPA (Defense Advanced Research Projects Agency), 73
De Bono, Edward, 144, 161
Decision-making, interview questions about, 89–90
Decision meetings, 142, 161
Decision trees, 22, 26–28
Dedicated, as a leadership attribute, 112
Deep fake technology, 256
Defense Advanced Research Projects Agency (DARPA), 73
Delayed compensation, 18–20
DeMarco, Tom, 124
DISC (dominance, influence, steadiness, conscientiousness) model, 16
Diversity
  of mental models, 172
  when hiring, 84–88
Dominance, influence, steadiness, conscientiousness (DISC) model, 16
Double bind, 118–119

E

Educational system, 273–276
Email, as a communication channel, 149
Empathy, as a leadership attribute, 111
Empowering your team, 57–58
Engineering triangle, 150n
Enneagram, 16
Enterprise salespeople, 194–195
Environmental Protection Agency, 257
Equity, negotiating in job offers, 243
ERG theory, 126
Ethics, 251–267
  career questions for, 15, 283–284
  fighting unethical behavior, 260–266
  as leadership attribute, 112
  risking unethical behavior, 257–260
  workplace, 253–257
Ethnic diversity, 85
Expectancy theory, 126
"Expert in your field," 33

F

Face-to-face communication, 149
Family
  career plan help from, 35
  career questions, 14, 280–282
  networking topic, 203–204
  in your network, 190
Feedback, negative, 147
Feibelman, Peter J., 33
Ferrazzi, Keith, 170, 203–204, 210
Ferriss, Tim, 58
FFM ("five-factor model"), 16

287

The Career Toolkit

Fiduciary responsibility, 131
Financial Conduct Authority, 258
Financial cost, 22n
Financial needs, career questions on, 14, 282
Firm skills, 2, 269
Fisher, Roger, 226
"Five-factor model" (FFM), 16
Five gorillas parable, 158–160
Five Whys approach, 160
Flow, 127–128
Foldit, 73
Follow-up messages, for networking, 199–200
Formal education, 276
Forming stage, in team formation, 129
The 4-Hour Workweek (Ferriss), 58
Friends, help from, 35, 190

G

Gateway connections, 196, 197, 209, 217
General Electric (GE), 98–99
Getting to Yes (Fisher, Ury and Patton), 226
Gilbreth, Frank, Sr., 57n
Glengarry, Glen Ross (film), 46
Goals, 11–13, 108, 136
Goal-setting stage, in negotiations, 226–227
Goldman Sachs, 258
Good for You, Great for Me (Susskind), 228–229
Google, 110
Grandin, Temple, 86–87
Gray areas, in negotiations, 236
Green: Creativity category (Six Thinking Hats), 145–146

H

Hanlon's Razor, 156–157
Hard bargaining, 234–235
HBDI (Herrmann Brain Dominance Instrument), 16, 178
Health, networking topic, 203–204
Heat of the moment, in negotiations, 232–233
Herrmann Brain Dominance Instrument (HBDI), 16, 178
Herzberg, Frederick, 126
Hierarchy of needs, 126
Hippocratic Oath, 251, 257
Hiring team
  cultural fit, 96–99
  defining the role, 78–82
  diversity, 84–88
  hiring triangle, 83–84
  interview questions for, 88–96
  trust in, 187–189
Hiring triangle, 83–84, 99
Hopper, Grace Murray, 113, 124
HR (human resources)
  career plan help from, 35
  in large corporations, 41
  limitations of, 75–78
  reward violations, 126–127
  in startups, 41

I

Illegal interview questions, 94
Image, crafting your, 181–183
Impact, career questions on, 15, 283
Imposter syndrome, 138–139
Inclusivity, in visions, 108
Industry
  compared to profession, 26
  learning about your, 54–55
Influence
  as leadership skill, 109–110
  in negotiations, 232
Influential leadership, 104–106, 114
Informational statements, 145
Initiative, showing in interviews, 71–72
Inspiring, as a leadership attribute, 111
Instant message, as a communication channel, 149
Intelligence, as a leadership attribute, 111
Interests, compared with positions in negotiations, 224–225
Intermediate-term career plan, 30
Interpersonal dynamics. *See* Communication; Ethics; Negotiation; Networking
Interviewing, 65–100
  airport test, 95–96
  from candidate's perspective, 66–78
  constancy of, 74–75
  extending networks with, 195–196
  as form of public speaking, 179
  from the hiring team's perspective, 78–99
  limitations of HR, 75–78
  preparing for questions, 70–71
  selling yourself, 68–69
  showing initiative, 71–72
  tone in, 69, 70
  trust in, 187–189
Interview questions
  analysis, 92–93
  assignment, 94–95
  communication, 90–91

Index

illegal, 94
personal preferences, 93–94
situational, 89–90
technical skills, 91
values, 88–89
Introductions, making, 211–213

J

Job description, 79–81
Job offers, negotiating, 242–248
Job requirements, defined by hiring team, 14, 278–280
Job(s)
    adjusting career plan when changing, 44–45
    learning your, 49–55

K

Kelling, George L., 261n
Kerth, Norman, 153, 155
King, Martin Luther, Jr., 106
Kohn, Alfie, 127
Kroc, Ray, 236

L

Lampert, Diane, 57
Lawler, Edward E., 126
"Lazy manager," 57–58
Leadership, 103–120
    alpha male myth, 117–118
    compared with management, 160–161
    developing your, 113–115
    double bind, 118–119
    and Machiavelli, 115–116
    obligations for, 131
    positional vs. influential, 104–106
    skills of, 106–113
Leadership development, 114–115
Learning
    about your customers, 54
    about your industry, 54–55
    about your suppliers/partners, 54
    your job, 49–55
    your role, 50–52
Leiserson, Charles, 3
Levy, Steve, 60
Lifestyle options, career questions on, 14, 280–282
Linear career path, 21
Listening, as a leadership attribute, 111
Lister, Timothy, 124
"Livestock Behavior as Related to Handling Facilities Design" (Grandin), 86–87

Location, negotiating in job offers, 244
Long-term career plan, 31
Loyalty, 46
"Lunch and learn" approach, 53–54
Luperfoy, Susann, 2n
Lying, in negotiations, 235–236

M

Machiavelli, Niccolò, 115–116
Mackay, Harvey, 193, 200–202
Mackay 66, 200–202, 216, 217
Malicious behavior, 260
Management, of people, 121–133
    compared with leadership, 160–161
    flow, 127–128
    motivation, 125–127
    obligations to your team, 131–133
    roles of managers, 121–124
    teamwork, 129–131
Management process, 135–162
    communication channels, 148–149
    Hanlon's Razor, 156–157
    imposter syndrome, 138–139
    improving, 153–160
    leadership vs. management, 160–161
    meetings, 140–148
    precepts of, 136–140
    project triangle, 150–152
    tasks in, 136–140
Managers
    career plan help from, 34
    obligations for, 131–132
    roles of, 121–124
    working effectively with your, 55–57
Marketer career decision tree, 27
Maslow, Abraham, 126
MBTI (Myers-Briggs Type Indicator), 16
McClelland, David, 125–126
McDonalds, 54–55, 236
McGregor, Douglas, 125
McVinney, Chuck, 86
Meaning, in communication, 167–169
Meetings
    agendas, 143
    Six Thinking Hats methodology, 144–148
    types, 141–143
    unplanned topics, 144
Mental diversity, 86–88, 97
Mental models, 169–178
Mentors, 35, 36–38, 63
Meta-statements, 145
MGA (Mutual Gains Approach), 223–224

289

Milken, Michael, 259
Miłosz, Czesław, 263
Models, of communication, 169–172
Motivation. *See also specific theories*
    expectancy theory of, 126
    as leadership attribute, 111
    when managing people, 125–127
Multi-issue negotiations, 222–224, 230, 241, 248
Multi-party negotiations, 241
Multi-round negotiations, 240
Mutual Gains Approach (MGA), 223–224
Myers-Briggs Type Indicator (MBTI), 16
Mythical man-month, 150n

N

National origin diversity, 86
Needs theory, 125–126
Negative feedback, 147
Negative goals, 108
Negotiation, 219–249
    analogies in, 221–222
    approaches for, 110
    disguised, 240–241
    for job offers, 242–248
    positions vs. interests, 224–225
    stages of, 225–234
    types of, 237–240
    unethical, 234–237
    zero-sum, 222–224
Networking, 185–218
    advanced techniques, 209–214
    business cards, 207, 215, 216, 217
    and communication, 170
    correct way for, 198–203
    as form of public speaking, 179–180
    introductions, 211–213
    people in your network, 195–198
    talking to strangers, 204–209
    trust, 186–192
    wrong way to, 192–195
Neurodiversity, 86n
Never Eat Alone (Ferrazzi), 170, 203–204
Nike, 51–52
N:N meetings, 141–142
Non-disclosure agreement, 71n, 265
Non-verbal channel, of communication, 148–149
Norming stage, in team formation, 130
Note-taking, for networking, 200–202

O

Occam's Razor, 156

OCEAN (openness, conscientiousness, extraversion, agreeableness, and neuroticism) model, 16
Oh, Sadaharu, 221–222
1:1 meetings, 141n
1:N meetings, 141
Opening offer stage, in negotiations, 229–231
Operating structure, 50
Opportunities
    adjusting career plan for new, 45
    creating your own, 72–74
Optimistic statements, 146
Ouchi, William, 125

P

Partners, learning about your, 54
Patton, Bruce, 226
Peers, career plan help from, 35
People operations. *See* HR (human resources)
Peopleware: Productive Projects and Teams (DeMarco and Lister), 124
"People with disabilities," 86n
Performing stage, in team formation, 130
Personality traits, as a component of job roles, 78–82
Personal needs, career questions on, 14, 277–278
Personal preferences, interview questions about, 93–94
Perspectives, viewing job roles from multiple, 52–54
Persuasion, power of, 109–110
A PhD Is Not Enough! A Guide to Survival in Science (Feibelman), 33
Phone calls, as a communication channel, 149
Physical diversity, 86
Planning
    as management role, 123
    in negotiations, 231–232
Politics, corporate, 60–63, 64
Porter, Lyman W., 126
Position, in negotiations, 224–225, 232
Positional authority, 104–106, 110
Positional leadership, 104–106, 113
"Post-mortem" review, 153
Post-negotiation deals, 233–234
Power of ideas style, 60–62
Power of person style, 60–62
PR, unethical behavior and, 259
Preventive visions, 108
Prime directive, 155

Index

Proactive, being, 57–58
Problem-solving, interview questions about, 89–90, 92–93
Professions
  compared to industries, 26
  risk of changing, 24
Project Retrospectives: A Handbook for Team Reviews (Kerth), 153
Projects, adjusting career plan when changing, 44–45
Project triangle, 150–152
Promotions, 15–16
Pronouns, avoiding in communication, 174
Publicity, to fight unethical behavior, 264–266
Public speaking, 65, 70, 178–180, 184
Punished by Rewards (Kohn), 127

Q

Qualifications, as component of hiring triangle, 83–84, 99
Questions, interview. *See* Interview questions

R

Racial diversity, 85
Rackham, Neil, 231
Rangnekar, Dwijen, 125
Raymond, Eric S., 86n
RCA (root cause analysis), 157–158, 160, 162
Record, right to, 263–264
Recordkeeping, to fight unethical behavior, 263–264
Recruiters, 193, 238–239
Red: Emotions category (Six Thinking Hats), 146–147
Regulatory agencies, 257–258
Reinventing You (Clark), 183
Relatability, in visions, 109, 110
Relationships
  trust in, 189–192
  value of in negotiations, 237–240
Repeating back, in communication, 174
Research and planning stage, in negotiations, 227–229
Respect, as a leadership attribute, 111
Responsible, as a leadership attribute, 112
Resto, Chris, 183
Résumés, 67–68, 77–78
Retrospectives, in processes, 153–156
Reviews
  annual, 43–44, 183
  periodic, of your career plan, 31–32, 43–44
Rewards, for employees, 126–127

Right to record, 263–264
Risk
  in hiring, 24
  minimizing, 168
  minimizing in communication, 174
  of unethical behavior, 257–260
  seeing in mental models, 169–172
Ritti, R. Richard, 60
Roles
  creating your own, 72–74
  hiring team's definition of, 78–82
  learning your, 50–52
  negotiating in a job offer, 242
Root cause analysis (RCA), 157–158, 160, 162
The Ropes to Skip and the Ropes to Know (Ritti and Levy), 60
Rorschach test, 173

S

Salary, negotiating in job offers, 246
Salespeople, 194–195
Sales strategy, 46
Scope, as component of project triangle, 151–152, 162
Securities and Exchange Commission (SEC), 257–258
Seldman, Marty, 60–63
Self-enforcing deals, 233
Selling yourself, 68–69
Senior managers, career plan help from, 34
Shared mental model, 173–174
Shell, Richard, 231, 237
Short-term career plan, 30
Signals, watching for, 59–60
Situation, Task, Action, Result (STAR) technique, 90
Situational interview questions, 89–90
Six Thinking Hats methodology, 144–148
Skills
  evaluating, 98–99
  firm, 2
  leadership, 106–113
  soft, 2
  survey on, 275–276
Social media, used for political influence, 256
Soft skills, 2
Speaking up, to fight unethical behavior, 261–263
STAR (Situation, Task, Action, Result) technique, 90
Start date, negotiating in job offers, 245

291

The Career Toolkit

Startups
  compared with large corporations, 40–42
  risks of pursuing, 22–24
Start with No (Camp), 230
Stewart, Potter, 96
Storming stage, in team formation, 129–130
Strangers, talking to, 204–208
Strategist, as a management role, 122
Summary, providing in communication, 174
Suppliers, learning about your, 54
Support, managers providing, 139–140
Survival of the Savvy: High-Integrity Political Tactics for Career and Company Success (Brandon and Seldman), 60–63
Susskind, Lawrence, 228–229

T

Talent management. *See* HR (human resources)
Talking 9 to 5 (Tannen), 118–119
Tannen, Deborah, 118–119
Teams
  building, 114
  empowering, 57–58
  fostering flow in, 128
  framework for, 129–131
  obligations to, 131–133
Technical skills, 16, 92
Text message, as a communication channel, 149
Theory X model, 125
Theory Y model, 125
Theory Z model, 125
Thinking modes, 175–178
Third-party resources, career plan help from, 35
Time
  as component of hiring triangle, 83–84, 99
  as component of project triangle, 151–152, 162
  during interviews, 71–72
  sensitivity of in negotiations, 232–233
Title, negotiating in job offers, 245
Toastmasters, 180
Tone, during interviews, 69, 70
Training
  in leadership, 114–115
  negotiating in job offers, 244–245
Transaction value, in negotiations, 237–240
Translator, as a management role, 123
Trust
  in hiring, 187–189
  in relationships, 189–192
  trustworthy leadership attribute, 112
Tuckman, Bruce, 129–131
Two-Factor theory, 126

U

Understanding, shared, 173–174
Unethical negotiating, 234–237
Unplanned topics, in meetings, 144
Urwick, Lyndall F., 125
Ury, William, 226
Users, 192

V

Vacation, negotiating in job offers, 244
Value claiming, 233
Value creation, 228, 233
Value(s)
  interview questions about, 88–89
  understanding your, 50
Verbal channel, of communication, 148–149
Video conference, as a communication channel, 149
Vision
  and career plan, 31
  as leadership skill, 107–109
Voicemail, as a communication channel, 149
Vroom, Victor, 126–127

W

Wealth, networking topic, 203–204
Weighting job requirements, 79–82
White: Information category (Six Thinking Hats), 145
Wilson, James Q., 261n
Women, in leadership, 118–119
Working effectively, 49–64
  in corporations, 58–63
  learning your job, 49–55
  techniques for, 55–58

Y

Yellow: Optimistic Support category (Six Thinking Hats), 146

Z

Zero-sum negotiations, 222–224, 246
Zone, being in the, 127–128